Additional Praise for *Defending Your Brand*

"Calkins has written a valuable management reference, illuminating the usually hidden but critical arts of effective defense. This worthy guide, brought to life with robust case examples, warrants reading by every manager who wants to succeed amidst the disruptive competitive forces of our capitalist system."

—M. Carl Johnson III, executive vice president, Brands, Del Monte Foods

"In tough times, the best offense is often a good defense. That's what makes this book so interesting and relevant."

—Dr. John A. Quelch CBE, Distinguished Professor of International Management, vice president and dean, CEIBS

"A must-read for marketers, Calkins's book offers strategic and tactical wisdom on how to deal with ever-increasing competition. While we all tend to concentrate on offense (increased sales and market share) *Defending Your Brand* focuses on an equally important but often-overlooked marketing aspect, defense (defending your brand and protecting market share). I'm buying a copy for each member of my staff."

—Rob Gallas, vice president, chief marketing officer, Museum of Science and Industry

"Creating a brand is hard work, but establishing a brand and maintaining its relevance is even more important. Understanding how to defend your brand against the competition is the difference between long term success and short term failure. Calkins shows how to keep brands on top by countering competitors' attacks."

—Daniel Hamburger, president and CEO, DeVry Inc.

"This is a great read for any marketing leader. *Defending Your Brand* outlines practical strategies for brand management in a focused manner, backed by relevant and compelling case studies. You'll walk away with applicable ideas for your business."

—Conrad York, vice president, marketing, Northwestern Mutual

"The purpose of any writing on brand management is to provoke a thoughtful debate on strategy and the resulting actions. Professor Calkins's discussions on defensive strategies deliver on that purpose."

—Kevin Newell, executive vice president and
global chief brand officer, McDonald's Corporation

"Insightful, provocative, and inspiring, this book provides a prism for executives and entrepreneurs to challenge even the most focused business strategies. Full of illustrative examples, we found ourselves preparing to fall into traps that we will now avoid. Tim nails it!"

—E. Douglas Grindstaff II, CEO, NuSirt Sciences, Inc.

DEFENDING YOUR BRAND

How Smart Companies Use Defensive Strategy to Deal with Competitive Attacks

TIM CALKINS
Kellogg School of Management

palgrave
macmillan

First published in hardcover in 2012 by PALGRAVE MACMILLAN® in the US—a division of St. Martin's Press LLC, 175 Fifth Avenue, New York, NY 10010.

Where this book is distributed in the UK, Europe and the rest of the world, this is by Palgrave Macmillan, a division of Macmillan Publishers Limited, registered in England, company number 785998, of Houndmills, Basingstoke, Hampshire RG21 6XS.

Palgrave Macmillan is the global academic imprint of the above companies and has companies and representatives throughout the world.

Palgrave® and Macmillan® are registered trademarks in the United States, the United Kingdom, Europe and other countries.

ISBN: 978–1–137–27875–3

Library of Congress Cataloging-in-Publication Data

Calkins, Tim.
    Defending your brand : how smart companies use defensive strategy to deal with competitive attacks / by Tim Calkins.
        p. cm.
    ISBN 978–0–230–34034–3
        1. Product management. 2. Strategic planning. I. Title.

HF5415.15.C26 2012
658.49012—dc23   2012012775

A catalogue record of the book is available from the British Library.

Design by Newgen Knowledge Works (P) Ltd., Chennai, India.

First PALGRAVE MACMILLAN paperback edition: January 2014

10 9 8 7 6 5 4 3 2 1

Printed in the United States of America.

CONTENTS

List of Exhibits   vii

An Important Note   ix

1   Introduction   1

2   The Threat   13

3   The Financial Challenge   29

4   Know Your Enemy   39

5   Competitive Intelligence   59

6   The Key Question   87

7   Planning the Defense   117

8   Stopping the Launch   137

9   Blocking Distribution   155

10   Limiting Awareness   173

11   Preventing Trial   183

12   Fighting Repeat   205

13   Defense Never Ends   219

14   Defensive Strategy for Innovators   235

15   A Cautionary Word about Competition Law   251

Acknowledgments   267

Notes   269

Index   281

EXHIBITS

1.1	Prevalence of defensive strategy	5
2.1	Successful new businesses	17
2.2	Quaker Oatmeal estimated P&L	19
2.3	Quaker Oatmeal risk	21
2.4	Evanston Oatmeal years 1–3 P&L	22
3.1	Dusty Chimney Sweep initial financials	33
3.2	Dusty Chimney Sweep revised financials	34
4.1	Positioning statement	43
4.2	Source of volume	46
6.1	Defense decision tree	94
7.1	New product launch process	120
8.1	Koblenz Classics Stoves financials	139
9.1	Super Shine year 1 financial proposition	156
9.2	Super Shine year 1 financial proposition: updated	157
9.3	Quandry Medical financials	162
10.1	Elbert Alpine Energy outlook	174
10.2	Elbert Alpine Energy outlook: updated	175
11.1	GTHR financial forecast: initial	186
11.2	GTHR financial forecast: updated	187
11.3	GTHR profits	187

AN IMPORTANT NOTE

THERE ARE TIMES WHEN THIS BOOK will make you uncomfortable. You may read about certain tactics and think, "That is so wrong. I can't believe someone would do that." Some of the approaches and strategies really push the boundaries of what is considered acceptable behavior. If you are an attorney, this book will certainly make you feel unsettled. Some of the techniques discussed in this book are highly questionable. Indeed, the entire topic is a bit of a minefield.

Nonetheless, defensive strategy is a major part of the world of business, and it's critical to any venture's long-term success. You may not approve of certain activities or tactics, but they happen, and they work.

Most of the tactics discussed in this book are legal. However, rules vary from country to country. An important point: before creating a defensive campaign, you should consult with your legal advisors. They can best guide you on the laws that pertain to competition in your specific business and country.

The examples in this book are all based on interviews and discussions with company executives. Few of the stories have appeared in media outlets, however, and the companies involved might deny their involvement. One person I spoke with about the topic was quite direct, explaining, "It's nothing I can talk about. They'd send a death squad."

While people don't like to discuss defense, it is critical to understand when to defend and how to create a defensive plan so that you can make smart decisions when under attack. No matter whether you're running a giant global brand or a small neighborhood café, you are bound to encounter a new competitor at some point. The long-term success of your business will depend on how effectively you respond.

Chapter 1

INTRODUCTION

YOU ARE UNDER ATTACK.

As you read this, people around the world are thinking up new ideas, looking for ways to get into your industry, and dreaming up schemes to steal your market share. Companies great and small are working on innovations and employing teams of talented people focused on bringing breakthrough concepts to your market. People launch thousands and thousands of new products every year; if you aren't facing a major new competitive threat today, there's a very good chance you will be soon. As business strategist Gary Hamel observed, "Every company is in a bare-knuckle fight to defend its margins, defend its position in the marketplace."[1]

This book will help you fight back.

If you're looking for a cheerful book about the power of innovation and strong brands—well, this isn't it. Instead, this book is a practical guide to the dark arts of marketing: the shadowy world of defensive strategy.

This book will teach you how to survive, and perhaps even thrive, when competitors attack. It will show you how to push them back and protect your market share by using a systematic approach. Fair warning: some of the tactics are not pretty; the most successful defense initiatives force your competitors out of the market and sometimes drive them into bankruptcy. Your legal advisors probably don't want you reading this book, and they may not want to see it displayed on your bookshelf. But knowing how to defend a business is essential in a world where competition is intense and new market entrants are attacking from all sides.

THE POWER OF DEFENSIVE STRATEGY

In early 2008, Kraft Foods, one of the largest food companies in the world, announced that it was launching a new product under its iconic dessert-topping brand Cool Whip. The new product, Cool Whip in a can, was a spray version of the traditional product, a creamy dessert topping. Prior to the introduction of this new product, Cool Whip had only been available in a tub and was generally stocked in the frozen desserts section of the grocery store.

The executives at Kraft had carefully planned the launch of the new product. The rationale was logical and clear: Cool Whip in a can would be more convenient and easier to use than the topping in the traditional packaging. As a result, people would use more; with a simple spray, customers might add Cool Whip to additional desserts or use more on each occasion. The new product would also increase the brand's store presence since it would be stocked in the refrigerated section of the store. And the new product had good margins, so it would increase profits. In many ways this was a very solid growth idea.

There was just one small problem: ConAgra.

ConAgra Foods, another global food giant, owned Reddi-wip, the leading brand in the category of spray dessert toppings, with a market share of over 50 percent. Reddi-wip was a very profitable, stable business for ConAgra. For Reddi-wip, the Cool Whip attack was a major threat; Cool Whip could potentially steal significant market share with its new product.

Reddi-wip and Cool Whip had long coexisted on store shelves, with Cool Whip in the frozen section and Reddi-wip in the refrigerated section. The brands didn't directly attack each other; Cool Whip focused on promoting new uses for Cool Whip, and Reddi-wip invested heavily in retail support to secure displays near seasonal fruit, where consumers often looked for Reddi-wip to jazz up their fruity desserts. Overall, the marketing in the category was functional but uninspired; the brands were firmly established with stable revenues and profits.

With the new product, however, Cool Whip was now directly attacking Reddi-wip. This changed the competitive game in the category. When news of the Cool Whip launch reached ConAgra, the Reddi-wip group sprang into action. Sergio Pereira, head of the business unit, created a cross-functional team of salespeople, promotion specialists, advertising executives, and R&D experts and set out to create what he called a ferocious defense. The team studied the situation and quickly built a defense plan that centered on creating awareness of the differences between Reddi-wip and Cool Whip and investing in deterring trial of the new product.

First, the Reddi-wip team identified a notable point of difference between Cool Whip and Reddi-wip: Cool Whip contained hydrogenated oil, while Reddi-wip was made with real dairy cream. The team talked with consumers and learned that people were concerned about hydrogenated oils; clearly, the fact that Reddi-wip was made with dairy cream was a significant benefit for consumers.

Second, the Reddi-wip team developed a new advertising campaign to communicate the difference in formulation and emphasize it. Reddi-wip notably attacked the core Cool Whip product, not just the new spray version. All of the marketing efforts featured the Cool Whip tub, the heart of the Kraft dessert topping product line.

A new print ad compared the two products by stating: "Cool Whip uses hydrogenated oil. Reddi-wip always uses real dairy cream. Which one will put a smile on your face? Nothing's more real than Reddi-wip."[2] A new television ad made the same point, featuring a waitress asking a diner whether she wanted oil (holding up the Cool Whip tub) or cream (holding up the Reddi-wip can). Reddi-wip secured in-store displays that delivered the same message and revised the graphics on its packaging to emphasize the "real" nature of its ingredients and to highlight the "less than real" ingredients used by competitors.

Third, Reddi-wip increased promotion and advertising spending, adding coupons and in-store promotional offers. In total, Reddi-wip spent much more to promote its product than Cool Whip.

The result of this forceful, integrated campaign: Reddi-wip clobbered Cool Whip. The Cool Whip spray product failed to meet sales objectives and struggled to maintain shelf space. At the same time, Reddi-wip sales grew, as did profits. Inspired by the success of the defense effort, the Reddi-wip brand managers changed all of their marketing efforts to support the "real dairy cream" positioning.

The Cool Whip attack turned into a significant win for Reddi-wip; the defense plan pushed back Cool Whip and brought life, energy, and a compelling positioning to the Reddi-wip brand.

WHY DEFENSIVE STRATEGY MATTERS

There are few certainties in the world of business, but here is one: if you're lucky enough to have a profitable, strong business, you'll attract a lot of competition. Reddi-wip certainly learned this when Cool Whip decided to directly attack its product. And when someone decides to attack *your* product, you are going to need to defend your business.

The topic of business defense is broad; it includes all the things a company does when responding to competitive threats. The difference between growth strategy and defensive strategy is quite simple. Growth strategy includes all the proactive steps you take to build your business; defensive strategy involves responding to your competitors' moves. Growth strategy consists of all the advertising, new product introductions, cost reduction efforts, and promotional offers that you create in a bid to increase market share, revenues, and profits. Defensive strategy is always a reaction to a real or perceived competitive threat. Offensive strategy is largely proactive, while defensive strategy is largely reactive. Companies *initiate* growth programs and offers; they *respond* to competitive attacks with defense plans.

Companies can defend against virtually anything. It is possible to defend against a new advertising campaign, a promotional offer, an online advertising program, a social media campaign, or a change in packaging graphics. A company that adjusts its advertising message to respond to a competitor's message is defending. A company that moves its price in response to a competitive move is also defending.

Defending your business is an essential part of management. Indeed, in some ways it's the most important part of running an established business. Leaders must constantly watch for competitive moves, especially from new entrants, and then respond appropriately to the threats. People get very excited about growth, but growth is just one part of the strategic mix. There's a strong case to be made for growth being the second priority, after dealing with competitive issues. You can't grow when your core business is eroding underneath you. As legendary football coach Bill Walsh observed, "Leaders who don't understand what their territory is and how to protect it will soon find themselves with no turf to protect."[3] Defense plays an important role in any competitive enterprise; a good offense is valuable, but a good defense is even more important.

Companies defend all the time; they study their competitors and adjust course accordingly. As Harvard professor Michael Porter points out, "In essence, the job of the strategist is to understand and cope with competition."[4] When a new entrant appears, the established players take action; they work to protect their business and slow the competitor's growth. Starbucks CEO Howard Schultz made the point in a recent interview, explaining: "When you love something and someone tries to take it away from you, you fight."[5]

Recently, I studied the prevalence of defensive strategy. I surveyed 93 executives studying in MBA programs in the United States and Europe. These individuals worked for companies all around the world, in both big global corporations and small local enterprises. On average, these students had 14.7 years of business experience; they were fairly seasoned business leaders.

The survey showed that more than 80 percent of companies defended at least occasionally and over 50 percent defended frequently or all the time. Twenty-eight percent of the students reported that their firm devoted more than 40 percent of company resources to defensive activities (see exhibit 1.1).

One of the more astonishing figures in business is the dismal rate of new product success. Even at a savvy company such as Procter & Gamble, as many as 80 percent of new products are disappointments. Some innovations are simply bad ideas, and customers predictably turn away. Many new products, however, are quite good; the quality is high, and the marketing support is solid.

Exhibit 1.1 Prevalence of defensive strategy

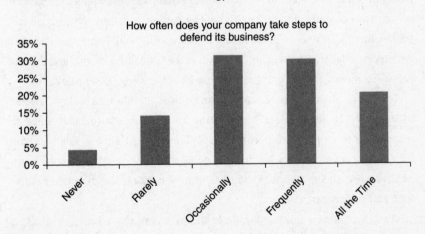

Source: Survey of 93 executive MBA students in the United States and Europe

Despite this, the new product never takes off; market share doesn't build and profits fail to materialize. Hellmann's salad dressings, for example, were a perfectly respectable line of products. Torengos was a very tasty tortilla chip, and Air Australia was a fine airline. All of them failed.

One of the key reasons new products fail is that the established players defend; they take action to make life difficult for the new entrant, and in doing so, they substantially contribute to the new product's demise. Many new products don't fail on their own merits; they are killed off by competitors mounting strong defensive campaigns.

THE INVISIBLE STRATEGY

Defensive strategy is an odd topic in the business world because it is rarely discussed. People talk about innovation all the time; stores are full of books on ways to be more creative and think up new ideas. People also discuss advertising strategy, social media campaigns, promotions, and public relations efforts. But defense? Well, defense just isn't mentioned very much.

I teach marketing strategy at Northwestern University's Kellogg School of Management. Every year, dozens of business leaders speak on campus, addressing a wide range of topics. One typical spring day I took the time to count up all the different events advertised with signs and flyers in Kellogg's main building, Jacobs Hall. I counted 26 different programs covering a wide range of topics, from new product strategy to raising cash for startups to developing strategies for using Facebook and Twitter. The CEO of Habitat for Humanity was giving a talk on "Building a Business, Constructing a Community, Following your Passion." An expert on Japan was speaking on "Japan in the Globalized World," and the vice president of marketing at golf giant Titleist was discussing "Laser Marketing."

Curiously, however, there wasn't a single presentation on any topic related to defensive strategy. There was nothing about competitive intelligence or responding to competitive new products. There wasn't anyone talking about using intellectual property law to fight competition or about employing competitive game theory to anticipate likely moves or about creating competitive financial statements.

And this wasn't a unique day. Over the past year, the number of speakers at Kellogg talking about defensive strategy was precisely zero. The previous year was exactly the same; there wasn't a single person talking about the topic.

A review of the agendas for marketing conferences reveals the same thing; people simply don't discuss defense.

The bookshelves are similarly bare when it comes to this topic. While there are many books on advertising and innovation and growth, there are very few on defensive strategy. The first book that comes up in a search on Amazon is *Defensive Football Strategies*. This is followed by *Soccer Strategy: Defensive and Attacking Tactics* and then *Rightful Termination: Defensive Strategies for Hiring and Firing*. There really aren't many books that focus on how companies can protect their business from competitive attack—on how companies can fight back.

The issue isn't that companies don't defend. Companies defend all the time, and at many firms defensive spending makes up a significant share of the overall spending and activity. The curious point is that people don't talk about it.

So why isn't defense discussed? Why is it a hidden topic in the world of business strategy?

THE DARK ARTS OF DEFENSIVE STRATEGY

Defensive strategy is a rough business; most people just don't like to discuss it in public. The goal of defensive strategy is really quite simple: to ensure that your competitor struggles and, if all goes very well, fails. If a new competitor is trying to enter your market, you want to push that company back and protect your market share. If your competitor happens to encounter some financial troubles due to your defensive efforts and is forced to go out of business—well, so much the better. In the best case, the competitor goes away and you make off with its creative ideas, using its innovative thinking to grow your own business.

Anyone in a competitive market has to fight hard; you should do everything you possibly can to protect your business. As Apple CEO Tim Cook observed about fighting a competitive battle: "We'll use whatever weapons we have at our disposal."[6] Football coach Bill Walsh makes a similar point: "You use the resources and remedies that are available within the boundaries of the law."[7] McDonald's founder Ray Kroc famously declared, "If any of my competitors were drowning, I'd stick a hose in their mouth."[8] British Airways CEO Roy Watts summarized the situation with remarkable candor: "Competition is about eliminating competitors, not about competition. That is what business is about. It is about the elimination of competitors."[9] Marketing strategist Jack

Trout observed, "Business is about war. It's not about better people and better products."[10] This is tough stuff.

Business executives are very comfortable discussing their company's latest new product launch; everyone loves to hear about the next big innovation. Executives also like to talk about new branding campaigns and new advertising spots, the latest human resource policy, and the creative office design. Innovative Facebook and Twitter campaigns make similarly attractive topics. These concepts are upbeat and exciting.

Even cost-reduction projects are safe topics for executives; there is nothing wrong with talking about efforts to increase margins. It is sometimes controversial to discuss laying people off, of course, but if done with a certain amount of sensitivity and grace, most people recognize that a bit of "rightsizing" is appropriate and necessary.

Defensive strategy is completely different; it is a polarizing topic that people rarely mention. For fairly obvious reasons, executives are reluctant to discuss how they plan to drive their competitors into the dirt, steal their ideas, and push them out of the market. It feels combative and offensive and somehow wrong.

Many defense strategies are rather ethically and morally questionable. If the broad concept of defense is delicate, some of the specific tactics that companies employ can make the stomach turn. Companies routinely engage in aggressive corporate intelligence campaigns, copy competitive products, file suits to distract and delay new entrants, and hire away key executives. As CBS marketing veteran Steve Yanovsky explained, "It isn't intended to be sporting. It's intended to save your business."[11]

Indeed, the entire area of defensive strategy brings up some rather substantial ethical questions. Is it okay to spy on your competitor? Is it proper to simply copy someone else's work? Is it right to damage someone else's product or brand by planting seeds of doubt? These are all complicated questions that present themselves when defensive issues arise.

Because the answers to these questions can be difficult, defensive strategy is rarely discussed by business leaders. The topic isn't elegant and it isn't inspirational. It isn't even clear if a good defense makes the world a better place; one could argue that preserving a business is critically important, and it certainly is. But people love entrepreneurs, and the idea that as an established player you're trying to stomp on innovative new competitors makes the idea of defense a more questionable proposition.

WHAT ABOUT THE LEGAL IMPLICATIONS?

Legal issues can often be particularly delicate when it comes to defensive strategy. While virtually everyone agrees that competition is healthy and good (and it is very reasonable that a company fights to win and keep customers), defensive strategy quickly gets into very complicated and sensitive legal terrain.

Many countries around the world have rules governing anticompetitive behavior. The theory is that society benefits from open competition but not from monopoly markets where competition is limited and one or two big players control the industry. Companies are routinely taken to court for anticompetitive behavior, and when they are found guilty, the punishment can be serious indeed.

Computer chip giant Intel, for example, was fined $1.45 billion in the European Union in 2009 for its efforts to limit competition—that is, essentially for efforts to defend its business. The European Union's top antitrust regulator, Neelie Kroes, stated at the time, "Intel has harmed millions of European consumers by deliberately acting to keep competitors out of the market for computer chips for many years. If we smell that there is something rotten in the state, we will act."[12]

The problem is that there are relatively few clear rules when it comes to defensive strategy. It isn't always obvious what is proper and what isn't. Competition is good, and almost everyone would agree that trying to hang on to your customers is a noble task. So when does defensive strategy cross the line? It's hard to know. Debating this point keeps lawyers busy and prosperous.

Since the world of legal affairs is gray and full of uncertainty, defensive strategy gets little attention. It is easier to ignore defensive strategy when in the public eye and focus on the more cheery and safer subjects of growth strategy and innovation. When statements related to defense can be quickly twisted to suggest a nefarious intent, executives avoid commenting at all.

The fact that defense is rarely discussed doesn't mean that it isn't an important part of business strategy. Indeed, defense is perhaps the most important strategy there is; protecting an existing business should be the top priority of a corporate leader.

USING THIS BOOK

Smart defensive strategy is incredibly powerful. A well-crafted defensive effort can push back a competitor and strengthen your business. This is a book about how tough, strategic companies defend. If you're a business leader, this book will show you how to protect your business in the face of tough competition. We'll highlight why defense is so important and then provide frameworks and ideas that will help you understand, assess, and react to competitive threats.

This book is primarily for people leading organizations, whether they're heading a company, managing a brand, or running a restaurant. The book applies to big companies and small companies, to for-profit and not-for-profit organizations. It doesn't matter whether you're running a plumbing business, promoting a brand of deodorant, operating a neighborhood café, or leading a small charitable organization or church. Anyone responsible for or involved in managing an enterprise has to think about defense because the world is full of competition, and with the rise of globalization competition in many categories will only increase. Defensive strategy is more important than ever.

The biggest defensive situations involve new product introductions; these are the moves that pose the most significant long-term threat to your company or brand. Because defending against new product launches can often pose some of the biggest challenges in business, this aspect of defensive strategy is the primary focus of this book.

This book is also useful for innovators, because it provides insight into what the established players are likely to do. Before introducing a new product, it is important to analyze the competition and consider how the established companies will respond to the launch and defend their business. It is important to think about what this defensive effort means for the new product introduction, then revise your launch plan accordingly. It's like a chess game: your job is to anticipate the next move of your competitor and then make sure your plan addresses that likely move—and the next move after that. Launching a new venture without thinking about how the established players will respond is naïve; you're assuming you're living in your own world, playing your own hand. This just isn't the case for most new products; existing players will see your launch and will likely respond. You must anticipate the defense and then develop a plan to overcome it or at least to survive as the defensive effort unfolds.

The book starts by reviewing why defensive strategy matters so much (chapter 2) and then looks at the financial challenge of defending (chapter 3). The next two chapters focus on learning about competitors and consider information needs (chapter 4) and competitive intelligence or ways to locate and work with information about competitors (chapter 5). The key question, whether to defend or not, is covered in the following chapter (chapter 6).

The next section focuses on developing a defense plan. It starts with planning the defense (chapter 7), then covers specific ways to defend (chapters 8 through 12). The following chapter highlights the importance of thinking about defense all the time (chapter 13). The focus then shifts to what all this means for innovators, people launching new products (chapter 14); that chapter highlights the challenges and explains how innovators should think about and deal with defensive efforts.

Stephen Calkins wrote the final chapter, which looks at the important topic of competition or antitrust law (chapter 15). He is professor of law at Wayne State University and a member of the Competition Authority of Ireland, and was formerly general counsel to the United States Federal Trade Commission and of counsel to the global law firm Covington & Burling, but he wrote this chapter in his capacity as an individual. Full disclosure: he is also my brother.

Chapter 2

THE THREAT

THERE IS NOTHING MORE IMPORTANT than protecting a profitable business; defending your brand must be your top priority as a manager. People love growth; they love finding new revenue and profit. But growth is priority number two. Focusing on new opportunities without defending the base puts an enterprise at serious risk.

A SAD BUSINESS STORY

The depressing story of Blockbuster video stores highlights why defensive strategy matters so much.

Computer programmer David Cook created Blockbuster in 1985. He noticed that people were generally unhappy with the existing movie rental options and developed a new video store concept that featured a large selection of titles and a computerized inventory tracking system.

Blockbuster quickly caught on; the business attracted and retained thousands of customers as it became the dominant force in the video rental industry in the United States. The Blockbuster management team added hundreds of locations in a bid to saturate the market, driving further growth. In 1994, less than 10 years after Blockbuster's introduction, Viacom acquired the chain for $8.4 billion, later spinning off the division as the growth continued. By 2004, Blockbuster had 48 million member accounts,[1] and in 2006 the chain had 8,360 stores and revenues of over $5.5 billion. The company had gross profits of $3 billion and a net income of over $50 million.[2] Blockbuster was an incredible success story.

Unfortunately, Blockbuster was slow to recognize the changes in the competitive landscape. In particular, Blockbuster failed to defend against the launch of two new competitors, Netflix and Redbox.

Reed Hastings created Netflix in 1997. The company focused on renting consumer DVDs and shipping them by mail. By doing this, Netflix didn't need to have physical stores located all around the country; this translated into dramatically lower operating costs than Blockbuster had as well as lower inventory expense. Netflix also developed an innovative pricing model. Instead of asking consumers to pay for each movie, Netflix charged a monthly subscription fee of $19.95. For this fee, consumers could rent three DVDs at any one time. When they were done with a DVD, they simply mailed it back and received another. This system eliminated late fees; Netflix customers could keep the movies as long as they liked. By contrast, Blockbuster relied heavily on late fees to build profits, much to the frustration of Blockbuster customers.

A few years later, the McDonald's Corporation funded Redbox. The new company focused on renting DVDs through free-standing automated kiosks, with the first Redbox outlets installed in McDonald's locations. The company later expanded to other sites. By using kiosks, Redbox was able to dramatically reduce operating expenses compared to Blockbuster. Redbox provided a more limited selection of movies, but the kiosks were very convenient for consumers and exceptionally economical: each movie rental was just 99 cents.

In the early 2000s, Blockbuster studied both Netflix and Redbox but dismissed the threats as inconsequential. Indeed, Blockbuster apparently had an opportunity to buy both companies and elected not to. Instead, Blockbuster focused on growing revenues and profits in its existing business.

Unfortunately for Blockbuster, both Netflix and Redbox caught on with consumers. Some movie watchers loved the variety and convenience of Netflix. Others loved the speed and economy of Redbox. By 2010 Netflix had annual revenues of $2.16 billion and pretax income of $269 million. Redbox had more than 26,000 kiosks nationwide, with revenues of $1.16 billion and operating profit of $193 million.

Things quickly unraveled for Blockbuster. As the growth of Netflix and Redbox became apparent, Blockbuster tried to defend, but efforts were too little, too late. The company created an online DVD rental service in 2004 similar to the one Netflix had and invested more than $500 million in the effort.[3] In 2008 the company launched a line of kiosks similar those operated by Redbox. But Blockbuster was far behind both companies; it had a struggling core business and two late and underresourced new products.

Blockbuster filed for bankruptcy in 2011. Its founder David Cook observed sadly, "It didn't have to be this way. They let technology eat them up."[4]

UNDER ATTACK

The moral of the Blockbuster story is quite clear. Be careful. If you are lucky enough to have a strong and profitable business, other people will want to get a part of it. Competition might not appear right away, but eventually people will notice your success and try to enter your market. As Mars vice president of marketing John Anton observed, "If things are going really well, somebody will try to copy you."[5]

The better your business, the more likely you will attract competition. As Intel CEO Andy Grove correctly noted, "The more successful you are, the more people want a chunk of your business and then another chunk and then another until there is nothing left."[6] One of the few good things about working in a difficult, low-margin business is that you don't have to worry too much about defense; people don't generally spend a lot of time trying to break into an industry that is not very profitable. You don't see a lot of new entrants in the world of salt or margarine, which are tough, low-margin categories.

The world is full of people thinking about new ideas and trying to develop successful new products. Large companies staff new product development departments solely focused on finding growth and expansion opportunities. Individuals dream up the next big thing, hoping to strike it rich. The classic image of an entrepreneur working from her dining room table to dream up the next great invention is not far from the truth; every year at Kellogg I meet with dozens of students pursuing entrepreneurial ventures while attending classes. Many of the ideas are terrible, of course, but a certain number are compelling. Marketing professor Phil Kotler notes, "There is a never-ending stream of new companies arising to serve markets in new ways. When patterns seemed set in the airline industry, along came Richard Branson with his

Virgin Atlantic Airlines and Herb Kelleher with Southwest. When patterns seemed set in the furniture retailing industry, along came Ingvard Kamprad and Ikea."[7]

The statistics for new product entries are staggering; every year, there are more than 150,000 new products.[8] That is a remarkable number of new ideas and new market entrants. As Ilya Gutlin, vice president of airport solutions at aerospace giant SITA, observes, "People are trying to get into your industry all the time."[9]

People launch new products because the financial rewards can be huge. There are just a few ways to legally make a fortune in the world. You can inherit vast wealth; you can win the lottery; you can become a rock star or a world-class athlete—or you can launch a successful new product.

This is how many of the world's wealthiest people made their money. Bill Gates, the second wealthiest person in the world according to *Forbes*' 2011 list, created Microsoft. Larry Ellison, number five on the list, created Oracle, and Lakshmi Mittal, number six, created steel company ArcelorMittal. The others on the list, such as Carlos Slim and Warren Buffet, made their money by investing, often in new ventures.[10]

With this sort of financial incentive, people work hard. They dream, they develop, and they imagine, and in most cases they are focused on established, profitable product categories.

This situation isn't likely to change any time soon; as long as people want to get rich, they will look for new products and innovative ideas. Indeed, it doesn't really matter how the global economy performs; when times are good, people innovate, buoyed by a ready supply of investment funds. When times are bad, people innovate, too, partly because the alternatives aren't very compelling. If you don't have a job, the opportunity cost of spending a couple years on a new product is modest indeed.

If anything, the level of competition is only going to increase as global technology and communication improve and transportation costs fall. Today, a company may find itself facing competitors from all around the world. Even just 20 years ago, the biggest competitive threats for most companies were local. Today, a competitor can arrive from halfway around the world in an instant. As marketing consultant Jack Trout points out, "The wars are escalating and breaking out in every part of the globe. Everyone is after everyone's business everywhere."[11]

NEW PRODUCT SUCCESS

Take a look at exhibit 2.1. What do all these brands have in common?

There are several things that connect all these brands, or at least many of them. All are successful and profitable. They have high brand recognition and are generally well regarded. Many of the companies are global, but not all. Many are consumer companies, but not all.

One key thing that connects all these companies is that they were late entrants to their respective industries. They were not the first player; there was someone in the market before they arrived. People were delivering packages before Fred Smith started FedEx, and people were wearing sneakers before Phil Knight started Nike. There were hardware stores before Home Depot and European airlines before Ryan Air.

All of these brands found a way to break into an existing industry. They were innovative companies, certainly, but they didn't launch completely new products and services. They didn't create new categories. They found a way to succeed in an industry that was already in place.

This means that for all these brands, the existing players in the industry failed to stop them. The established players didn't defend successfully. The companies that were in place, serving customers and making sales, were unable to block these new entrants. British Airways couldn't stop Ryan Air. Pampers couldn't stop Huggies. Zocor couldn't stop Lipitor. General Motors, Ford, and

Exhibit 2.1   Successful new businesses

Acuvue	Lululemon
Apple	Nike
ArcelorMittal	Pepsi
Cirque du Soleil	Petco
Crest	Ryan Air
Dyson	Stouffers
FedEx	Toyota
Home Depot	Virgin
Honda	Wal-Mart
Huggies	Whole Foods
Lipitor	Zara

Chrysler together couldn't stop Toyota and Honda. The existing players either chose not to defend or were unable to do so successfully.

The reason to learn about defensive strategy is to ensure that this doesn't happen to you and your business.

THE ECONOMICS OF DEFENSE

New entrants can cause significant financial damage to an established company. For this reason, there is an enormous economic incentive to defend. When companies cede market share to new entrants, the financial hit is often startlingly big. Even a small reduction in market share can lead to a meaningful reduction in revenue and, in turn, a serious decline in profit. Understanding this dynamic is critical to appreciating the importance of a strong defense.

Two things make this financial hit particularly significant. First, fixed costs are not likely to change significantly when a new competitor appears; a company doesn't usually move to a smaller building, significantly cut corporate overhead, or close production facilities if a new entrant manages to gain a small portion of a market. As a result, each lost sale translates into a bottom-line hit since the fixed costs don't decline with sales volume.

Second, the financial impact isn't a onetime event; if the new entrant is successful at gaining a foothold in the market, the volume losses will continue for many years. There will be a profit hit in year one, certainly, but there will also be a profit hit in years two and three, and this decline will continue into the future. Financially, defensive situations need to be evaluated as perpetuities since the financial pain will go on for years to come. Indeed, things might actually get worse over time. Once a new competitor is established in a category, it will, of course, seek to grow. This growth will lead to further investment and growth, as the competitor invests in the business.

The financial risk of a new entrant is much larger than it initially appears, and this leads to one of the great pitfalls in business: established companies often underestimate a competitive threat.

Consider oatmeal. This is a large, established category in the United States. Total retail sales were about $900 million in 2009, and the category leader was PepsiCo's Quaker Oats with retail sales of about $500 million, or a market share of about 55 percent. We can make a few rough assumptions and create an income statement for the business quite easily; let's assume Quaker Oats has

Exhibit 2.2   Quaker Oatmeal estimated P&L

Retail sales	$500 million
Quaker revenue	350
Cost of goods sold	140
Variable margin	210
Advertising	30
Trade spending	40
Consumer promotions	20
Market research	5
Overhead	30
Operating profit	85

revenues of about $350 million (retailers take about a 30 percent margin) and operating profit of $85 million, or a 24 percent operating margin. It is a nice, profitable business (see exhibit 2.2).

Imagine that one day a new entrant called Evanston Oatmeal appears, attempting to enter the oatmeal category. This new competitor has a good product and ample financial backing. The new entrant will spend heavily on advertising, consumer promotions, and in-store merchandising. Analysts anticipate that Evanston Oatmeal will capture 10 percent of the oatmeal category.

What is the financial risk to Quaker?

On first glance, the new entrant appears to be a fairly modest threat. With a few reasonable assumptions, we can quantify the threat. Let's assume a few things:

- The new entrant ends up with the projected market share of 10 percent.
- All of the sales come from market share gains, with no significant impact on the size of the total oatmeal category. This is a reasonable assumption; people aren't likely to eat more oatmeal simply because there is another oatmeal brand on the market.
- Quaker loses proportionately or at a "fair-share" rate. So Quaker loses 10 percent of its sales. One could argue Quaker might lose more, since it is a branded product like the new entrant as opposed to a low-price brand. But one could also argue Quaker will lose less since it is a strong brand and presumably has loyal customers.

With these assumptions, it is then easy to calculate the financial hit to Quaker by simply looking at lost unit sales and marginal profit. Quaker will see sales decline by 10 percent, or $35 million, and with a 24 percent operating margin, the total financial risk is $8.4 million. This is a big number, certainly, but not alarming.

Based on the risk calculation above, Quaker could spend up to $8.4 million to defend the business. Put another way, it would make financial sense for Quaker to spend up to $8.4 million in the defensive effort, assuming that the spending would eliminate the competitor.

But the loss to Quaker is actually much greater than this. Indeed, the $8.4 million is a deceptively small number; it doesn't come close to representing the actual risk. There are several factors the simple calculation above does not address.

One issue is that the profit loss will be much greater than calculated due to fixed costs. Using operating profit margin in the calculation assumes that fixed costs, such as overhead and marketing spending, will fall as revenue declines. So if revenues decline by 10 percent, then marketing spending and overhead will follow along accordingly. This is a faulty assumption for two reasons. First, it isn't likely that the introduction of a competitor will result in lower overhead costs; these are largely unrelated events. Second, Quaker shouldn't cut marketing spending now that it has a new competitor to deal with. Strategically speaking, cutting spending at the moment that a new competitor shows up would be exactly the wrong move for Quaker. Instead, Quaker will need to increase marketing spending given the new competition.

To better consider the financial risk, then, it is best to use the variable profit margin, not the operating profit per unit. Using variable profit captures the full impact of the volume loss with the assumption that overhead and marketing spending remain fixed. Making this small shift substantially increases the financial risk; it goes from $8.4 million to $21.0 million (see exhibit 2.3).

This updated risk calculation is certainly more accurate. But this calculation still significantly understates the risk. A key problem is that the calculation reflects just one year. If Evanston Oatmeal is able to enter the market, the loss isn't just a one-year issue. The losses will continue to compound year after year. Looking at just one year is the wrong way to think about situation.

Exhibit 2.3   Quaker Oatmeal risk

	Original Calculation	*Updated Calculation*
Quaker revenue	$350 million	$350 million
Loss to competitor	10%	10%
Revenue loss	$35 million	$35 million
Margin	24%	60%
Profit impact	$8.4 million	$21.0 million

To fully capture the risk, then, it is essential to quantify the long-term impact. In essence, the risk should be treated as a stream of losses, stretching out into the future. The correct way to value a stream of payments it to do a net present value calculation, discounting the future sums back, taking into account the cost of money. If we assume a discount rate of 5 percent, then the risk dramatically expands from $21 million to *$420 million* ($21 million divided by the 5 percent discount rate).

Yet, even this extraordinary number doesn't fully capture the potential losses. Once the new entrant is established, for example, it will try to grow by stealing more market share. If it is successful, Quaker will suffer further losses, and with more competition, Quaker might find it difficult to increase prices or reduce costs, creating further financial issues.

The potential losses are staggering. Quite simply, Quaker has an enormous incentive to defend against Evanston Oatmeal. This isn't an $8.5 million problem; it is a problem substantially bigger than $420 million. To be sure, we could adjust the risk to factor in the odds of success. After all, it isn't certain that Evanston Oatmeal will be successful. When we do, the total falls somewhat; if we assume the odds of Evanston Oatmeal succeeding are 50 percent, then the adjusted risk drops from $420 million to $210 million. Either way, the number is huge; Evanston Oatmeal is a tremendous threat to Quaker's profitability.

This is almost always the case for established brands; losing a small amount of share to a new entrant can result in a major financial hit. The math isn't complicated, but it is compelling.

In this particular case, and in many situations involving new products, Quaker has a much larger financial incentive than the new company; the volume lost to a new entrant by the established company is worth more than the new entrant's gain.

If we look at the new entrant's financials, the picture is likely to be quite mixed. Before the new entrant can even get started, it will have to secure placement in grocery stores, and this is likely to cost at least $1 million per item in slotting funds (payments to retailers). If the product line includes six items, then the amount rises to $6 million. In addition, to support the business launch, the new entrant will have to invest significantly in advertising (perhaps $20 million) and consumer and trade promotions (perhaps each to the tune of $10 million). That's $46 million in initial investment.

So if the new entrant is able to capture 10 percent of the oatmeal market as projected, the financial picture looks quite grim indeed; the company will lose $13 million in year one if we assume it has a cost structure similar to that of Quaker Oats, and this calculation ignores any fixed costs, such as sales and legal expenses.

This grim picture isn't unusual; new products always require significant spending in the early years. The logic, of course, is that later on spending can be scaled back while still maintaining market share, so profits will appear in year two and grow in year three.

In total, then, the new product is profitable over time as the initial losses are offset by subsequent gains. If we again employ a 5 percent discount rate and assume the business stabilizes at the profit levels of year three, then the new business has a financial value of $275 million.

Exhibit 2.4   Evanston Oatmeal years 1–3 P&L

Market share	10%	10%	10%
Retail sales (million)	$90	$90	$90
Evanston Oatmeal revenue	63	63	63
Cost of goods sold	25	25	25
Variable margin	38	38	38
Advertising	20	15	7
Trade and consumer promotions	20	16	12
Slotting fees	6	–	–
Market research	5	3	3
Overhead	–	–	–
Operating profit	−13	4	16

The new product launch, however, is worth much less than the losses incurred by the established business. The established business is looking at a financial hit of at least $420 million, but the new business is worth only $275. From a financial perspective, the established player has a very significant incentive to defend and can spend much more money defending than the new entrant can spend trying to succeed.

The financials highlight two important points. First, established players should take competitive threats seriously. Responding to and limiting the damage that competitors cause is an exceptionally important task; the downside is enormous even if a competitor can only steal a small market share.

Second, defenders can and usually should financially overwhelm new entrants. A company defending its business can spend far more than a new entrant funding the launch. The financial advantage goes to the defender.

THE MOTIVATION GAP

As we've seen, in many cases the established player has more to lose than the new competitor stands to gain. In theory, this means that the defensive effort should outweigh the attack and the new competitor should face a difficult fight indeed.

This doesn't always translate into action, however, since the two companies are looking at very different situations in terms of motivation. People launching a new product have a huge incentive to succeed, while the people in the established business often have much less motivation to defend.

A new entrant is frequently led by entrepreneurs who started the company and invested their own time and money. These entrepreneurs have a significant stake in the outcome of the venture; if things go well, they stand to make enormous amounts of money. Conversely, if the venture goes poorly, the individuals might lose everything they have invested, financially and otherwise.

Even in a big company, the individuals leading a new product effort have a huge incentive. If the new product succeeds, they will be regarded as heroes, and their careers and bonuses will be enhanced. If the new product flops, they will have to deal with the sometimes unpleasant consequences. They may not lose their own funds, but they may lose their jobs or at least a portion of their bonuses.

Established players, on the other hand, are not quite so motivated when it comes to defending, so they often don't respond to threats with urgency.

Defenders most likely have a comfortable job running a solid business with good sales and profits. The team is big, ownership of decisions is diffused, and while the financial results matter, they do so only to a certain degree. These executives are, of course, motivated by profit results, but they are not likely to be fired up by one year's performance. In a big business, losing $5 million in profit to a new entrant would be an issue but only a fairly minor one in the grand scheme of the business.

This creates a huge motivation gap. Defenders should be highly motivated given the extraordinary risk they face, but they often aren't. Entrepreneurs, on the other hand, are exceptionally motivated.

There is a fundamental misalignment between motivation and financial reality. The new entrant is usually much more motivated than the established player, despite the fact that the established player has a greater financial incentive. This disconnect creates an opportunity for an innovator and a risk for the defending company. Any company facing a competitive threat needs to be sensitive to this dynamic and create urgency where defense is concerned.

DEFENSE VERSUS GROWTH

Growth is important, but defense, especially of established and profitable brands, matters more. Focusing solely on growth and failing to defend is a very risky approach.

People love growth. Business leaders focus relentlessly on finding opportunities to increase revenues and profits. In a recent survey, the Conference Board, a global business research firm, asked CEOs to rank various business priorities. The top priority was, not surprisingly, business growth.[12] Procter & Gamble's CEO Bob McDonald succinctly captured the point in a recent interview, saying, "We've got to grow; that's the main thing."[13] Brad Kirk, CMO at Jergens, made a similar point in his book: "The first imperative of every organization is growth."[14]

It's clear why people focus on growth; that is what they have incentives to do. Investors are attracted to companies that gain value over time; this is how investors make money—buy low and sell high. The value of a company, in simple financial terms, is the present value of future cash flows. Logically enough, people running companies are *supposed* to focus on growth, increasing the cash flows and in turn building the value of the business. Simply maintaining profitability is rarely sufficient; managers don't get big bonuses for preserving the status quo. In some ways, running a highly profitable business is a particularly big challenge because the leadership team has to find ways to increase profits even more. As investor and *Financial Times* columnist Luke Johnson observed in a recent column, "An obvious truth dawned on me recently: all the really successful investments I've ever made have achieved great returns because the underlying companies enjoyed high growth."[15] He titled the column "There is Only One Way to be a Success."

And so managers focus on growth. They create new advertising campaigns, reduce costs, and develop innovative social media efforts, all designed to get more customers or to get current customers to buy more products and services. I recently reviewed the marketing team charter for a major telecom company. The document clearly spelled out that the team's mission was to enable the company to meet or exceed its annual goals.

The problem is that managers get so focused on growth that they neglect defense. I recently did a study with one of my research assistants looking at corporate annual reports. We analyzed the use of words, in particular the use of "growth" words versus "defense" words. The study included the 2010 10-K filings of the top 25 companies in the Fortune 500. When counting "growth" words we included terms such as *grow, growth, build, innovate, innovation, innovative,* and *increase.* To find "defense" words we looked for terms such as *maintain, defend, protect, preserve, defensive,* and *respond.*

The results were striking: growth words were used far more than defense words, by an 80–20 margin. Indeed, the top 25 companies used growth words 7,141 times in total, but defense words just 1,746 times. The most-used word was *increase,* with 4,867 occurrences. *Defend* was used just 155 times, and *defensive* was used just 21 times.

Emphasizing growth over defense is usually a mistake for a very simple reason: the downside risk. Every growth initiative carries some risk because it might not work, and it is a problem when it doesn't. An advertising campaign that fails to deliver the expected market returns is an issue. Revenue will fall below plan, and profits will likely suffer. You might need to cut spending to try to get back to the target. If things don't work out, profits may actually decline a bit, and you might not receive your full bonus.

Similarly, an unsuccessful new product launch is a setback for the organization. New products almost always require a major investment of time and money. A new product that fails is a disappointment and a financial setback. It is also discouraging for the team.

But in the big picture, the failure of a growth initiative isn't that big a deal. If the advertising isn't working, you can develop a new campaign that will work better or get a new advertising agency and start over entirely, and next year you will have a lower financial base to compare against, so you are positioned for success. If a new product fails...well, most new products fail, so it's really not much of a surprise. It was a long shot in any event. You can just get to work on the next idea. The downside risk of growth initiatives just isn't that big. In the worst case, you fail to grow and have to come up with something new for next year.

Defense is completely different because the downside is enormous. There is no room for error; if you fail to stop a competitive threat, you put the entire company at risk. Indeed, once a company lets a competitor into its market, it can quickly enter a "doom loop," where the existing business begins declining, forcing the team to scramble in a bid to prop up the core business, often while cutting spending in the process. This opens the door for the competitor to grow even more, thus increasing the problem and creating a downward spiral.

Simply stated, focusing on growth at the expense of defense is a dangerous approach. As marketing consultant Jack Trout noted, "The desire for growth is at the heart of what can go wrong for many companies."[16]

THE BEST DEFENSE IS THE BEST DEFENSE

You don't have to spend much time in strategy meetings before someone comes up with this bit of wisdom: a good offense is the best defense. The problem is that this just isn't true when it comes to defensive strategy. When you are being attacked, the best *defense* is the best defense.

Offensive strategy and defensive strategy are completely different. When you're playing offense, you're looking for ways to grow share, volume, and profit. When you're playing defense, you're focused on stopping a competitor. These are very different tasks.

A company trying to grow profits—playing offense—will look for smart, prudent moves. The company might try to enter an adjacent market, for example. Or the company might offer a slight discount to customers for purchasing a certain amount above and beyond customary order quantities. Marketing spending will be scrutinized to ensure that incremental spending is justified by the additional sales. People will study the return on investment.

A company playing defense will do very different things. The company will likely shelve the geographic expansion and focus on the core business. The firm will increase promotional offers and reward customers for loyalty and simply maintaining purchase rates. Spending will be much higher and more aggressive. The coupon in the Sunday paper might well be shockingly large, perhaps $1 instead of the usual 25 cents.

Defense is a distinct task; it is the job of addressing new competitors and fighting back. It's important not to confuse defense with growth; the goals are different and the approaches are different. Given the stakes, however, the defensive effort always matters most. Intel CEO Andy Grove understands this point: "I believe that the prime responsibility of a manager is to guard constantly against other people's attacks and to inculcate this guardian attitude in the people under his or her management."[17]

Defending the business is a leader's most important responsibility.

Chapter 3

THE FINANCIAL CHALLENGE

DEFENSIVE STRATEGY IS FUNDAMENTALLY A financial challenge. You know your competitor is trying to achieve some financial goal. Your challenge is to do everything in your power to ensure that this doesn't happen.

At the core, business is about financials; an organization has to make the numbers work if it is going to succeed. This is true in the for-profit world and in the not-for-profit world; ultimately, the enterprise has to find a way to generate cash and cover the bills, ideally with a bit left over at the end of the year.

The financials matter enormously when considering a defensive situation; the numbers shed light on the risk you face, and more important, the numbers provide an opportunity. If you can convince your competitors that attacking you is not a good financial idea, they will stop.

IT'S ALL ABOUT THE MONEY

Companies launch new products in order to make money; this is why people dream up new ideas and bring them to market. This seems like an obvious point, but it is critical to remember when you are in a defensive situation.

As we've already noted, there is a tremendous financial incentive to bringing big new ideas to market; a successful new product launch can lead to remarkable financial returns. If a new product had no hope of making money, people wouldn't launch it. As Bob Parsons, CEO of the web-hosting company Go Daddy, observes, "Let's face it. We're all in business to make money."[1]

This means that behind every new product is a set of numbers, a financial proposition supporting the idea. We know that the new product may not be profitable in year one, but in the long run the financials have to work. When asked recently about a potential new product idea, Reed Hasting, CEO of Netflix, commented truthfully, if somewhat sarcastically, "Well, we're inclined to do things that are profitable for us."[2]

The proposition isn't always a formal set of numbers, prepared in a business plan format. Many organizations develop formal propositions behind each new product launch, with a detailed set of financial projections justifying the financial commitment. Some of these documents can be 30, 40, or 50 pages long, filled with elaborate calculations and projections. But other companies skip this step, moving more on gut feelings and rough estimates jotted on a slip of paper.

Regardless of the format, however, there is a financial belief in the new venture, an expectation that financially things will work out well in the end for the new product, and that this will lead to profits.

This doesn't mean that every new product is expected to deliver the same financial returns. Some people are fine with very modest figures while others need to see quick and dramatic results. A proposition with a rate of return of 5 percent may not be very attractive for one company but could be highly attractive for another company. A pharmaceutical company, for example, will not be particularly fired up about a product with a 40 percent variable margin. But an office supply company might find that simply irresistible.

Timing can vary substantially. Some companies, especially public companies, have a relatively short time horizon; initiatives must pay off quickly to make sense. Taking a financial hit for many years is rarely a way to succeed in a public company where shareholders are pushing for immediate returns. Other companies take a much longer view, and losing money for five or even ten years might be acceptable if the long-term returns justify the investment.

More important, the particular new venture in question might be just one part of the big picture. Larger companies often have vast portfolios of products and businesses, and this can impact how they view a particular new product launch. A company may launch a new product to fill out a product portfolio; the new item might have little hope of ever making money, but the portfolio in total will benefit financially since the sales organization can now sell a more complete line of products. Alternatively, a new product launch might be designed to establish a presence in a particular market in the hope that this presence could then lead to the successful launch of another, more profitable product.

In the end, however, there is always a financial proposition at the core of every new product, a reason to launch it and invest in its development.

For someone defending a business, this insight leads to two very important questions.

QUESTION #1: WHAT DO THEY SEE?

If someone is entering your market, you know they have a set of numbers supporting the move. They see an opportunity to be successful and capture a portion of your market; this has to be true, otherwise they would not be launching the product. People don't do things for no reason, and successful business people don't do things that have no hope of making money.

Therefore, the question you should ask is this: What numbers are they looking at? Clearly, there is a financial rationale to the move. What is it? What do they see?

If the answer isn't readily apparent, you have to look again. There is some set of assumptions that makes the concept financially viable. So what does your competitor see that you don't? When someone is attacking your market, there's a very good chance that they see something you might have missed or overlooked. This might be a unique segment of customers or a different business model. People who enter a market from the outside bring a fresh perspective; it is quite possible that the new entrant identified an unmet need in the category or a broader trend that backs up its move.

By trying to understand a competitor's financial proposition, you may learn that they are onto something, perhaps a big and compelling opportunity. If you can identify what they're seeing, it could be great opportunity for you, too, since great ideas can come from anywhere.

If a competitor's launch makes no apparent sense, it usually means that you don't understand what's going on. People just don't make irrational moves, at least not frequently. At this point it is worth bringing in someone with an outside perspective to look at the situation and try to figure it out. Understanding what your competitor sees is essential in order to develop an appropriate and effective response.

QUESTION#2: HOW CAN WE DESTROY THEIR FINANCIALS?

The second question you must ask is just as critical: How can we destroy their financials? Since every new product is based on a financial proposition, the defensive challenge is clear: destroy the proposition. If you can ensure that the competitor's financials no longer work, then they will give up and stop attacking you. As Harvard professor Michael Porter observed, "If a new entrant is denied its targets and becomes convinced that it will be a long time until they are met, then it may withdraw or deescalate."[3] Paul Groundwater, vice president of marketing at Trane, the heating and cooling division of Ingersoll Rand, echoed the point: "You have to undermine their economics."[4]

There must be a reason for a company to invest time and money in a new venture. With a strong defensive effort, you can impact your competitor's financial situation. Eventually they might come to the realization that the new product isn't working, and they will then move on to something else. For example, British retailer Tesco attempted to enter the US grocery market in 2007. The effort was met with a stiff defense from US retailers. After losing an estimated £700 million ($1.1 billion), Tesco was forced to reevaluate the entire initiative. The question for executives at Tesco: would the new venture ever generate a positive financial return?[5]

More important, if you're trying to push back a competitor's new product by undermining its financial projections, remember that perceptions matter most. Financial propositions are based on assumptions about the future, and these assumptions are based on perceptions and forecasts. The defensive challenge is to convince the people responsible for the new product that the venture will not work.

It might be counterintuitive, but focusing on financial reality is not always the best approach. Ensuring your competitor delivers weak results is a good thing, of course. But weak results won't necessarily make the competitor go away; it could secure more financial backing and carry on. The real challenge is getting your competitor to *believe* that they won't or can't succeed at the venture. As long as they believe the financial proposition will work, they will keep going. Once they believe the financial proposition just isn't going to work out, they will stop.

Destroying a competitor's belief in its financial proposition seems like a rather daunting challenge, but it really isn't. Here's an example. Let's assume you're the only chimney sweep in a small mountain town with 3,000 homes. It happens to be a town where every home is required to get a chimney cleaning

Exhibit 3.1 Dusty Chimney Sweep initial financials

	Forecast
Total market size (homes per year)	3,000
Anticipated market share	25%
Sales per year (homes)	750
Price per job	$100
Revenue	$75,000
Truck lease	$15,000
Insurance	$10,000
Marketing	$20,000
Profit	$30,000

each year to prevent chimney fires and decrease the risk of forest fires. You hear that a new chimney sweep is planning to open up shop in your market. Let's call your new competitor Dusty Chimney Sweep. You know Dusty has just a few expenses. The company will be leasing a truck for $15,000 per year, and it has to carry insurance that costs $10,000 per year. You also know that your competitor will have to spend about $20,000 on marketing expenses, such as online ads and brochures. You've also learned through some small-town gossip that Dusty is planning on getting 25 percent of the market, or 750 homes per year, at a price of $100 per cleaning. This is $20 below your price.

Financially, then, your new competitor has a reasonably attractive proposition; he will make about $30,000 per year if things go well—a decent wage (see exhibit 3.1).

You have little interest in seeing a new competitor open up in town, so you want to convince Dusty to think about finding a different town on the other side of the mountain. What can you do?

The single best way to get him to give up is to damage his financial proposition. Probably the simplest approach is to cut your prices dramatically. If you cut your price from $120 to $80, you will create a very significant issue for Dusty. If he cuts his price in order to remain $20 below yours, he will presumably still gain market share, but he won't make any money. If he keeps his price at $100, he will get much less market share, perhaps just 10 percent. With a market share of 10 percent, he will lose money. Either way, your competitor now has a problem (see exhibit 3.2).

Exhibit 3.2   Dusty Chimney Sweep revised financials

	Initial Forecast	New Forecast A	New Forecast B
Total market size (homes per year)	3,000	3,000	3,000
Anticipated market share	25%	25%	10%
Sales per year (homes)	750	750	300
Price per job	$100	$60	$100
Revenue	$75,000	$45,000	$30,000
Truck lease	$15,000	$15,000	$15,000
Insurance	$10,000	$10,000	$10,000
Marketing	$20,000	$20,000	$20,000
Profit	$30,000	–	($15,000)

You could also increase your marketing dramatically. This will force Dusty to match your increase or plan on getting a smaller market share. In either scenario, his financial proposition weakens significantly.

Cutting your price or increasing your marketing spending are moves that will have a direct impact on Dusty. Perhaps these moves won't necessarily stop the launch entirely, but they will reduce its attractiveness.

This is exactly what the major airlines did to British carrier Laker Airways in the 1980s. Sir Freddie Laker founded his namesake airline in 1966. Laker was a small company for many years and focused on its charter business. The company began to expand during the 1970s and began regularly scheduled service. Laker was one of the first true discount airlines; it significantly undercut the fares of the established airlines, such as British Airways and Pan Am. In 1977 Laker started flying across the Atlantic, and in the early 1980s it announced plans to dramatically expand service further.

Concerned about the growth of Laker, executives at Pan Am took action and simply matched all of Laker's fares. Other established carriers followed, and prices fell across the industry. The impact was dramatic. As Freddie Laker remembers, "The ding-a-ling stopped ringing. The phones didn't ring. And our load factor dropped like a stone."[6]

As passenger counts declined, Laker began to lose money. Freddie Laker couldn't convince investors that the business would ever become financially viable. In 1982 the company filed for bankruptcy. A BBC documentary about

Laker concluded, "Laker Airways was murdered and chopped into little pieces."[7]

SLOWING THE FINANCIAL MOMENTUM

A defense plan doesn't have to completely destroy a competitor's financial proposition to be effective; simply weakening and slowing the new product provides an enormous benefit because it diminishes the new product's momentum.

Momentum is a powerful force in any endeavor, and this is especially true in the world of business and new products. When a new item gets off to a strong start, everything is positive. Revenues come in above plan, so variable profit is higher than expected. As a result, the team can increase spending, investing more in the launch while still delivering the same profit result (or, as is often the case for a new product, the same financial loss). The incremental spending might take the shape of more advertising, more promotional deals, or a more aggressive push into channels of distribution. All this incremental spending fuels additional sales and growth, which generates more cash that can be invested in the business. A very positive cycle then is set in motion, with each success leading to further success.

There is an important psychological aspect to this, too. When a new product has a strong start, people inside the organization get excited about it. This leads to positive buzz as people see the success materializing. The sales force then gets fired up about selling the new item, and the product development group is energized, focused on creating a follow-up success. The momentum builds and carries people along.

The reverse dynamic also occurs, however. Falling below plan can send a new product into the dreaded financial "doom loop." If the new product starts slowly, with disappointing initial sales, the financial picture will look worse than planned; with slow sales revenue, variable profit will be below plan, and the business will lose more money than expected. This will force the new products team to do one of two things: cut spending in order to deliver the planned profit or accept a lower profit figure. Both options are unappealing.

If the new products team decides to cut spending, for example, on advertising, promotional offers, and trial events, the new product can quickly lose momentum. Sales were soft even with the planned spending, so cutting the spending will slow sales even more, sending the product even further below plan, forcing yet another round of cuts. This can lead to a spiral, where further cuts in spending lead to weak results and then further cuts in spending and weaker results. Momentum slows and sales decrease. Eventually the business loses steam.

On the other hand, if the new products team decides to reduce the financial targets in year one, then the project is off to a weak start. It is tempting to just push the profits off into the future, concluding that profit will be bigger than planned in year three, thereby offsetting the miss in year one and protecting the overall project returns. But this logic doesn't really work and a sharp financial manager will question the move, asking why year three returns will be higher than expected when year one returns are lower. Projecting a dramatic increase in profits far in the future is always a red flag when looking at new product opportunities. Indeed, if a product gets off to a slow start in year one, it is likely to miss plan in year two and year three as well.

If the team simply reduces financial targets, perhaps concluding that year one results will be worse than planned, then the overall financial attractiveness of the proposition diminishes. If the company was counting on a 15 percent rate of return, and the new product now falls to an 11 percent rate of return, then the appeal of the entire venture weakens. At some point, if the return declines enough, the company will have to recognize that the proposition simply doesn't make sense and should be shelved.

Poor results can create a psychological problem, too. People get discouraged and focus on other things. The sales team pushes other, more promising products. People start pointing fingers, trying to pin the failure on someone else to protect their career prospects.

If you are defending your business and market share, the implication is clear: failing to defend increases the risk that the new product will be able to set up a positive momentum cycle, leading to increased investment over time and a growing problem. This is a scary proposition. Defending, however, can put pressure on the new product's financials and force your attacker to reassess the venture. A good defensive effort can reverse the momentum and turn it in your favor.

The key point: a defense effort doesn't need to completely destroy the attacker to be effective. Simply slowing the launch can provide an enormous benefit and diminish a competitive threat.

THINK ABOUT THE NUMBERS FIRST

It is hard to overemphasize the importance of financials for defensive strategy because ultimately your attacker will succeed or fail based on how the numbers work out.

For this reason, it is critical to start with the numbers when considering a defensive situation. You have to understand what your attackers see and then identify ways to impact their financial situation.

Chapter 4

KNOW YOUR ENEMY

GOOD DEFENSIVE STRATEGY IS GROUNDED in information. Before you can properly react to a competitive move, you have to understand it and determine what it means to you. A military general needs information to develop a battle plan, and a business leader needs information to assemble a defense plan. As Willie Pietersen, former CEO of Tropicana, observed, "In every competitive arena, including business, you must know your enemies in order to defeat them."[1]

What isn't obvious is exactly how much information you really need to create an effective defense plan. There are the basics, of course—the what, when, and where. But there are many other critical pieces of information to identify and gather; the list is long and varied. To truly understand a competitive situation you need to dig deep.

START WITH THE BASICS

There are a few things that immediately come to mind when considering a competitive move. Many of these are obvious. What is this threat, anyway? When will it appear? Who will be making this competitive move? If you take the time to analyze and answer the basic questions, then you can get an initial feel for the situation.

WHAT'S THE REAL THREAT?

Competitors can make all sorts of different moves, so the initial step is to figure out precisely what you are facing. Is this a new product launch? If so, what sort of a new product is it? Or is this a new marketing push on an existing product? Again, what is this initiative about? This initial scoping is where everything begins.

Fleshing out the reality of the situation is often not as easy as it seems. A competitive threat may appear as just a rumor. A salesperson might report that a customer saw a prototype from a new competitor, or a supplier might tell you that someone contacted her about securing material for a new production line. It is sometimes clear that a competitor is working on a new product but not at all clear what that product is. Indeed, you can be certain competitors are always working on something, but knowing what that something is may not be easy.

Understanding what a competitor is thinking about is most difficult early in the development process, when the company itself might not even know. A year before a product hits the market, the new product development group might still be figuring out all the details, and it will be difficult to nail down precisely what their plans might be.

TIMING IS EVERYTHING

Timing is a particularly critical issue. When will this threat materialize? It's hard to formulate a defense without knowing the answer to this question. The defense plan for a product launching in June will be very different from the defense plan for a product launching in December. But timing is often more complex than it seems. On the surface, timing is a direct question: when is the hotel opening? When is the product available for sale? But things are rarely this simple because there are critical timing milestones before and after the launch, and you can interrupt a product's success at any stage of the game.

For a product in development, the critical information is *where* the competitor is in the development process. Is the competitor just considering the new product idea? Or is the product in testing? Has the competitor invested any capital yet? When is the go/no go decision date?

After a product launches, timing is still important. When are the key milestones? Is this just the first phase of a multiphased launch? What are the key dates for deciding on the expansion?

Every new product has a certain pacing in terms of launch timing, and this matters too. How is the competitor planning to stage the introduction? Is the spending concentrated early on, to quickly build awareness and start trial in order to drive significant sales quickly? Or is the launch slower, with spending spread over time with a slower sales buildup? This is an important question because it has an impact on how defense money should be spent; defensive money spent too early will fail to block the launch plan while defensive money spent too late might be miss the critical window—the moment of opportunity.

I recently worked with a company based in an African country that was formulating a defense plan against a new market entrant. The competitor was definitely on the way; this was quite certain because my client could see that the competitor was constructing a new factory. But the timing of the launch wasn't at all clear. Would the competitor start selling the product in March? Or would the competitor wait until September? This lack of clarity was a major obstacle in formulating a defense plan; it was clear that a defense would be critical, but it wasn't clear when that defense should hit the market.

WHERE WILL THE LAUNCH OCCUR?

Understanding the geography of a launch, the "where," is another important question. Where is the product appearing?

There are three basic ways to introduce a new product in terms of geography. One option is to begin in a narrow geographic region, perhaps a single city or town. A company introducing a new product in Germany, for example, might decide to just launch in Berlin or a smaller city like Koblenz. Another option is to go national and cover the entire country at the same time. A final option is to go global and reach multiple countries at the same time.

For the company launching the new product, there are pros and cons to each of these options, of course. The basic trade-off is risk and reward: the larger the launch, the larger the opportunity and the greater the risk. When you're the defender, the geography question is essential; you have to fight where the battle is being fought and capitalize on opportunities. A small launch requires a very different response than a larger national or global launch.

WHAT'S THE PRODUCT'S POSITIONING?

Positioning is the heart of marketing strategy, so understanding a competitor's positioning is essential when you need to defend against a new product launch.

Positioning defines how a product or service competes. This is a core question for any company; a basic lesson in marketing is that you can't be all things to all people. It is essential to stand for something in particular. Trying to make everyone happy with the same product or service will almost always produce an unsatisfactory outcome; you will make everyone just a little bit happy. But this is a very dangerous position, because competitors can delight particular groups of customers and leave you without a sustainable business.

Anyone being attacked by another company should ask a very simple question: What is my competitor's intended positioning?

In almost all cases, a product or service will have a defined positioning. It might not be written out in the classic format that the marketing professors teach at Kellogg or Harvard, but the company presumably has an idea of who the product or service is for and how it will differentiate itself from competing products. While companies use different formats to in their positioning, there are usually four very important elements: target, frame of reference, primary benefit, and key attributes.

The *target* is the ideal customer: Who is the brand for? Most important, the target isn't everyone who will buy a brand; it is the ideal customer, the core group.

The *frame of reference* defines the competitive set. The frame explains what a product actually is in terms of its competitors' offerings. This part of positioning is often overlooked, but it is a critical question.

The *primary benefit* is the heart of a positioning statement. This is the most important reason for the target to buy the product. The key thing to remember when considering primary benefits is that there should be just one; a brand can't be many things.

The *key attribute* provides a reason to believe the primary benefit; it is a support point. While there is usually one primary benefit, there may be several key attributes supporting the benefit. Very often a key attribute is a particular figure, perhaps "30 percent more effective" than competing products or "18 percent fewer side effects."

Positioning can be summarized in a positioning statement, a short sentence that summarizes the four key questions (see exhibit 4.1).

The Schick Quattro, a men's razor with four blades, might have the following positioning: *To men who want the very best in their lives, Schick Quattro is the brand of razor that provides the closest shave because the Schick Quattro is the only razor with four blades.*

Exhibit 4.1   Positioning statement

To (target), X is the brand of (frame of reference) that (primary benefit) because (key attribute).

Positioning matters because it has a huge impact on a product or service. For example, a car positioned as the fastest sports car will likely have a high price and all of the marketing communications will reinforce the idea of speed. Similarly, a product positioned as environmentally friendly will likely have a low carbon footprint and be recyclable with green packaging.

In a defensive situation, understanding each part of your competitor's positioning is critical. The target is exceptionally important because this defines the battlefield. Who is the competitor trying to reach? Is it environmentally concerned young adults? Is it wealthy retired people? This has big implications; if a competitor is pursuing your customers, then the risk is of course very high. Alternatively, if a competitor is going after a very different target group, the risk is seemingly lower.

The frame of reference is also important, because this defines the playing field and sheds light on the competitor's thinking. A frame that overlaps with your frame suggests a direct attack. A different frame might indicate the competitor is pursuing a different market or looking at the industry in a very different way.

The primary benefit and key attributes are also important; these define the competitor's proposition. If you know how your competitor will be promoting its product, then you have an opportunity to counterattack it with your own marketing efforts.

Positioning is in many ways the heart of every new product; thus, it is very difficult to evaluate and respond to a competitive attack without understanding the positioning of the competing product.

UNDERSTANDING THE 4 PS

One of the core marketing frameworks is the four Ps — the four things to address when marketing any product or service. The four Ps are *product* (the actual product or service offered), *pricing* (the total cost to customers), *place* (the distribution channel), and *promotion* (the advertising and sales effort). For any product, the four Ps should be consistent with the positioning: each part should reinforce the product's core value proposition. Understanding each of the four Ps is essential when considering a defensive effort.

PRODUCT

The first P, product, is a basic and somewhat obvious area for investigation. What is the new product, anyway? What does it do? What is it made of? What are the product specifications? How well does it work? If your competitor is introducing a technical product, this P is particularly important.

Product can also apply to a service business, though in this case the product would be the service offering. What precisely is the service? What do consumers experience? What are the different parts of the service experience?

It is important to look beyond the product itself to understand the full offer. If the product is paired with a service, for example, what is the total proposition? What is the customer support situation?

PRICING

The second P, pricing, is similarly critical. What is the price of the new product or service? Is the price higher than that of other players in the category or lower? What is the pricing structure? Is pricing by unit or by a monthly fee? Are there volume discounts or bundled offers? Are there exceptional credit terms? Are there additional fees or charges?

As with an examination of the product itself, it is essential to take a broad look at pricing in order to understand the various elements. For example, an airline may charge a low price for a ticket but then charge extra for services such as checking luggage, changing flights, or upgrading to business class. Similarly, pricing might be low initially during a product's launch period but higher in the long term.

PLACE

Place, or distribution, is another critical area for examination, and one that is all too often overlooked when considering defensive efforts. Every product has a distribution strategy; if you can understand precisely how the product is flowing from the company into the market, you will have a basis to mount an effective disruption technique. When it comes to distribution, there are actually three different things to watch.

First, how does the product actually flow to market? Is the company managing its own distribution? How is the product being shipped? Second, what is the selling process? Is the company using its own sales force? If so, who are they, and what are the capabilities of the sales organization? How big is it? What is its structure? Are the hires seasoned players? Moreover, very often a new entrant will rely on brokers to handle the sales process. Is the company using agents and dealers? If so, who are they?

Third, what sort of financial arrangements are being offered to the distribution channel? Are there very large bonuses for achieving certain sales targets? How much of an incentive is being offered to retailers? Very often a new player will offer a higher margin to support initial sales.

PROMOTION

Finally, it is essential to be familiar with competitor's plans to promote the product. How will the competitor build awareness and drive trial? There are several particularly important aspects to this element.

The first question is total spending. How much is the competitor investing in the effort? And, even more important, how does this compare to spending in the category? A competitor spending at a much higher level than existing players is certainly a larger threat than someone with a minimal amount of marketing investment.

Another important question is the message. The message will presumably be consistent with the positioning, emphasizing the key benefit and attributes. But how will the competitor promote? What will be the tonality?

Finally, it is important to think about media. How is the competitor spending? What tactics are receiving high levels of support? Understanding the mix of media spending is important because it will shape the eventual defensive effort. Knowing that a competitor will be investing heavily in social media, for example, is useful information.

SOURCE OF SALES VOLUME

When examining a new product's entry into your market, it's critical to ask: Where will the new product draw its volume from? This question is significant because it sheds light on the risk and opportunity posed by the new entrant.

Sales always come from somewhere; revenue doesn't just materialize out of the sky. A new product that achieves annual sales of $100 million stole sales from another player in the economy. As economists like to point out, everything balances in the end.

When considering source of sales volume, the first question to consider is share versus category. The sales of any product will be a mathematical function of two things: the size of its category multiplied by its percentage of market share. This is the case for unit sales and for dollar sales. The unit sales of a product will be unit sales of the category multiplied by the company's percentage (in units) of market share. The dollar sales of a product will be dollar sales of the category multiplied by the percentage (in dollars) of market share. Gillette's razor sales in Thailand, for example, will be total razor sales in Thailand times Gillette's percentage of market share. This equation is just simple math.

For a new product, understanding this math is critical. Will sales come primarily from category growth—incremental to the existing category—or will sales come primarily from market share? This simple distinction leads to two logical follow-up questions.

If the new product will get sales from outside the existing category (by essentially growing the industry), then the question is, where will these new sales come from? They might come from existing customers using more of the category in total, or they might come from new users to the category. This distinction matters, because if the new entrant is attracting people from outside the category, then your volume risk is smaller but your competitor might have identified a growth opportunity.

If an increase in market share is likely to be the main source of volume, the critical question then becomes which existing brands will be affected. If the new product is likely to have sales of 50,000 units, with market share the primary source of volume, then the question is this: Who will lose market share to this new product? Will it be *your* product?

Whether the volume is coming from inside the category or outside the category, it is important to understand which customers will respond to the new

Exhibit 4.2   Source of volume

Sales = Size of Category x Market Share

product idea. Is it just a select group? Who is it? How valuable are these customers to you?

Understanding the likely source of a new product's sales volume will be important in assessing the competitive risks and in formulating the best response; from this analysis it is possible to determine if a new entrant is a threat, an opportunity, or a nonissue.

SUPPLY CHAIN

Understanding a company's supply chain is another critical way to identify areas of focus in a defensive effort. Every product has a supply chain: materials must be sourced, converted into the finished product, and then shipped to market. This part of a product's lifecycle is critical because the supply chain has a major influence on costs, capacity, and flexibility.

Supply chains can vary immensely. At the one extreme, a new competitor might construct a new factory to produce its new product. This suggests a high level of financial investment and commitment to the idea, because it is not cheap to construct new factories. At the other extreme, a new competitor might be relying entirely on outsourced production, this minimizing its investment.

Especially in manufacturing, the supply chain can have an enormous impact on costs, which can vary dramatically. Production in a low-cost country like China brings with it a favorable cost position, which provides flexibility in terms of margins. Production in a country with higher costs has similarly significant implications; higher costs mean the competitor must be planning on setting high prices or securing high sales volumes that deliver profits despite a small profit per unit. The mix of fixed and variable costs is also important. A supply chain with high fixed costs will force the company to generate significant volume, and capacity utilization is critical. Alternatively, capacity with high variable costs and low fixed costs is more flexible, at least from a financial perspective.

Every supply chain has a certain amount of capacity. Knowing that a competitor has high capacity has major implications; this suggests the company is optimistic about the product. It also suggests that the company will be under pressure to utilize the capacity. High capacity usually brings with it low costs.

Supply chains also have a certain amount of flexibility. Some supply chains can vary production significantly with little notice, while other chains have long lead times and limited flexibility. A company that relies on production in China and transportation by ship will have fairly low flexibility; it can't quickly ramp up production given the long lead times. Alternatively, a company with local production and ample capacity can quickly adjust production levels to meet demand.

Supply chains also matter for services, though in this case the issue isn't the actual chain of production; it is the set of processes behind the service delivery experience. What types of people is the company hiring? What incentives are provided for the customer service team? Are the salespeople based locally or overseas? Has the company hired its own employees, or is the company relying on contract employees?

Knowing the supply chain behind a new product or service is critical for evaluating a threat and plotting a proper defense. For example, marketer Paul Groundwater formulated a defense plan for a brand of pudding snacks based on a key supply chain insight: the new competitor had outsourced production. This meant the company hadn't invested heavily in the new product and could abandon it without incurring a significant financial write-off. He noted, "We were convinced if we could lean on them enough, they would have an easy exit." Based on this insight, he assembled a strong plan that blunted the competitive launch. As he had anticipated, the competitor then dropped out of the market.

UNDERSTANDING THE MOTIVATION

Learning about the details of your competitor's move is important, but it is just the start. To truly assess a competitive threat it is critical to uncover much more information about the larger context of the threat: *Why* is this competitor doing what it's doing?

WHAT'S DRIVING THE BEHAVIOR?

A simple life lesson: it is difficult to impact someone's behavior unless you understand why they're acting the way they are. It's difficult to get your children to act differently, for example, unless you can appreciate the motivations behind their current behavior. It's difficult to get your boss to put you in charge of an important new project if you don't have a sense of her point of view.

This lesson is enormously important, too, when it comes to defense. You have little chance of impacting a competitor's behavior unless you understand what is driving the behavior. For this reason, one of the most important things to understand when evaluating a competitive move is the motivation behind it. If a competitor is launching a new product, it is important to evaluate why they are launching the new product. What are the goals? What is motivating the decision? The surface answer is often pretty simple: most companies are trying to grow profits and be successful. This answer is also of little use. You have to go deeper.

WHAT ARE THE GOALS AND OBJECTIVES?

If you're able to deeply understand the objectives and goals behind a launch, then you can make important decisions regarding your defensive strategy. It is reasonable to think that a competitor wants to increase profits; that's a pretty common objective. But a more significant question is, by how much do they want to increase profits? A new product launch that targets annual profits of $7 million is a very different situation than a new product with a target of $400 million.

It's also important to ask when the company expects the initiative to become profitable. A new product launched with significant short-term profits is a very different sort of threat than a product with a long time horizon before it becomes profitable.

Keep in mind that profit is not always the objective for a new product launch (or at least profit from that particular item). Companies launch products for many reasons; for example, the new product may be designed to support an existing product, perhaps by completing a product line and offering a full suite of options. In this case, there are few profit expectations for the new product. Indeed, the new product might never make any money; the launch might be purely to support another product in the mix. Alternatively, a new product might be primarily defensive in nature, so what appears to be a new product is actually just a small move in a bigger and broader competitive battle.

WHAT'S THE CORPORATE CONTEXT?

A new product should always be considered in the larger context of a company; this is the only way to fully understand the motivations that led to the introduction. What else is happening inside the company that has had an impact on the launch?

Sometimes, there might be political motivations behind a product launch. The politics could be internal or external. Internally, a product might be satisfying the demands of an obstinate but influential senior executive. For example, in some companies, the sales force wields enormous power, and if the head of sales demands a new product, it is quite likely that he will get it. The new product might make little financial sense but that won't necessarily stop it.

External political factors also could drive a new product launch. If government leaders in a country request a new product, then a company dependent on the goodwill of those leaders will probably seriously consider introducing it. This is the case particularly with environmentally friendly products, where societal pressure might force a company to launch a product it might otherwise not have introduced.

The Italian pasta company Barilla provides an important lesson in the importance of understanding objectives. In the 1990s, Barilla made a significant move into the US pasta market. The company began importing and selling more products and invested heavily in marketing to build the brand.

Someone analyzing the launch might have assumed that Barilla was attempting to drive short-term growth, with a typical two- or three-year planning horizon. But they would have completely misread the situation. Barilla is a privately held, family-owned company. The family patriarch, Pietro Barilla, had capably run the company for many years and led its expansion to become the largest pasta company in Italy. The next generation in the family decided that they would take the company to the next level by growing it in the United States and making it one of the largest companies in that market. The US expansion wasn't motivated by short-term financial returns at all; the move was part of a generational shift. The company leaders had an exceptionally long time horizon.

DON'T ASSUME EVERYONE THINKS AS YOU DO

One of the great risks when considering a defensive situation is that companies often assume a competitor has similar objectives and is looking at the market in a similar way. For example, executives at a company accustomed to 30 percent gross margins or an 18 percent return on capital might well assume that a competitor is looking for similar returns. This is an enormous mistake; it is the first step toward misunderstanding a competitive threat. As consultants Kevin Coyne and John Hurd observed in a recent *Harvard Business Review* article, "Companies often mistakenly assume that everyone measures success in the same way. This explains why many of our clients claim that their competitors are 'irrational.'"[2]

Paper giant Boise Cascade, for example, aggressively invested in the commercial office products distribution industry in the 1990s. This industry was exceptionally challenging; it is difficult to make a lot of money distributing pens and printer supplies. But for Boise Cascade the office products business was very attractive; while margins were somewhat modest, they were much better than returns in the company's core paper and wood pulp businesses.

Understanding goals is particularly challenging in a global market because culture has an impact on strategy. People in different parts of the world think differently about competition and success; understanding a competitor's perspective and mental framework is critical. The US military, for example, uses an ancient board game to help understand how China views strategy. People have played the game *wei qi*, also known as *Go*, for more than 2,000 years in China. The game is based on long-term strategy, not quick wins. David Lai, a professor at the Army War College, believes that understanding the game sheds light on how Chinese leaders think. He observed, "*Go* is the perfect reflection of Chinese strategy thinking and their operational art."[3]

WHO'S REALLY ATTACKING ME, ANYWAY?

Understanding *why* your competitors behave as they do is the first step to a deeper understanding of what's really going on. A closely related and equally important question is figuring out *who* is really doing the attacking, both from a corporate perspective and from a personal perspective. Obviously, you'll respond differently depending on who is involved.

WHO: THE COMPANY

When you're facing a competitive threat, it is essential to understand the competitor. An attack by General Electric is very different from an attack by Samsung and very different from an attack by a brand-new start-up company. The need for defense and the type of defense will vary substantially depending on who you are dealing with.

One major issue to consider is financial resources. Is the company profitable, well funded, and strong? Or is the company struggling? A company with deep pockets generally poses a potentially bigger threat, assuming, of course, that the new product launch is a priority. A company that is financially weak is vulnerable, which creates significant opportunities for defense.

If the competitor's existing businesses are doing well, the company may be able to invest heavily in the new product launch. As marketing veteran Paul Groundwater observes, "You have to know their P&L and where they are making their money."[4]

A company's other resources are also important. Generally, the question is what assets the company has to leverage in support of the new product introduction. A company with a massive and motivated sales organization, for example, could potentially deploy it to help the new product. Similarly, a company with extensive manufacturing knowledge or sourcing expertise could bring these capabilities to the new product.

Another issue is ownership: is the company public, private, or government controlled? Public companies often have ready access to capital. At the same time, public companies must regularly report earnings, in many countries on a quarterly basis. Public companies also must pay attention to their stock price; while executives may claim not to care about short-term stock price moves, it is almost impossible for them to ignore this issue given the heavy use of stock-based compensation in many companies. If a CEO has 500,000 options with a price of $50, she would lose $2.5 million on paper if the stock fell from $65 per share to $60 per share. And if the stock falls below $50, the entire value of the options is gone. It is difficult to resist this sort of pressure.

Private companies may have a much longer time horizon. One of the advantages of being a private company is that there is frequently less need to focus on short-term results; private firms don't generally release quarterly earnings, and there is no stock price to worry about. This allows some private companies to focus on the future. Of course, this isn't always the case; some private companies are owned by people with a short-term horizon, and other private companies have so much debt that the focus, by necessity, is on short-term returns.

Government-controlled companies pose an entirely different sort of threat. With these companies the goals may be closely tied to government policy and objectives. For example, maintaining high levels of employment might be a top concern, since government leaders want to keep people busy and feeling productive. In this case, the government might prop up what otherwise is a struggling business. Alternatively, if expanding into a particular sector of the economy is a national priority, the government might support a company financially.

Government-owned companies also might have tight connections with pol-icymakers. This is potentially a significant factor; if a company is closely linked to the people who set a country's policies, it is highly likely that the policies will end up being very favorable for that company. In China, for example, state-controlled enterprises are a major force; anyone competing with one needs to seriously consider the long-term outlook.

In 2011, *The New York Times* profiled a Chinese entrepreneurial company that was competing with a government-sponsored enterprise. Not surprisingly, it wasn't going well. Reporter David Barboza observed, "The usurping of pri-vate enterprise has become so evident that the Chinese have given it a nick-name: *guojin mintui*. That roughly translates as 'while the state advances, the privates retreat.'"[5]

WHO: THE PERSON

Behind every business initiative there is a person, someone who owns the ini-tiative and is responsible for its success. So who is it? And once you know who it is, what are the implications?

Understanding the personal dynamics is particularly important and an often overlooked part of defensive strategy. In some situations there is just one person to focus on, and in other cases there may be several. But the question always is the same: Who am I dealing with?

This question is specific: you want the name of the key person. Saying, "We are being attacked by a bunch of Brazilians" is not all that helpful. Brazil is a huge country, and it's difficult to generalize about someone's behavior simply based on country of residence or origin. You need to know the specific indi-vidual. As Sun-Tzu observed, "In general, as for armies you want to strike, the cities you want to attack, and the men you want to assassinate, you must know the names of the defensive commander, his assistants, staff, door guards, and attendants. You must have your spies search out and learn them all."[6]

Knowing the specific person behind a competitive attack is important for several reasons. First, we know that people learn through trial and error, often repeating themselves when things go well. This is one way we learn; we try something, and if it turns out well, we do it again. Or we try something and it goes poorly, and we stop doing it. So if you know the person attacking you, it is possible to understand what this person has done before, and this can help you predict what he or she is likely to do next. As consultants Kevin Coyne and John

Horn observed, "By studying your competitor's past behavior and preferences, you can estimate the likelihood of his responding at all, identify the responses he is likely to consider, and evaluate which will have the biggest payoff according to his criteria."[7]

Knowing the person also gives you a sense of the threat you face. For example, if you learn that your foe, a Chinese executive name Hua Cheng, is a star performer in the company, you now can fairly safely assume several things. First, you can assume that this is a high-priority project for the company. If she is a star, then it is likely she wouldn't be working on the project unless it was important. Second, you can assume that Hua has significant resources at her disposal. She has credibility in the company, so she will probably have access to investment dollars. She will also probably have time; the company may well give her the benefit of the doubt if things start slowly and will continue investing in the new product over the long term. Third, you should probably be a little nervous; if Hua is as good as she seems, then the threat might be significant; the new product might be a very good idea with real potential. You should be very concerned.

Suppose, however, you find out that Hua Cheng is not a star performer; instead, she is a bit under pressure. Perhaps she just oversaw two failed product launches, and all of her former managers and champions have left the organization. Indeed, some people think that she won't last long at the company.

This information is enormously significant. Perhaps most important, Hua isn't likely to have much internal credibility, so she is likely on a short leash. Senior management isn't likely to give her a lot of autonomy. She probably has access to limited resources with a short time horizon.

A defense plan would look very different in these two scenarios. If Hua is indeed a star performer, a strong defense is incredibly important because the threat is large. The defense effort will need to be substantial and prolonged; it won't be a quick or easy fight. On the other hand, if Hua is on a short leash, the need for a defense is less critical and the plan would be different; a strong initial defense that gets the new product off to a slow start might be sufficient. If the new product falls behind plan, then senior management might quickly step in and declare the new product a failure. "Oh no, here we go again," senior management might think: "Let's end this quickly." Then Hua is fired and a new manager installed in her role, someone who has no vested interest in the new product and might shut it down. In terms of your defense, then, your mission is accomplished.

It's also critical to understand the personalities involved so that you can be aware of potential personal issues that might play a role in the situation. Business leaders are supposed to be rational, strategic individuals who always operate in the best financial interests of their companies. In reality, however, personal dynamics can absolutely interfere with this logical thinking or at least shape how people view things.

Many industries are fairly small; there are only so many people in the world who know how to sell commercial airplanes, for example, or frozen pizzas. In each industry, there is very good chance that the players involved in a competitive situation know each other. They might have worked together at some point along the way, or they might have served together on an industry committee. They have read many of the same articles and spoken with the same customers.

Personalities matter. If the two people leading brands in a competitive battle fundamentally don't care for each other, then this dynamic will play a role; both players might fight particularly hard just to attack the other person. Similarly, both companies might be reluctant to give up and hand the other person a perceived victory. The battle might even get vicious, with companies making personal attacks on the other players. Alternatively, if the people leading the initiatives are friends, the battle is likely to take a different turn; things are not likely to get ugly.

OTHER IMPORTANT PIECES OF INFORMATION

Beyond all these critical pieces of knowledge about your attacker, the list of questions goes on and on; there is a lot to learn about a new competitive player.

FINANCIALS

Every new product is based on a financial proposition. To formulate the defense plan, you want to know what the proposition is. What is the competitor looking at? What are the financials? You can be relatively certain the financial figures make sense, somehow. If you can figure out precisely how it all works, you can understand an enormous amount about the launch. You can also understand the motivation behind the launch and how to stop it.

Uncovering the financial forecast might seem like a daunting task; it is possible to learn many things about a new product, but the P&L isn't likely to appear. Companies keep this sort of information very private.

In truth, however, figuring out the financials isn't that difficult. Indeed, if you know the expected sales of a new product and the pricing, you can then fairly easily calculate the revenue. If you can figure out the supply chain and production costs, both fixed and variable, and the planned marketing expenditures, you then basically have the income statement for the new product. If you add in the capital investment and commercialization costs, figures that you can estimate fairly easily, you have a good sense of the overall financial proposition for the first few years. Based on some trend calculations, you can then develop the likely business proposition.

Will you create the exact P&L? No. Your calculations will be off, and they'll probably be off by quite a bit. But you don't need to be perfect; you just need to be fairly close. This will give you a sense of the financials of the business.

It is quite easy to check your work. Do the financials make sense? Is it apparent why the company is launching the new product? If the projected financials don't work—that is, if it isn't clear how the proposition makes sense financially—then you are probably looking at the numbers the wrong way and are missing something. Ultimately, people do things for a reason; if you can't see the reason, then you probably don't quite understand what is going on.

INTELLECTUAL PROPERTY

Intellectual property, such as patents and trademarks, plays a major role in defensive strategy; many competitive battles are primarily fought in court. For this reason, understanding your competitor's intellectual property in terms of strengths and vulnerabilities is critical.

The first step is to determine what intellectual property your competitor plans to leverage. In most cases this will involve looking at patents and trademarks. Has the attacker filed for patents and trademarks? What are they? How strong are they? If the attacker has an innovation and very strong patents, then any defensive response will need to take this into account. If the attacker doesn't have significant patents and trademarks, then the defense effort can be very different.

The second step is to identify areas where the new entrant may be vulnerable. Does the new product violate any of *your* patents or trademarks? Are there grounds to make a case?

Intellectual property is rarely a black-and-white situation; patents and trademarks are subject to interpretation. The important point is *relative strength*. If a competitor is clearly violating one of your patents or trademarks, then the defense plan may focus largely on this. If the issue is gray or if the infringement is weak, then the opportunity may be smaller.

THE LEGAL AND REGULATORY ENVIRONMENT

Every industry faces a set of laws and regulations. Understanding the existing regulations, and the regulatory bodies behind them, is an important part of the process of researching a defensive threat.

There are three things to focus on in this area. First, what are the existing regulations that impact this industry? Second, can you impact the regulations? A company that has influence with key regulatory bodies has the ability to shape the competitive environment, potentially encouraging lawmakers to pass regulations that might work to its advantage. Third, how does the new product comply with existing and potential regulations?

In some cases, the competitive environment is set; there are laws and regulations in place and little opportunity change them. It is important to know this, because then defensive opportunities in this area are fairly small. In other cases, however, the competitive environment is more fluid: laws are changing and regulations are evolving. Understanding the opportunities in this area is essential.

OTHER PLAYERS IN THE INDUSTRY

Defense is rarely a one-on-one situation. In most categories there are many competitors. While most of the competitive intelligence work concerns the new entrant, it is also important to assess the other players in the category. How will the new entrant impact other players in the category? Will they see a major impact? Or are they likely to be spared volume losses? Your source of volume analysis should include other competitors in the market. If one of your competitors is likely to suffer major losses to a new entrant, for example, there is a risk and an opportunity. The risk is that the competitor will do something radical in the course of defending that might have an impact on your business. The opportunity is that while the competitor is battling the new entrant, you may be able to gain market share at its expense.

Second, how will the other players in the category react to the new entrant? Will the other players defend? And if they defend, how significant will the defensive activities be and how will they impact your company?

Understanding the coming competitive battle will highlight opportunities and risks. For example, a small niche player in a category might initially think there is no need to defend against a mainstream launch. But once it becomes clear that the other leading players are likely to defend, with major investments in sales and advertising, the risk is clear; the smaller player could well get caught in the cross fire of the larger competitive battle.

THE CHALLENGE

It is easy to become overwhelmed when considering the amount of information you need to assess a competitive threat and develop a defense plan. The list of questions you need to answer is extensive indeed.

But information is critical; without data it is impossible to create a strong plan. Most important, you will never know everything. The challenge is to learn as much as you can in an expeditious manner and then focus on action.

Chapter 5

COMPETITIVE INTELLIGENCE

IT'S ONE THING TO MAKE a list of all the information you should gather in order to evaluate a competitive threat and formulate a defense plan. But getting the actual information in your hands is quite another.

Uncovering competitive data is a challenge and a rather delicate matter. But business intelligence is one of the keys to success when it comes to defensive strategy. Anyone with a thriving business must constantly look for and learn about competitive threats, sniffing out information anywhere it can be found. Companies with strong competitive intelligence capabilities have an edge; they can defend at appropriate times in optimal ways.

THE CHALLENGE

Competitive information is critically important, but getting it is not easy. Many companies work very hard to limit the information that enters the public domain, so learning about a new product launch is a major issue.

Even when you come across data from your competitors, it can be difficult to determine whether it is credible. If a customer tells you that your competitor has a new product with a cycle time of 80 minutes, do you trust the information or not? If a competitor publicly announces that it will spend $50 million on advertising, do you believe them? You'd like to, but of course there is no reason to assume that your competitor is telling the truth. It could be a bluff or a boast or simply an unrealistic forecast from an overly optimistic product manager.

The challenge of gathering competitive intelligence is most profound when a competitor has a new product in development. As a company works on a new idea, information is usually very hard to find. In part this is because people closely guard this information, and in part it is because the company hasn't yet finalized all the launch details itself and doesn't even know what's happening.

Once a product hits the market, the basic product specifications are apparent, as is the pricing, the distribution strategy, and the core marketing message. But even at this point, much is still unknown. What are the plans for year two? How much will the manufacturer spend in the second quarter? Are there new product variations in the pipeline?

In time, of course, things will become clear. You will eventually find out what the competitor has planned for year two and year three. You will see the advertising creative and the website. You will learn about the supply chain and the pricing.

The problem is that by the time things are clear, the opportunity to defend is limited. As a competitor enters a market and gains traction, it becomes harder and harder to defend. By the time you realize you have a major problem, it is often simply too late to address it. As we've learned, Blockbuster largely ignored Netflix and Redbox for many years. By the time Blockbuster fully understood the threats, it was in a difficult spot; the momentum had shifted, and the company never recovered.

While gathering competitive information is a challenge, it isn't impossible. With creativity, energy, and skill, you can learn about what competitors have planned. And it should be your top priority if you think there's even a possibility that you're facing a defensive threat. As Procter & Gamble CEO John Pepper observed, "I can't imagine a more appropriate time to be talking about competitive intelligence than right now. For I can't imagine a time in history when the competencies, the skills, and the knowledge of the men and women in competitive intelligence are more needed and more relevant to a company."[1]

WHERE TO LOOK

There are many ways to find competitive information. The list below highlights a few of the most common techniques. However, the list is not complete; it is designed to be just a thought starter. There are many other approaches that you will undoubtedly uncover in your quest.

STUDY THE COMPETITOR'S PRODUCT

One of the very best ways to learn about a competitor that has entered a market is simple: buy the product and study it. You want to become a customer and experience the product. If you're worried about a new restaurant opening in town, go have dinner there a few times and watch what happens. If you want to learn about a new type of detergent, go buy it, use it, and examine it. In most cases, the basic proposition will soon be clear; you will easily learn about the new entrant and the 4 Ps: product, price, place, and promotion.

As you soon as you locate the competitor's product, the first P—product—is apparent. You can see it, feel it, and examine it. You can take it apart and see what it is made of. More important, your engineering and purchasing teams can study it. In the technology industry, for example, companies routinely crack open competitive products to see what is inside. Similarly, companies in the auto industry buy competitors' cars and then pull them apart, studying each element to determine the quality and cost.

The second P, pricing, is also generally apparent once the product is on the market. What is the price? What are the deals? What are the contract terms? This information is essential to know and fairly easy to get once the product hits the market.

Place, or distribution strategy, is also usually easy to see. Where is the product being sold? Is it sold through direct sales or through a broker? If it is sold in a retail store, where precisely is it showing up? To understand the distribution strategy employed by a competitor, it is critical to involve your sales organization; they will likely be able to assess the competitor's approach.

The final P, promotion, will eventually become clear as the marketing campaign kicks off. If the competitor is using television ads, it is easy to see the executions; just monitor the major networks. Similarly, it should be easy to locate brochures or visit the new product's website.

Studying a competitor's product is a common and productive form of competitive intelligence. But there is one very significant problem with this approach: it is late. You can get the information only when you get your hands on the product. And in many cases this occurs after the product launches or, in the case of the marketing effort, after the product has gained significant distribution and the marketing campaign begins. In most cases, this is simply too late; you will have lost your best defensive opportunities. For this reason, studying a competitor's product is a good approach but never sufficient.

LISTEN TO SENIOR EXECUTIVES

One of the very best ways to learn about a company is to listen to its leaders. Virtually every senior business executive gives talks in public. They speak at industry associations and investor conferences, high school graduations, and charity events. Every year, for example, hundreds of them visit Kellogg to talk about the latest developments at their company. Communication is part of leadership, and most executives are happy to discuss what is going on in their firms.

These talks are very important sources of competitive information. When your competitor's CEO is giving a speech at Harvard, you should listen to it. If she is giving a recruiting talk at Wharton, sit in if you can, or have one of your former interns sit in. If he is presenting at an industry analysts' conference, listen in.

Of course, there are many things that won't be in a CEO presentation. Senior executives are generally smart and savvy people, so they won't rush to reveal huge amounts of competitive information. Don't expect to learn precise spending levels or details on key technological challenges. Things like launch dates, innovative marketing efforts, and sales incentive programs generally won't be mentioned.

But there will be much useful information in a senior manager's presentation. For example, what are the company's priorities? Why is the company entering a particular market? What is the big-picture strategy? What are the expectations? All of this is important information for evaluating the threat and deciding on your defense.

What *isn't* said is often as important as what is said. If a CEO is giving a speech and doesn't mention a particular new product, you have to ask yourself why this might be the case. It could be that the product is a major secret, so the company is keeping it very quiet. More likely, the product just isn't that important; it isn't a big priority, or it isn't an initiative the CEO is confident about.

LOOK AT THE COMPETITOR'S FINANCIALS

Understanding a competitor's financials is a key task when evaluating a threat. Getting this information is sometimes quite easy. Public companies, for example, file extensive quarterly financial reports showing the income and cash flow statements and balance sheet. Companies that have a narrow range of products are particularly transparent; the financials are presented with great clarity.

Once you're able to find the financial information, it is important to understand it in detail. What is the overall financial position of the company? Is the company leveraged and has sizeable debt? Or is the company well capitalized?

Does the company have some products that are performing exceptionally well? Are these products likely to continue to do well? If so, the company may be able to redirect profits to the new line of products.

TALK TO SUPPLIERS

In many industries companies rely on the same suppliers, so a particular vendor will work with several competitors. In the pharmaceutical industry, for example, many companies will work with Becton Dickinson and Catalent Pharmaceuticals. In the watch industry, many companies purchase movements from Swatch. In the food industry, many companies work with International Flavors and Fragrances. As a result, suppliers know a great deal about what the different players in the industry are up to. Suppliers often know about new products long before the items hit the market, and you can learn a great deal from these firms.

Suppliers are always in a bit of a delicate spot, torn between two opposing forces. On the one hand, suppliers want to make their existing customers happy. Protecting customer confidentiality is a big part of maintaining relationships, so suppliers will be reluctant to divulge competitive secrets. On the other hand, suppliers also want to secure new business; they are driven by financial incentives, too. An enthusiastic salesperson will want to discuss a nifty new technology in a bid to get new business.

Purchasing departments and supply chain managers play a critical role in the competitive intelligence area; an alert and experienced purchasing manager can learn many things about competitive products. Every time people from your purchasing department walk through a supplier warehouse, they should be looking around, checking out the different products. When visiting the company that prints your labels, for example, your purchasing person should pay attention to what other labels are stacked up in the warehouse. If she notices a different sort of label for a competitor, she should take a look or snap a photo—and then ask about it. "Hey, look at that! I haven't seen that before. Is that a new product? Something they are testing?"

Suppliers sometimes intentionally provide competitive data in a bid to strengthen a relationship or generate new business. They need to drive growth and profits so they have an interest in publicizing their latest achievements. It is very tempting for a supplier to spread the word about its latest technological innovations.

On other occasions, suppliers unintentionally reveal competitive information. They might leave a purchase order on a desk or inadvertently include competitive data in an analysis of bids. Such accidental disclosures can be extremely useful too.

CONTACT DISTRIBUTORS

In many industries, the best source of competitive information is the distribution channel. Distributors often carry products from many different companies. In the United States, for example, Best Buy sells technology products from a variety of manufacturers. In Europe, Media Markt carries many different brands. As a result, these players have an extensive knowledge of the various competitors in the industry.

Of course, the particular players will vary based on the industry. For fast-moving consumer products retailers are particularly important because they carry almost all the top products. Indeed, securing retail distribution is one of the great challenges of launching a new product. In the financial services world, financial advisors are key players. In many business-to-business markets distributors are important.

While the players vary, one key dynamic is almost always true: the channel will hear a great deal about a new product launch well before the product actually hits the market. In many categories, it takes weeks or months to get the product into distribution. As a result, the channel knows about every new product well in advance.

Distributors often have access to detailed launch plans. To break into the channel, a competitor will frequently show distributors the full launch plan: advertising spending, promotion spending, pricing, and discounts. In some cases, the information will also include key pieces of customer research—perhaps concept scores and in-home test results. Securing distribution can be difficult, so new entrants have a big incentive to share information to prove that the new product will sell.

Of course, getting distributors to share information can be difficult. For this reason, it is important that your sales organization is always out building relationships with key players in the channel. Going golfing with a distributor might seem like a waste of time and money, but the relationship-building effort can pay off. After a long day on the links, a supplier might well provide some data when casually asked, "So have you heard anything from GE, Dave? What are they up to these days, anyway?"

USE TRADE SHOWS

Trade shows are incredibly fruitful places for competitive intelligence. Indeed, it is hard to imagine a better setting for learning about your competitors.

The role of a trade show is to give the key players in an industry an opportunity to interact, so competitive data flows with particular speed. Often, if you simply sit back and listen to the flow of information, you will learn a tremendous amount about what's going on in your industry and about your competitors.

If you want to find out what a particular company is doing, just stop by their trade show booth and look around. What products are on display? What are the representatives discussing? Visiting a competitor's booth is of course a bit delicate, so you must approach the task with care. First, just walk by the booth and observe what's happening. Some very basic observations are illuminating. Is the booth in a prominent place? How big is it? Is the booth active and exciting, or dull and boring? Are people stopping by? The answers to these questions shed light on the spending and investment behind your competitor's booth as well as on potential customers' reactions to it.

After you've observed the booth, stop in and look around. What's on display? What do the signs say? Who's staffing the booth? If there are product samples, pick one up. If there are brochures or takeaway materials, grab one or two.

If you're particularly daring, you can ask a few questions. What is this new product, anyway? When is it launching? Are there volume discounts for large orders? Where is it produced? The company representatives staffing the booth shouldn't provide a lot of information to a competitor, but they might. At a large show, it is difficult to keep track of precisely who is who, and asking everyone to display company ID before entering the booth discourages traffic and defeats the purpose of the booth.

Honesty is essential, so if someone asks what company you are with, you must respond truthfully. If they then ask you to leave, you should, of course, depart. If they ask you not to take pictures, you shouldn't.

But there's no need to broadcast your affiliation, either. So before stopping in, you should probably put away your company ID badge. Similarly, if your briefcase has your company logo embroidered on the side, leave it in your hotel room.

Information at trade shows doesn't just flow in the booths. Indeed, every interaction can be scrutinized. Company presentations are exceptionally informative, as are award applications. A company trying to win an industry prize will often assemble a robust dossier on its activities.

Remember, though, that everyone at a trade show knows the basic situation: competition is everywhere. So be very careful about the information you gather; it might be real, but it could also be misleading. Companies sometimes release information designed to obscure and confuse competitors.

CONFER WITH INDUSTRY ANALYSTS

In virtually every industry there are analysts who study the different competitors. Sometimes these are people who create reports that they then offer for sale. More often, they are industry financial or stock analysts who are investigating investment opportunities.

Industry analysts are exceptionally valuable sources of information for several reasons. First, analysts are generally smart people, often trained at top business schools. They think logically and analytically. Second, analysts are outsiders, so they are free of at least some of the biases that can cloud judgment. People working for a company can believe in its products with blind faith. People working for a competitor will tend to dismiss competitive threats. An analyst, however, is an outside, neutral party. Some people have observed that analysts are not as objective as one might hope; there are certainly cases where analysts have a vested interest in boosting one particular company or another. Still, on balance an analyst brings an outsider's point of view, and this is valuable. Third, analysts work on the task at hand: understanding the potential for new products. Their goal is to understand a business exceptionally well and in the process identify investment opportunities. An analyst studying an industry can uncover insights by conducting independent research to verify company data.

As a result, anyone facing an attack should look at what the analysts are saying. Are they excited about the new product? What information are they looking at? Have they done studies of their own?

Fortunately, much of this research is readily available. Some investment reports are free, and others are available for a small fee. It is worth the investment. Still other reports are not public, but through connections it is possible to get access to the information and data.

TALK WITH CURRENT AND FORMER EMPLOYEES

One effective but controversial means of competitive intelligence is to speak with people who currently work for your competitor or, perhaps more promising, people who used to work for your competitor. As insiders, these individuals have an in-depth knowledge of the situation at the company, and they will likely know the issues, the company's capabilities, and the people involved.

The ideal person to reach is the product manager; this is the person closest to the details of the launch. This person likely knows the all-important details of the thinking behind the new product and the tactics supporting it.

But many people at the company have valuable information to share. A sales representative can provide insight into the morale of the company, the internal buzz, the launch details, and the sales plan. A market research manager will be familiar with the customer insights behind the product and the test results. A summer intern can provide useful information, too, since she may have sat through a number of critical meetings about the product and might know the key people. Even if these individuals didn't work on the specific product, they will likely have interesting and valuable insights into how the organization works and what might be driving the launch.

Current employees are the most valuable sources of information since they are there at the moment. Current employees *shouldn't* provide information that is valuable to competitors, and companies go to great lengths to prevent important information from slipping out. But it still happens. Sometimes current employees reveal something they think isn't important, but it actually is. The start ship date, for example, might seem like an unimportant fact, but in truth it is an absolutely essential piece of the puzzle for a competitor. The name of a key supplier might similarly seem unimportant but is useful to you as defender.

Former employees are a more promising source of information, since they have moved on and don't currently interact with the company threatening your market share. Executives try to prevent these individuals from revealing competitive information, just as they do with current employees. But it's much tougher to do this; once an employee leaves, the company has less power over the employee and less contact.

There are several ways to reach out to current and former employees. It is important to note that many people are required to sign confidentiality agreements. You should be aware of these and respect them. If you are at all unclear about what you can do, it is best to consult with your legal team. The simplest approach is to simply ask questions and hope they answer. In most cases they shouldn't respond and won't. But if you ask, "So, when will that product be available in Turkey?" you might actually get an answer. Similarly, the question "Where do you source your widget 741?" might lead to fruitful responses.

You can ask people questions in many different forums. You can call them on the phone, meet with them at an industry conference, or talk at a college recruiting event. You could send the company an e-mail or call the 800 number. For example, one brand manager who was concerned about a new product his competitor had in a test market in Ohio simply called the competitor's customer service number and asked when the product would be available in California. The helpful customer service agent replied cheerily, "Oh, that product will be in stores in California by October." You can even invite your competitor's employees in to interview for a high-profile position, with the hope that they will provide insights. The candidate will have a big incentive to discuss all of his notable achievements in the course of the interview. A more extreme move is hiring your competitor's former employees.

Talking with your competitor's employees is a controversial form of competitive intelligence. There is a fine line between being appropriately aggressive and innovative with your competitive intelligence efforts and being unethical or doing something illegal. One particularly important rule: never be dishonest and never misrepresent yourself. If someone asks you who you work for, you must reply honestly. Similarly, when asked why you want to know something, you need to fully disclose your reason for asking.

WATCH JOB POSTINGS

A good way to learn about a company's new efforts is to follow help-wanted ads. Seeing what sort of people a company is hiring can tell you a lot about what it is focusing on.

When a company enters a new market, it needs people and usually lots of them. The company will need marketers, market research experts, and developers early in the process, and then it will need customer service reps and salespeople as the product gets closer to launch. The obvious people to target are people with experience in the industry. If you are entering the industrial pump market in Germany, for example, it is best to recruit people who know this market. Similarly, if you are launching a new artificial knee, you will need to locate some medical device sales reps with contacts and expertise in the industry sector.

If you see a company trying to hire people with experience in your industry, you can generally assume it is planning to enter your market or is at least considering it. The scale of the hiring sheds light on the scope of the threat; a company hiring 200 salespeople is obviously a much bigger threat than a company hiring just one or two.

Some job posting activity is easy to see. Many companies list their job openings on their company web site, making the information readily available. Other job posts are less obvious. A company using a recruiting firm, for example, will be a bit more opaque than a company just relying on public posts. Still, the information is available. Ideally, your own employees can provide information; if they get a call from a headhunter about a new job, they should pass that information along to you (of course, this assumes they are happy in their own job and not looking to jump ship to your competitor).

Job posts are a very common but often neglected source of information. Even CEOs use the technique; Bill Gates, then CEO of Microsoft, apparently studied Google job postings in 2003 and was alarmed to see that Google was hiring developers skilled in operating-system design. He then alerted his people, sending an e-mail warning: "We have to watch these guys. It looks like they are building something to compete with us."[2]

USE SOCIAL MEDIA AND THE INTERNET

The rise of the Internet provides remarkable opportunities for competitive intelligence. Blogs, message boards, and social networks are important tools that open vast opportunities for learning. Indeed, it is now easier than ever to find out what a competitor is doing.

Simply reading your competitor's blog is a wonderful source of data. As Jonathan Schwartz, President of Sun Microsystems, explains, "Many senior executives at Sun, including me, have blogs that can be read by anyone, any-where in the world. We discuss everything from business strategy to product development to company values. We talk about our success and our mistakes."[3] There is nothing better than a competitor blogging in such a fashion.

Corporately authored blogs are interesting, but these posts are often so tightly scrutinized by lawyers and public relations professionals that the infor-mation isn't very useful. Individual blogs are more important. For example, if you know that Susan Roberts is overseeing the launch of a new product into your market, finding her blog would be a very positive development indeed.

Blogs provide certain types of information. Susan isn't likely to post detailed new product launch plans; she won't discuss pricing, timing, or advertising strategy. Of course, there's a chance she might discuss these things, but it isn't likely. However, she might well provide her thoughts on industry trends. This is instructive information; it sheds light on how she's thinking about the market and new developments. If the blog is more personal, Susan might discuss the stress of balancing a demanding job and a family. This is also instructive; it provides insight into how she is feeling and how hard she is working.

Bulletin boards can be even more useful. In many industries there are public forums where people in the industry discuss trends and developments. These posts are often anonymous, so people may feel free to voice opinions. Café Pharma (www.cafepharma.com) is an example of an industry-specific pub-lic bulletin board. The site is frequented by sales representatives in the phar-maceutical industry. There are forums on hundreds of different topics; there is a place to post comments on Amgen and another place to post comments on Eisai. The comments can be crass and vulgar, but they are sometimes very insightful. People are free to voice opinions about new products and the execu-tives behind them. Weaknesses in a product's clinical trial results, for example, are discussed and debated openly.

Social networks also present a very rich source for intelligence; indeed, the rise of networks is changing competitive intelligence entirely. Facebook, Twitter, and LinkedIn are three examples.

LinkedIn, the business-oriented networking site, is a fine place to begin. On LinkedIn people essentially maintain a résumé. A typical profile includes current job title, prior job titles, education, professional associations and rec-ommendations, and a list of contacts. The basic information on LinkedIn is valuable; there is no simpler way to determine who is working on a project than to look here. You'll learn about your competitor's experience, and how fast the executives involved are moving up in the company. You can also figure out if you are connected to them in some fashion, perhaps through a mutual acquaintance. LinkedIn opens up a world of opportunity for learning about the individuals at a competitive firm.

Facebook is perhaps the most intriguing opportunity for competitive intelligence. On this site people post remarkable amounts of information, from photos to links to random observations about the world. The network operates on the idea of "friends"; you have to be approved as a friend to have access to a person's information. Competitors will often be your friends. Silvia Lagnado, for example, CMO at Bacardi, admits, "I also use Facebook for business and have competitors as friends."[4]

If you can become your competitor's friend, you have access to personal and sometimes professional information. People sometimes post confidential information on Facebook. One Israeli soldier, for example, posted on Facebook that he was about to go on a raid, disclosing the timing and the location.[5] People shouldn't do this, of course. But you don't need obviously proprietary information to learn something useful. If someone is traveling all around the country going to big cities, you can assume there is something happening. In some industries, simply learning that a competitor is traveling to a certain city is important; there may be just one notable customer or industry expert in that town.

Social networks are powerful sources of information because they are public, which makes them accessible, and because people post often and quickly. Anyone writing a book or magazine article will be very careful; they will write it, and then rewrite it, and then look at it a few more times before submitting it. As a result, meaningful competitive information isn't likely to show up. On a social network, however, people post messages more freely and quickly, and this increases the odds of someone posting something useful to you.

Monitoring the Internet is fast becoming a core task in the world of competitive intelligence. Social media monitoring is critical to identify new threats early on and to learn about emerging problems. For example, Randy Hlavac, CEO of Marketing Synergy and a professor of integrated marketing at Northwestern University, tracks a number of different competitors. He explains his approach; "I monitor hundreds and hundreds and thousands of blogs and microblogs, forums, bulletin boards, social sites as well as news aggregator sites."[6] Listening to Internet chatter sheds a bright light on competitive moves.

DO MARKET RESEARCH TESTS

A good way to learn about your competitor is to talk with your customers. An even better approach is to do formal and rigorous market research studies of your competitor's product.

Companies often spend substantial amounts of money on market research. These studies, both qualitative and quantitative, reveal how customers are thinking. Much of this research investment is intended to create growth strategies. A company will often do substantial consumer research before airing a new advertising campaign, for example, perhaps beginning the process with a round of focus groups to help refine the communication brief and then using quantitative studies to evaluate different creative ideas. Similarly, most new products are grounded in a robust set of market research studies, evaluating the appeal of the concept, delivery of the product, and overall purchase interest.

Market research can also shed light on defensive threats. This is an often overlooked opportunity. Every piece of research you do on your own product can be done on your competitor's product. If you're unsure about the appeal of the competitor's new product idea, for example, you can do a concept test on that new product. One of the easiest ways to resolve internal debate about the merits of a competitor's idea is to put it in front of customers.

Doing market research on a competitor's product is enormously helpful because it provides a credible outside assessment. Managers all too often misunderstand what a competitor is doing and then underestimate the threat. Market research studies, however, provide an objective assessment.

A best practice is to use the same techniques to study the competitor's product as you use to study your own product. If your company relies heavily on concept tests, for example, field a concept test on the competitive product. This will ensure that the data you have is comparable. How does the new product stack up against ideas that you've been working on?

The biggest challenge in doing market research on a competitor's product: you might not have access to the product in time to be useful. To field an in-home use test, for example, you have to give people the product and let them use it. But if you can't get a large number of the competitor's product, you can't do the test. Once the product hits the market, you'll have access to it, of course, but by that point the optimal opportunity for defense may have passed.

Remember, though, that many types of research don't require the actual product. You can easily do a focus group with customers without a product.

You can field a concept test without a product. You can do ethnographic studies without a product. The lack of a product doesn't mean market research isn't a good opportunity to learn about the threat you face.

MONITOR PROMOTION RESERVATIONS

Many promotional vehicles promise category exclusivity. The companies that distribute coupons along with the Sunday newspaper, for example, will only run a coupon from one company in a particular industry, so the coupon for one shampoo doesn't appear next to a coupon for a competing shampoo.

This opens up an important area for competitive intelligence. Every time a promotion opportunity is not available for purchase, it means that another company has reserved the space. This has bigger implications as well, because as marketers embrace integrated marketing, one promotion technique is usually paired with several others, such as a big advertising push or public relations effort.

In many categories, this is exceptionally useful information; it tells you precisely what a competitor is about to do. In one defensive situation, for example, the defending company was able to identify the exact dates of the new entrant's promotional events and then preempt each one.

WATCH REGULATORY AND LEGAL FILINGS

Every government has certain rules and regulations, and companies must comply with them. Many of these regulatory filings can provide useful competitive data. Above all, this information is likely to be accurate, since submitting false reports to the government is not a smart thing to do.

Perhaps the most obvious place to look is among patent and copyright filings. Companies have a big incentive to file for patents and trademarks because intellectual property can be exceptionally valuable. In most countries, these documents are public; they are readily available for scrutiny. In the United States, for example, it is easy to search current patents and trademarks and applications through the US Patent and Trademark Office's website (www.uspto.gov). This information can shed considerable light on a company's plans. What patents and trademarks did it file for?

Trademarks can be particularly instructive when learning about brands. If a company files a trademark to use a particular brand name in a new category, you can be fairly confident that it plans to expand into that market sector, since it isn't generally possible to maintain a trademark unless you actually use it.

Other government documents can be useful too. A company in Latin America used import records to learn what a new competitor was bringing into the country. A food company in the United States looked at Occupational Safety and Health Administration (OSHA) filings to understand the equipment in a competitor's plant; one filing noted that an employee had sliced his finger on a particular type of machine. From this the company learned about the competitor's production process.

Several years ago, the brand team for Minute Rice was puzzled when Uncle Ben's introduced instant rice, directly attacking Minute Rice's core business. The Uncle Ben's product was of exceptionally high quality; the Minute Rice team couldn't determine how it was technically possible to manufacture such a product. So the executives at Minute Rice dispatched several people to visit the small town where Uncle Ben's was producing the new item. During a visit to the local town hall, the Minute Rice team obtained the environmental discharge records of the factory Uncle Ben's was operating there. By studying the effluent reports, they were then able to figure out that Uncle Ben's was using a particular type of chemical in its manufacturing process. This solved the puzzle.

BE OPEN TO SURPRISES

Competitive information will often simply pop up; something happens, and then—*voilà!*—the information is available. This can depend on a bit of luck. The key is to be open and alert so that when the information shows up, you recognize it.

In 2009, for example, a product team at one of the world's largest pharmaceutical companies was very worried about a new competitive product. By reviewing company statements and published clinical research studies, the established player knew that the new entrant would be launching in the next twelve months, assuming it received government clearance. It was not clear, however, how the competitor would promote the new product. How would the company talk about it? What was the target market? This information was important; it is hard to defend when you don't know what the competition is doing.

So a marketing manager started searching around the Internet, looking for any useful pieces of information. And eventually he located all of the competitor's promotional materials, months before the new product actually appeared.

It turned out that the competitor had hired a promotional firm to produce the materials, a fairly common approach in the industry. The promotional firm then hired a freelance graphic designer to work on the project, also a common approach. At the end of the project, the freelance graphic designer, eager to enhance his portfolio and secure additional work, posted the materials on his personal web site as part of his portfolio of work. It was available for all to see, including, as it turns out, the competitor.

A more astonishing story comes from Europe, where one of the major consumer goods companies was highly concerned about the launch of a competitive new product. The executives at the defending company were in the dark; they didn't know all that much about the product, the launch timing, or the promotional plan.

Everything changed one day, however, when a product manager at the defending company came across a publically available presentation the attacking company had made to industry stock analysts. He was going through the PowerPoint document, and as he moved his mouse across the screen, he started clicking on different elements. When he clicked on one of the charts in the presentation, something wonderful happened; a linked spreadsheet popped up, which contained all of the new product's financial projections: sales, costs, marketing spending, profit, trade discounts, and all the rest. The information transformed the defensive effort because the established player now knew exactly what the competitor was about to do.

It is impossible to plan for things like this, of course. But being alert, watchful, and drawing up a competitive intelligence plan can provide wonderful insights into a competitor's plans.

LEGAL AND ETHICAL BOUNDARIES

Competitive intelligence is a very delicate area, so it is critical to approach the task with sensitivity. The key question is this: What is appropriate behavior?

It is easy to push the bounds of competitive intelligence. Information is valuable, sometimes exceptionally valuable, so people may do extraordinary things to get it. One food executive, for example, was eager to learn about a competitor's new product efforts. She was a volunteer at her child's local elementary school, so she arranged for the class to visit the competitor. She went along as a chaperone to see what she could find out and encouraged the children to ask a lot of questions about new product development.[7] This sort of behavior makes most people very uncomfortable, and rightly so.

The world of competitive intelligence can quickly transition to pure espionage. H. Keith Melton specializes in the field. He notes that some companies are exceptionally aggressive, spying relentlessly on competitors. Governments engage in corporate espionage, too. He explains, "Businesses still spy on businesses, of course—they always have. It's not uncommon for companies to plant employees for intelligence gathering. But intelligence services around the world are also spying on companies, on a vast scale. Intelligence services, after all, exist to advance the national interest—and for many nations, that job includes spying on other countries' industries."[8]

Companies can employ very sophisticated techniques to gather information. Melton notes that "if I can get hold of your phone for 30 seconds, I can swap in a look-alike battery with a chip that will record your calls and transmit them to me." In some countries, the situation is particularly challenging. According to Melton, "If you leave your laptop in your hotel room, expect that the hard drive will be copied."[9]

There are two basic questions to consider when it comes to competitive intelligence. First, what is legal? Operating within the constraints of the law is a given. Many countries have laws that impact the gathering of competitive intelligence; this clearly limits what you can do. It is critical to work with your legal team to learn about the rules and avoid potentially illegal behavior.

Second, what is ethical? Something might be technically legal but still improper. It might be simply wrong, or it might be a public relations risk, with the activity making the company look bad in the public eye if it becomes known.

The problem with competitive intelligence is that situations enter the gray zone very quickly. Is it okay to hire your competitor's former employee? If you know someone is bound by a confidentiality agreement, but the person appears to be willing to tell you valuable information, can you listen? If an unknown person walks up to you and hands you a piece of competitive data, can you use this information? When I was in the corporate world, our fax machine would sometimes turn on and print out competitive information. We didn't know where the information was from, and we always debated if it was ethical to use it, or if we could even trust it.

The answers to many questions regarding competitive intelligence are not clear. I often give my business school students this hypothetical question: You find yourself sitting next to a competitor on a plane flight. Is it okay to look at her computer screen as she works on a presentation? Most of my students say that it isn't okay. But Ariel Kaminer, who writes an ethics column at *The New York Times,* takes the opposite view, explaining, "Companies vying for the same customers are engaged in explicit, mutual, ongoing competition. They are not just allowed to peek over their rival's shoulder, metaphorically speaking; they are also supposed to. Not trying would be irresponsible."[10]

The questions get more complicated as you operate across cultures and countries. Are you held to the standards of your home country or to those of the country where you are doing business? What if your competitor operates with a different set of standards? Should you simply resign yourself to always being at a competitive disadvantage or play by the local rules even if they go against your standards?

There are no simple answers to these questions. Sweeping generalities are not particularly helpful; there is a delicate balance in all of this. Some companies have a policy that they will only look at information a competitor has consciously released to the world through official channels. This is an honorable approach but also a bit foolish. Your competitors are likely to be far more aggressive; why put yourself at an obvious competitive disadvantage?

My advice is to follow two rules. First, you should involve your legal department when engaging in competitive intelligence activities. Your lawyers should be familiar with the laws governing competitive intelligence in your area, and they can provide guidance on the level of legal risk. You should follow their recommendations.

Second, use common sense. If you're uncomfortable with a particular approach, you probably shouldn't pursue it even if it is technically legal. Similarly, if you think your competitive intelligence activities would look inappropriate if written up in an article in *The Wall Street Journal*, then you probably shouldn't be pursuing them. And if you think your CEO would have trouble justifying the actions if queried about them in a news conference, then you shouldn't be doing them.

For example, executives at Procter & Gamble should have considered this before sending someone into to the trash dumpster at competitor Unilever to look for documents. The dumpster exploration later came to light, with P&G sheepishly returning the documents and firing three employees.[11]

It's also important to note that using outside resources doesn't change the legal and ethical restrictions. If you hire a firm to help you gather competitive intelligence, you have to be certain that it won't do illegal or unethical things in pursuit of this information. You can't hire someone to go shoot someone for you, and you can't hire a firm to engage in unethical competitive intelligence.

USING THE INFORMATION

The challenge of competitive intelligence is that the information rarely arrives in a logical, organized fashion. Many people who attend business school get hopelessly spoiled doing business case studies. In a typical case study, students are given all the critical information in a nicely typed and formatted document. The challenge is simply to use the data to think through the question and formulate a response. Indeed, students are usually told not to do external research but just to use the information provided. In fact, some students even get angry when told that they *can* do external research. I taught a case study recently where I let students do external research, and several students were quite annoyed. "That wasn't fair," they complained; "One team found a lot of information we didn't. How could we compete with that?"

The problem is that in the real world you aren't handed a case study with all the information nicely laid out in such a fashion. The information trickles in, much of it incomplete and often contradictory. One day you might receive a report about a competitor testing a new idea, and then two days later you might get another piece of information suggesting that the competitor is looking at something completely different. And then the following week another report arrives claiming that the first report was correct after all.

Figuring out what your competitors will do is inherently a difficult task; you won't know for sure what they'll do until they actually do it. One problem is that you'll never have all the data you think you need; even a mole buried deep in a company won't know the entire picture, what each player is thinking, and how all technology involved is progressing. A more fundamental problem is that companies often don't know the final plan either. Plans change. The launch plan for a certain product could change several times as the idea moves through development. Executives can accelerate or push back launch dates. Technology projects can succeed or fail. Financial results are never precisely on plan; if the results are particularly good, then the company might have the resources to invest more in a new product launch. But if results are weak, then the company may well scale back or cancel the new product.

Competitive intelligence is a bit like investing; you will never be completely right. The goal is to get close and then manage the risks.

Two approaches to working with competitive information are particularly important and worth considering: building competitors' financial statements and game playing.

BUILDING COMPETITORS' FINANCIAL STATEMENTS

Every company has a set of financials, and if you don't understand your competitor's numbers it is hard to defend correctly. Defensive strategy is ultimately about money, so it is critical to have a sense of your competitor's financials.

The problem is that you will rarely locate a competitor's financial plan for a new product. Companies generally don't broadly distribute new product financials. You shouldn't count on locating this type of data, regardless how hard you might search for it.

It is very possible, however, to *construct* your competitor's financials from other known data. By working with what you know about the industry and your competitors, you can make reasonable assumptions and develop a rough set of numbers. And by looking at the trends in the industry and your competitor's statements, it is then possible to extrapolate the numbers for the future.

To get a very rough-cut look at your competitor's financials, you can start with the size of the industry or category. How big is the market? Then apply a market share forecast, ideally derived from something the competitor said, to get a unit sales figure. Use the competitor's pricing information to get revenue figures and then apply customary discounts and credits. For cost, make some assumptions based on your cost position and your understanding of your competitor's supply chain. Assume marketing spending, such as advertising and promotions, based on what you have learned about the competitor's launch plan. Add some direct overhead, based on your assessment of how the company is staffing the new product group. And then see what happens to profit.

You can take the same approach to develop a cash flow forecast based on your knowledge of the competitor's necessary investments. If you know your competitor is building a factory, for example, you can add that to the projections.

Once you have a rough P&L, it is important to then test how sensitive it is to your assumptions. You can be very confident that your P&L is incorrect, so it's useful to spend some time exploring the levers that change the numbers. If your market share projection is low, for example, what happens when you increase it by one point? If your competitor's product cost is 5 percent lower than you figured, what happens to the projections?

Will this be perfect? Of course not; it will be an exceptionally rough swat at the numbers. But even a rough set of numbers can be very illuminating. If you project that your competitor will have profits of €750 million, then you know this is a very serious launch. Alternatively, if your competitor is losing significant money during the launch, then you can assume that the financials must improve at some point in the future or that there is something else going on.

GAME PLAYING

One of the most important approaches to working with competitive data is game playing. The basic concept is to have individuals or teams assume the role of different industry players, then ask them to make some decisions and watch what happens. One team plays the hand of company X, a different team plays the hand of company Y, and a third team plays your company.

The concept behind game playing is simple: people are predictable. If you give different people the same incentives and the same situation, they are likely to act in a similar way. Game playing exercises can be incredibly elaborate, with large teams and detailed decisions. This approach is robust and very insightful; you can develop a deep understanding of what is likely to happen.

For example, under the leadership of CEO Jack Welch, GE embraced this approach in the 1990s when trying to understand the threat posed by the Internet. Welch later explained the approach: "We put together separate teams, in many cases housed in different buildings, to analyze potential Internet-based models that could do to us what Amazon.com was trying to do to book-selling."[12] He continued, "With typical revolutionary fervor, we designed these units as 'destroyyourbusiness.com' teams (DYB). The goal of the DYB teams was to define a new business model for our existing businesses, without getting interference from those in the business who had been doing it 'the old way."[13] Simple exercises are also useful. Having a single product manager play the role of one of your competitors can provide valuable insights; by spending just a few hours you can learn something about how a competitor might proceed.

The challenge in game-playing exercises is to push on to implications. Understanding what a competitor is likely to do will be helpful if you can then project how it will impact your business and then think about how you should move in response.

ORGANIZING FOR COMPETITIVE INTELLIGENCE

So who actually does the work of finding competitive intelligence? Who is responsible for studying the competition and finding and organizing the key information? This is an important question because one thing is very clear: it doesn't just happen. A good competitive intelligence effort takes time and money. Setting up a social media monitoring system, contacting suppliers and distributors, and tracking legal filings takes dedication and concentration.

The problem, of course, is that a busy business executive isn't likely to focus on researching competitors on a regular basis. It's difficult enough to keep track of your own business, let alone some potential competitor that might be planning to launch a new product in another country. This is partly why people are so often surprised by competitive actions; they don't have time to study competitors and so they don't see the fairly obvious signs.

So who does the work?

There isn't one perfect solution; it depends on company resources and the importance of the business. A company with deep pockets should invest heavily in competitive intelligence if a profitable business activity is likely to face competitive threats. A small company with a struggling core business, on the other hand, won't be able to invest as much.

There are three basic ways to organize for competitive intelligence: rely on the business team, have a dedicated competitive intelligence group, and use external resources.

RELY ON THE BUSINESS TEAM

The simplest approach to competitive intelligence is to rely on the business team. In many cases, this will be the brand or business manager responsible for the product. In the job description, competitive intelligence should be clearly spelled out as a priority and a key part of the job requirements.

There are clear advantages to this approach. Most important, there is a solid link between the business team and the competitive intelligence. The information that turns up will be seen and considered by the people closest to the business. This reduces the chance that an important piece of data will be overlooked because the people who gathered it didn't know what it meant.

The challenge, however, is that the business team may not have time to focus on the task. Anyone who has run a business knows that the job is incredibly demanding; there are many tasks to be managed and many people to be satisfied. A product manager juggles urgent calls from the sales force, meetings with the promotion agency, and updates for senior management. On top of this, the product manager is supposed to come up with creative ideas for new products and new marketing approaches and to learn all about her customers. In this sort of environment, competitive intelligence is likely to take a back seat. It's very difficult to do great intelligence in an hour. Reading an article in the *Financial Times* is fine, but it's just scratching the surface. Talking with a competitor's sales rep at a conference is useful, but to really get insights you want to talk to six or more of them.

If the business team is responsible for competitive intelligence, two things are essential. First, the team must have adequate resources. Second, expectations must be clear: competitive intelligence is important. This aspect of the job should factor into year-end personnel reviews. Perhaps the worst thing you can do is assume the business team will be doing a lot of competitive intelligence and then give them no incentive to do it.

HAVE A DEDICATED COMPETITIVE INTELLIGENCE GROUP

Many companies have a dedicated competitive intelligence team, a group of people whose role is to study competitors, sort out what they are doing, and then brief the business managers. Some companies even have a dedicated team in each market, for example, one team in Brazil and another team in Japan.

This approach has an obvious advantage: with a dedicated group the work will get done, and assuming the team is strong, the work will be of high quality. A dedicated team can pursue leads, foster relationships with key analysts and industry players, and develop a robust picture of a competitor.

There are three challenges to keep in mind with this approach. The first is cost, because having a dedicated competitive intelligence team will require a considerable investment in personnel costs and in support funding. For example, the team will want to invest in attending conferences, visiting different locations, and purchasing research.

The second challenge is staffing; how do you get great people when you need them? Competitive intelligence is difficult and important, so you need talented people in the group. The need for competitive intelligence staffing will likely vary, however, depending on the situation. There are times when competitive intelligence is a top priority. For example, when you know a new competitor is gearing up for a launch, it is essential to find out quickly what is about to happen. At other times, however, there is less of a need; the task then is mainly monitoring.

To staff a competitive intelligence team, you will either need to hire very talented people directly into the group, perhaps from consulting firms or business schools, or you will have to create a career track where individuals with high potential rotate in and out of the department.

Finally, you need to ensure there is a good link between the competitive intelligence team and the business team. If the competitive intelligence group becomes isolated, it can do more harm than good. Its insights might never get to the business team, where things actually happen, and the business team might ignore competitive intelligence, confident that there is a dedicated team responsible for this activity.

HIRE EXTERNAL RESOURCES

Many companies hire external firms to help them monitor threats in the market. Competitive intelligence is big business; industry trade group Strategic and Competitive Intelligence Professionals (SCIP) claims worldwide spending on competitive intelligence exceeds $2 billion.[14] It is also apparently quite profitable. In 2010, Marsh & McLennan sold Kroll, its competitive intelligence unit, for $1.13 billion.[15]

The world is full of consulting firms, many of whom specialize in competitive intelligence; thus, every company should consider whether hiring an outside firm is the best approach for its situation. Firms are skilled at the task. One such firm, Phoenix Consulting Group, hires former government intelligence officers. The firm gets its name from a covert operation run in Vietnam, the Phoenix Program.[16]

Using a consulting firm to solicit competitive intelligence makes good sense for a number of reasons. First, the external firm will give competitive intelligence the attention it requires; if the external firm is hired specifically for this purpose, it will clearly focus on the challenge and address it with energy and vigor. Second, a consulting firm will usually have talented people working on the project. Many consulting firms hire from the best business schools and pay top salaries. That means they have great people working on projects; people who are smart, perceptive, and dedicated. Third, a consulting firm, especially one that specializes in competitive intelligence, may have some unique capabilities. A firm that does many competitive intelligence projects will know how to get the task done, whom to talk to, what sources are most valuable, and where time and money will yield the best return on investment in terms of locating useful information.

Perhaps the biggest single obstacle to using an outside firm is cost; competitive intelligence is time-consuming and thus can be expensive. It is very easy for a project with a top firm to cost $100,000 per week if the project team is staffed with junior analysts, a manager, and a partner. This sort of expenditure will cause many firms to pause and perhaps skip the project.

The money is often well spent, however. Firms need to know what the competition is doing; it is difficult to formulate a response without a deep understanding of the threat. If you're not set up to do competitive intelligence internally, relying on an external firm is the only option remaining. The other option, skipping competitive intelligence entirely, is not a promising approach; competitors don't go away simply because you choose not to study them.

There is another potential issue to consider when using external firms; the information you gather may be shared with other players in the industry, and in the worst case, your information will be shared with your competitors. Consulting firms take great pains to prevent this from happening; firms create so-called Chinese walls to separate teams working for different companies. Firms also sign strict confidentiality agreements, pledging not to divulge any information to your rivals. Through these precautions, most firms presumably manage to keep information private.

But the reality is that information tends to flow. If you hire a consulting firm to learn about Chinese computer company Lenovo, you have just educated the consulting firm about Lenovo; the firm will apply these insights when working on its next project. And that project could be from Lenovo, or it might be from another firm in the industry. Consultants are under pressure to sell projects and deliver good results, just as you are. Firms will use all of their skills and capabilities to win projects and delight clients. So proceed with caution.

One important aspect to consider is ethics. Before engaging a competitive intelligence firm, it is important to review guidelines for the approach. How will the consultants proceed? What sorts of activities are appropriate? What isn't appropriate? Ignoring the question of ethics is never the best approach, because you're then relying on someone else's code of conduct. What might be appropriate for one company is not appropriate for another, and a risk that might seem small for a consulting firm could be reckless for a major global firm.

ADDRESSING THE NEEDS

Ultimately, a competitive intelligence structure should match the business needs. The need and urgency for competitive intelligence will vary over time; competitive intelligence may not be particularly important one month and then incredibly urgent the next.

A well-established brand with few direct competitors won't generally require a massive intelligence apparatus. A traditional, regulated local electric utility, for example, won't need a huge team studying competition because there simply isn't a lot of competition to study. Similarly, the team managing Heinz ketchup, facing limited competition and a stable market, won't need to devote 50 percent of its time to competitive research; there aren't a lot of notable competitors in ketchup and certainly not a lot of new ones.

Things change dramatically, however, when a threat appears. When non-regulated electricity providers emerge and attempt to establish a position in the market, there is a dramatic need for intelligence. The task immediately leaps to the top of the established player's priority list. Who are these companies? What are they up to, anyway? Similarly, if a big company like Nestlé announced plans to launch a product in the ketchup category, Heinz would need a completely different approach to intelligence.

For this reason, it isn't likely that a company can embrace just one approach to the task; a structure that is completely sufficient at one point may be woefully inadequate a bit later. Flexibility is essential.

THE NEVER-ENDING TASK

The need for gathering competitive intelligence never ends. It is impossible to know precisely what your competitor is about to do; the situation changes as the competitor moves and adjusts to changing business and economic conditions.

Some people find the task of gathering competitive intelligence fundamentally overwhelming; it is simply too big and too difficult to address. The unknowns are enormous and the uncertainty is huge. The fact that competitive intelligence is difficult and vast, however, is not a reason to ignore it. Some information is better than no information. Competitive intelligence is a critical part of defending a business; you will never know everything, but you have to learn what you can.

Chapter 6

THE KEY QUESTION

THE WORLD OF BUSINESS IS full of astonishing stories about companies that led their industry and then stumbled when they failed to respond to competitive threats. When faced with a competitive attack, the executives decided not to defend and then suffered the consequences. For this reason, the key question—whether to defend or not—is critically important.

Harley-Davidson, the legendary motorcycle manufacturer, is an example of a company that faced a competitive attack and missed the opportunity to defend. The story ends well, as today Harley-Davidson is one of the world's leading brands. The company is financially strong, with sales of $4.9 billion in 2010. More important, the Harley-Davidson brand is distinctive; for motorcycle enthusiasts, there's nothing quite like a Harley. The brand has high consumer awareness and a core group of loyal followers. Over the past 50 years, however, Harley has had some rather significant ups and downs, including a major defensive miss.

Harley-Davidson was founded in 1903 in Milwaukee by three men: William S. Harley, Arthur Davidson, and William Davidson. Over the next fifty years, Harley grew to become the dominant player in the US motorcycle industry. In 1959 Harley had virtually all of the motorcycle market, a remarkable accomplishment. Motorcycle riders at the time were a rough crowd: bikers, the military, and the police.

In 1959 Honda entered the US motorcycle market. After a slow start, Honda embraced a rather bold strategy. The company decided to target a completely different group: college students. To support the strategy, Honda developed a small, inexpensive motorcycle, a simple 50 cc machine. Honda built new dealerships that were clean and bright, with lively colors and friendly service. After running a contest to find an advertising slogan, Honda eventually settled on this: "You meet the nicest people on a Honda."

How did Harley respond? The company decided to do very little; Harley didn't defend aggressively. There were probably several factors behind this decision. First, Harley thought Honda wasn't a credible player. A 50 cc machine isn't much of a motorcycle if you're used to building huge motorcycles. To Harley executives, the Honda motorcycle probably seemed more like a bicycle. Second, Honda wasn't a huge threat at the time. Honda was a small company targeting a very different group of customers with a completely different product. Few people were going to choose a Honda over a Harley or even compare the two products. Third, it would have been very difficult for Harley to defend against Honda. To copy Honda's move, Harley would have needed to invest a huge amount of money to create a new brand, a new retail environment, and a new manufacturing process.

Harley's decision not to defend gave Honda the opportunity it needed. Honda took off and went on to become the leader in the motorcycle industry, selling thousands and thousands of motorcycles. Inspired by Honda's success, other Japanese companies entered the US motorcycle market. Harley stuck to its core business as its market share declined and the competition grew stronger.

Harley eventually began a serious defense strategy. In 1978, for example, the company introduced a small, inexpensive motorcycle: the 49 cc Harley-Davidson AMF Roadmaster. By this point, however, the competition was far too strong.

By 1982, Harley was in a very weak financial position. The company was losing money and had just a 4 percent share of the US motorcycle market, lagging far behind industry leaders Honda (37 percent), Yamaha (25 percent), Suzuki (16 percent) and Kawasaki (14 percent).[1]

A number of years later, Harley eventually rose from the dead, phoenixlike, and became a vibrant, successful brand once again. But it took a millions of dollars, a new branding strategy, and government tariffs. Harley almost vanished because it failed to defend when a new entrant took over its market.

It is easy to look at the Harley story and conclude, "Well, these folks were out to lunch. What were they thinking?" But that view is a bit too simplistic.

Harley made very rational decisions; the Honda threat was slow to develop. The risk looked small at first, and defending would have been costly. The company's mistake was not revising its defense decision as the threat grew; Harley needed to recognize the risk as it took shape and take action to fight back.

DEFEND OR NOT?

Anyone facing a competitive threat must address a simple but critically important question: Do we need to defend?

This very basic question sets the stage for the entire defensive battle. If the decision is to defend, then the focus moves quickly to the next stage: developing the actual defense plan. If the decision is not to defend, then the business carries on its usual activities while monitoring the threat.

The decision is a difficult one. It's easy to make fluffy generalizations when it comes to defense, proclaiming, "We will fight every competitor, every time. We will never allow a new entrant to steal our market share," or "We don't defend. We never have and we never will. We just concentrate on serving our customers." These sweeping statements are rarely helpful for a manager facing a defense decision. The decision is just not that simple even when you've studied the threat in detail. As Procter & Gamble CEO A. G. Lafley observed, "The analysis never tells you the answer. The best it can do is to inform your judgment."[2]

There are reasons to defend and reasons not to defend. Before making the decision, it's critical to think about both sides of the question.

REASONS TO DEFEND

There are many reasons to defend a business. Indeed, if there is a competitor directly attacking your business, defending will often be an obvious decision. Below are some of the reasons why you might consider an aggressive defense when faced with a threat.

PROTECT SHARE AND PROFIT
The biggest single reason to defend a business is to protect market share and profit. Losing market share to a new entrant can be an enormous problem, one that quickly translates into a major financial blow. Preventing loss of market share is a critical task indeed.

A defense plan can protect a business in two ways. First, the plan can limit the new entrant's share gains, minimizing losses to the existing business. This is the most common defense effort. Second, the defense plan can ensure that the new entrant steals share from other players in the category, not from your business. As one marketing executive explained about a defense plan, "We wanted to push the pain onto other players in the category."[3]

AVOID A LONG-TERM PROBLEM

Competitive problems can grow over time. Letting a new company get a foothold in your business can create a long-term issue; by defending today you can address today's problem and prevent an ongoing concern.

A new business that gets up and running in an established category can create all sorts of problems for the existing players. The new entrant might come up with additional innovations or decide to discount prices aggressively in a bid to grow. The company might decide that directly attacking your business is the best approach, launching advertising that features product comparisons or drawing attention to negative aspects of your brand. The company might hire away your best people.

The more successful a product is during launch, the greater the long-term problem. The bigger the player, the bigger the problem you will probably face.

The best time to damage a new player is when the company is just starting out and is most vulnerable. New products are usually very dubious business ventures initially; most new products lose money early on while companies invest in driving awareness, distribution, and trial. Resources are tight; the financials looks grim.

Most new products are also surrounded by skeptics and vultures. People look for weakness. Everyone knows that most new products will generally fail, but they just don't know when. So they watch a new product launch with a sense of doom, knowing that the venture will likely not make it.

This is very true in big companies, as executives warily watch the new product, looking for any sign of weakness; this might suggest it is time to cut the investment. You don't want to throw good money after bad.

All of this makes new products highly vulnerable. At the slightest sign of weakness, the venture might collapse; executives might abandon ship, the sales team might lose faith, and funders might decide it is all hopeless.

Of course, everything changes once the new product has managed to deliver some success. With a good year under a product's belt, people begin to believe.

The new venture's leaders can make a strong case that things are working, claiming that this particular new product provides a rare opportunity to create a powerful, big business. "This is going to be the next Apple," they proclaim. People want to join the team. Distributors fight for the opportunity to carry the product. Investors are now eager to help fund the new business.

If things really get going, the new company can create a buzz of success, engaging with bloggers and writers, many of whom will tell the remarkable tale of success to the world. Momentum, once it picks up, is a powerful force for a new business. It's hard to stop it once it gets rolling.

By defending your own business against a new entrant in the early stages, you can stop the new product's momentum in its tracks, reducing the risk that the new player will be able to get started and grow into an even bigger problem down the road. As Duke basketball coach Mike Krzyzewski observed, "A little negative thing must be dealt with immediately—before it becomes a big negative thing."[4]

DEFENDING USUALLY WORKS

One of the most important reasons to defend is very simple: defense programs generally work. In the world of new product launches, playing defense is much easier than playing offense. So if you decide to defend, there is a very good chance that the time and effort you sink into the defense will yield positive results. It will be a strategic win.

Launching a new business isn't easy. You have to break into the distribution channel and then attract customers, make them aware of your product, entice them to try it, and then convert that initial trial experience into repeat purchases. The status quo works against new products; if customers don't change, then the new product isn't successful. People have to make a shift to embrace the new item.

Defending is easy in part because you are working to *prevent* people from changing. This is not all that difficult because you're trying to get people to do what they're inclined to do anyway. The status quo works in the defender's favor.

As a result, the odds of success go up; there is a great chance you will get the desired effect if you're playing defense. And this will translate into a high return on investment, the holy grail of business and marketing spending.

One major reason new products fail is that the established players capably defend their business, thereby contributing to the new product's lack of success.

SEND A SIGNAL

Defending a business is never pleasant; it takes time, energy, and money to defend well, and usually, at least at first, it feels like you're making little progress. When defending, you're fighting to protect what you have; you aren't moving ahead.

But one of the very best ways to avoid future competitive attacks is to deal decisively and immediately with companies choosing to attack you. The logic is simple: if your competitors know that you will defend aggressively, they will take that fact into account when thinking about entering your category by launching a new product. They'll have to plan to spend heavily in order to overcome your likely defense. This in turn makes it harder to justify launching the attack in the first place, since ultimately the numbers behind a new product proposition have to work. As Harvard professor Michael Porter notes, "How potential entrants believe incumbents may react will…influence their decision to enter or stay out of an industry."[5]

Sending a signal is harder than it seems, of course, since there is no guarantee that future attackers will remember how you defended years ago. For this reason, an overt defensive effort is sometimes the best approach, calling attention to the defense plan as it rolls out and then highlighting your competitor's failed launch.

CAPITALIZE ON A GOOD IDEA

Another good reason to defend: your competitor might have a good idea. New product ideas come from everywhere, and it's quite possible that your competitor has identified a promising opportunity. By defending you can take advantage of your competitor's fine thinking, capitalize on the concept, and avoid being left behind. John Krenicki, CEO of GE's energy unit, sees this as a big issue and opportunity. He outlines his worst-case scenario: "One of my competitors runs a play where they create a $10 billion business, and I slept through it—I'd say that's a disaster. I worry about that a lot."[6]

People only launch a new product if they believe it will be a success, so you can be certain the challenger is optimistic about the new product. That company has likely done significant consumer research to confirm its great idea. The idea might be appealing, or at the very least the consumer insights behind the idea might be valid and important. Guy Laliberte, founder of Cirque du Soleil, brought fresh thinking to the circus world. Chip Wilson, the creator of

Lululemon, correctly identified that yoga was a hot area for growth, and John Mackey, the driving force behind Whole Foods, understood that people would pay a premium for organic and natural foods they felt good about buying.

If your competitor has a good idea, the rationale for defending gets much stronger. First, the threat increases, because a competitor is likely to steal market share and have a big impact on your business. Second, the new product isn't likely to fail on its own; you will have to do something to stop it. Third, you can adopt the idea, perhaps launching a similar product to get a piece of the new opportunity.

LEARN AND GROW

Defending a business is exciting and dynamic. Many executives embrace the moment. They may establish a "war room" where the defense team meets to plot strategy and monitor execution. Many create colorful project names for the defense effort. One business leader called his defensive effort "Project Heisman," reflecting the goal to push away a competitor just as a running back might push away a lineman. Another executive who was defending against a competitor's new potato salad dressing product called the initiative "Project Spud."

Defense is also an opportunity learn and grow; a business under attack must take extraordinary measures. This makes it a wonderful learning opportunity. As J. Willard Marriott, founder of the Marriott Corporation, observed, "Adversity gives us opportunities to grow. And we usually get what we work for. If we have problems and overcome them, we grow tall in character and the qualities that bring success."[7]

MANAGE YOUR CAREER

Defending is often the right thing to do for the business. It can also help you personally. Behind every business decision is a person managing her or his own career. Executives encourage people to focus on the company and be confident that company success will translate into personal success. But this is a naïve approach. People always need to balance two goals: concern for the business and concern for their own future prospects.

In terms of a career move, defending is almost always a better choice than not defending. When you're under attack by a new entrant, you can choose to defend or not to defend. In either case, there are two possible outcomes: the new product will be a success, or the product will be a disappointment. It is worth considering the impact of both potential outcomes on your career.

If you decide to defend, then both outcomes will probably help your career. If you defend and the new product fails, you can claim success. You can happily announce to your team and senior management, "We did it! It worked!" And then you can schedule the big celebratory party. If you defend and the new product succeeds, you can also claim success, saying, "Well, we didn't stop them completely, but we surely made the right decision. Think how bad it would have been if we hadn't defended!"

If you don't defend, however, both outcomes don't help your career. If you don't defend and the new product fails, then you probably made the right decision, but the situation becomes essentially neutral for you personally. It wasn't a bad decision, but it also wasn't a dramatic step forward. You didn't do anything, after all. People rarely get rewarded for *not* doing something. Proclaiming, "We didn't make a bad decision last year!" is hardly the basis for company awards and promotions.

Conversely, if you don't defend and the new product succeeds, then you have a very significant career issue: you were the person who made the wrong decision and let the new entrant into your category. This sort of black mark can do lasting damage to a career. Twenty years later people may wonder, "So, who was running this business when Smith & Jones entered the category, anyway? Boy, they really screwed that up." People still look back with scorn at the team of people leading Merck's cholesterol-lowering drug Zocor when they were faced with competitor Pfizer launching Lipitor. Merck did little to defend, and Lipitor became the category leader in terms of sales and market share.

Defense has yet another career benefit: you get financial freedom. Anyone running a business knows that there is incredible pressure to deliver the

Exhibit 6.1   Defense decision tree

Your Decision	What Happens	Impact on Your Career
Yes	Attacker Fails	Very Positive: "We did it!"
	Attacker Succeeds	Positive: "Good thing we defended!"
Defend?		
No	Attacker Fails	Nothing
	Attacker Succeeds	Disaster

numbers. When I was running brands at Kraft, the head of my division, Carl Johnson (now executive vice president at Del Monte Foods), took me aside one day and gave me a piece of good advice. He said, "Tim, good numbers do not guarantee your success. But bad numbers will get you every time." And he was right, of course; if you are running a business, you have to deliver.

When a company is under attack, however, the financial situation is completely different. If a big new company enters your market, the financial picture immediately gets worse. You will lose market share if you don't defend, and then revenue and profit will fall; your original plan is no longer going to happen. If you defend, you may retain market share, but you'll have to spend much more than originally planned. Either way, you're in a new financial situation, and you should be held accountable for a different set of numbers.

In a curious way, this dynamic is a positive for a manager. When under attack, you likely won't be held to the original profit targets since they are now completely unrealistic. This frees you to make some bold moves; you can do what needs to be done without worrying about the financial impact. At the end of the year, you'll miss your original targets almost certainly but for a very obvious reason: the competition attacked, and you did what needed to be done. Only a most unreasonable and difficult manager wouldn't take that into account when considering year-end bonuses.

Defensive situations also provide an opportunity for a manager to demonstrate leadership. People are generally rewarded for being aggressive and taking action, and defensive situations are all about taking action. A manager leading a defensive situation can rally the troops.

In the end, a good defense is wonderful career opportunity. The choice is simple (defend!), and the goals are fairly easy to hit; you take the necessary action to protect the business. Unfortunately, managers don't make this choice as often as they should, to the detriment of their businesses and their careers.

REASONS NOT TO DEFEND

While the reasons to defend are compelling, there are definitely situations where *not* defending is the best move. There are a number of very valid reasons why defending might not be the best approach.

THE THREAT IS TOO SMALL

If a new product poses a very small risk to your business, it may not be necessary to launch a major defensive effort. In many categories, there are numerous new products every year. As a result, it's impossible to defend against everything; you must pick and choose.

Defense is costly; it takes lots of time, money, and attention. A weak defense is unlikely to succeed, and it's difficult to mount a strong defense with a limited budget. So it is important to compare the cost of defending with the risk of not defending. The biggest factor when making this decision is the size of the threat.

A new product may enter your category and have little impact on your business; thus, the immediate risk is limited. In this case, you have a valid reason not to defend (as long as you are certain that not defending immediately won't harm your business in the long run). For example, the new product might be targeting a very different customer segment. If you market to senior citizens, a new product targeting kids isn't likely to be a major risk. Similarly, a new marine pump for oil tankers won't be a big issue if your product is for recreational fishing boats.

Alternatively, the new product might be targeting a different geographic market, such as a different country or a different city. A company launching a new beer in Colombia isn't a huge, immediate threat for a beer company in Japan. Similarly, a new Italian restaurant in London obviously isn't a major concern for a restaurant in Sydney.

A new product with very limited funding isn't likely to be a big short-term threat, either. A person making a salad dressing in her garage will not be a huge problem for Clorox, a company that produces millions of bottles of Hidden Valley Ranch salad dressing every year.

YOU HAVE LEGAL CONCERNS

Defense is a tough business. The tactics are sometimes questionable, and the entire concept—preventing your attacker from being successful—is a bit controversial. There are times when you would like to defend, but due to external forces, you simply cannot.

One major concern is legal regulations. In many countries, government regulators actively try to identify and then limit actions that are considered anti-competitive. If you are at risk in this area, then you may not be able to defend your business even when the rationale to do so is otherwise compelling.

Generally speaking, a company is most at risk from antitrust groups if the company has more than a 70 percent market share. If you have a dominating presence in your industry, then regulators may scrutinize your actions, making it unwise to defend overtly.

In general, if you have a dominant share of what might be considered a logical market, then be very careful when considering a defense. Microsoft, for example, shouldn't be developing elaborate defense plans on its main products or holding employee seminars on the topic. Microsoft already has an enormous share, perhaps 90 percent of the operating system market. Anyone with 90 percent of a market must be careful about antitrust accusations. Indeed, government regulators in both the United States and the European Union have already gone after Microsoft. So Microsoft shouldn't be formulating aggressive defense plans; it would invite more government scrutiny and possibly even severe fines and regulations.

Similarly, Google shouldn't be focusing on defensive strategy since government officials in several countries are now scrutinizing the company in light of its remarkably high share of the search engine market.

THERE IS A SIGNIFICANT PUBLIC RELATIONS RISK

If defending your business would look bad in the public eye, you may not want to move forward. It's worth considering the type of company you would be defending against before you mount an all-out counterattack.

If the company attacking you is a sweet, gentle company that everyone likes, executing an aggressive defense to squash it would be a risky move. In the United States, for example, food giant Nabisco shouldn't spend millions of dollars attacking the cookies sold by the Girl Scouts, a nonprofit group. Similarly, if a respected war veteran is opening a restaurant, the restaurant next door probably shouldn't mount a particularly pointed defense; the story may well come out in the media, making the defender look bad.

There's an old saying that "there is no bad press," but in this case the saying is wrong. You can do enormous damage to your own brand if you defend against a beloved company without considering all the implications. Indeed, one of the ways a new entrant can fight back is to draw attention to your defensive plan.

YOU DON'T CARE ABOUT THE BUSINESS

A very simple rule of thumb: you shouldn't spend a lot of money defending a business that you don't care about. This is fairly obvious. Defense takes time and money, so if you don't mind losing market share and revenues then there isn't any point in defending.

There are two scenarios where this might be the case. First, a company may be planning to exit the business entirely, discontinuing the product, and shutting down the division. This happens fairly frequently in the world of business, as senior executives pull the plug on struggling business units. Cisco, for example, shut down the Flip business in early 2011. In this situation, Cisco wasn't particularly concerned about the launch of competitive products; there was no need to defend Flip.

Second, the business might have limited profitability, or, worse, it might be losing money. In this case, there may be little financial incentive to defend. The costs of defending are high, but in these cases the rate of return from protecting the business will be very low. The Parkay margarine brand, for example, makes little profit for parent ConAgra. There is no reason to spend a lot of money defending a business that isn't really profitable in the first place.

One thing to watch, of course, is fixed expenses. If a business has substantial fixed costs, then volume is important. In this case, a business might have little operating profit, but each unit of sales helps cover the fixed costs of the business. In this case a defense might be necessary to maintain economies of scale of the business.

YOU WANT A COMPETITOR

Paradoxically, there are times where you might actually want a competitor. In this case mounting a defense wouldn't make any sense since you hope the new entrant succeeds.

So who would actually want a competitor? Given all the trouble competitors cause, isn't it always better to have fewer of them?

In general, having more competitors is a bad thing; it puts pressure on a business and makes it difficult to build profits. But in certain cases an additional competitor actually helps. In an emerging category, for example, an existing player might welcome a new entrant because the new entrant might help build the category. Establishing a new category is a huge challenge. You must create awareness, figure out how to distribute the product, set the appropriate pricing, communicate the benefits, establish a favorable set of standards and regulations...the list goes on and on. Having a second company in the market is sometimes very helpful for developing a category. Eli Lilly, for example, would likely have welcomed the launch of a competitor as it rolled out Xigris, the first FDA-approved treatment for severe sepsis, because getting physicians used to diagnosing and treating sepsis was a sizable task.

A company launching a new technology in an established category might welcome competition as well. The new entrant would provide additional momentum to the launch and give the technological innovation more credibility.

Another obvious area: if you're being scrutinized by government regulators and accused of acting in an anticompetitive manner, then a new competitor would be a welcome development. It becomes at least one piece of proof suggesting that you do not have monopoly power. If a company wanted to launch a new operating system that competed directly with Microsoft Windows, for example, Microsoft would likely be quite pleased. Similarly, if someone entered the chip market, Intel would likely be delighted. In both cases, the new entrant would help refute accusations of monopoly power and anticompetitive behavior.

YOU HAVE MORE COMPELLING OPPORTUNITIES

Since no business has an unlimited budget, there are always tradeoffs, and sometimes the opportunities facing a firm outweigh the competitive risk.

In most cases, when a threat appears, the defending company pivots from a focus on offense to a focus on defense. This is very appropriate, since the attack is very urgent and very important. Most of the spending becomes defensive in nature, and growth initiatives are put aside temporarily. Taking on too many initiatives is never a good idea; it is highly unlikely that a company will be able to launch a major new product while also defending aggressively.

Delaying a growth initiative is a tough decision. Financially, it's a setback since you won't receive any of the benefits of the growth initiative. The impact of this can extend over several years. For example, in year one, the new branding program was probably a financial drain, as the costs outweigh the benefits. But after several years the branding effort should be paying back with improved customer loyalty and pricing leverage.

The decision to delay a new product launch is particularly frustrating because there's no guarantee you'll be able to launch the product later. Trends in the market may change, or a competitor might launch the idea before you're able to pull it off. If you wait, it may never happen.

When confronted with a decision about defending, ask yourself: what is the trade-off? What will we give up? What might we gain? There are times when the growth opportunity significantly outweighs the competitive threat, and in these cases defending wouldn't make sense. Be careful with the calculation, however; it's human nature to value your idea more than someone else's idea, so you may underestimate the competitive risk.

YOU CAN'T WIN

There are also times when you can't successfully defend; the competitor is so strong, and your position so vulnerable, that the odds of a successful defense are very small. In these situations, it may actually be better to retreat rather than to fight a battle you're destined to lose.

While defense efforts generally have a strong chance of success, they don't *always* work. There are many things a defender can do, but sometimes these efforts are insufficient. The competitor may have far more money than you can bring to bear, and then even your strongest defense will be insufficient. Or the competitor may have developed a product that is dramatically better than yours and may have protected it with so many patents that you are not able to match it. Or the competitor may have lower costs and be willing to sell at a price you can never approach.

If a defensive effort is not likely to work, it may be better to gracefully retreat than fight a losing battle. Defense takes money and time. Throwing your resources at a failed defensive effort might actually reduce your ability to do other things down the road; you might expend your financial reserves fighting the losing battle. As business school professors Ron Adner and Daniel Snow observed in a recent *Harvard Business Review* article, "Militaries have long regarded retreat as a legitimate—and responsible—strategic option."[8]

Chicago retailer Seigle's provides a good example of this. Seigle's was a large hardware store near downtown Chicago, on the corner of North and Clybourn Avenues. It was a busy, successful store, providing good service and a reasonable assortment of products. One day, home improvement giant Home Depot announced that it would be opening an enormous new store two blocks away from Seigle's. The new store would have hundreds of parking spaces, low prices, and a vast selection of products.

The managers at Seigle's analyzed the developing situation and then made a rather bold move: they retreated. Months before the Home Depot store opened, they announced that they would be closing Seigle's. And they did. They liquidated the inventory, sold the real estate, and moved into the commercial building supply market, opening a new location in the suburbs of Chicago.

The leadership team at Seigle's made a tough but smart decision. They presumably concluded that there was no way they could compete against a huge corporate power like Home Depot. Even their strongest defensive efforts would be insufficient because they couldn't match Home Depot's pricing, parking, or selection. By retreating, Seigle's was able to minimize the financial damage. This allowed the company to move into a completely different market.

IBM employed the same strategy on a bigger scale in the personal computer industry. Faced with a growing number of competitive threats, IBM executives assessed the options and eventually concluded the best option was to simply exit the industry; it would be simply too difficult to hold back the attackers. IBM sold the business to Lenovo in 2004, in hindsight a very savvy move. As CEO Samuel Palmisano said in a recent interview, "We've lasted 100 years, because we never limited ourselves to a view of a particular product."[9]

There are many ways to retreat. A company can simply exit a market, as IBM and Seigle's did. Alternatively, a company could sell out to the new entrant, capturing the value of the acquisition and also the value of the avoided defense. Or a company could concede a segment of the industry to the new entrant, deciding not to contest the launch and planning for a smaller business going forward.

Recognizing these situations is difficult, but anyone contemplating defense must evaluate the odds of success and be certain that fighting a defensive battle is better than retreating.

WRONG REASONS

It is important to note that many of the reasons why people don't defend are actually based on flawed logic; they seem like valid reasons, but the strategic thinking just doesn't work. Below are some examples.

YOU WILL VALIDATE THE DEFENDER'S IDEA

When I ask people for reasons not to defend, one of the first answers I usually get is this: "If we defend, we will actually help the attacker because we will validate the idea and give it credibility."

On the surface, there is a certain degree of logic in this; a very public defense, one that attracts a lot of attention, might well create additional interest in the competitor's idea and perhaps increase its sales. In addition, by taking extraordinary steps to respond, you indicate that the idea is promising and exciting, and this, too, helps the attacker.

But this concern is easily addressed by adjusting the type of defense. There are many ways to defend. A company can defend in a very dramatic fashion and draw lots of attention to the battle and the competitive product. But it's also possible to mount what is essentially an invisible defense, where people don't notice the defensive campaign at all. A particularly generous coupon in the Sunday newspaper might be an effective defensive tactic but it won't help the competitor. Additional advertising spending won't on its own indicate that you are particularly concerned about the threat. Similarly, launching a different new item into the market won't help the new entrant; it will just create clutter.

The desire to avoid drawing attention to a competitor should be a factor when planning the defense, but it isn't a reason not to defend at all.

THE COMPETITOR HAS A BAD IDEA

Simple logic would tell you that there's no need to defend against a fundamentally bad idea. If the competitor has a clunker of an idea, why bother to defend against it? It will die a natural death on its own; there's no need to help it along.

But this logic is flawed. Indeed, there are several very compelling reasons to defend against a bad idea. First, by defending you can protect your short-term sales and kill the new product quickly. Companies may continue investing in a new product for a very long time, clinging to the hope that it might work someday, and very often the spending gets more reckless as time goes on. If initial sales are weak, there is a temptation to just throw more money at the new product, and this can distort a market and damage your business: remember, people believe they are right. Killing a new product quickly is a significant benefit.

Second, sending a signal is very important in defense. If you don't defend against some big new products, you send a very odd signal: you defend sometimes but not all the time. This inconsistency will likely lead to more attacks down the road.

Third, and most important, the competitor's bad idea might actually be a good idea. You just might not understand it. You might not know all the details behind it. Or perhaps the product isn't yet quite perfect; it's just the first version. Again, people tend to think they are right, so when a new product appears in your market, your first instinct will be to declare that it isn't a good idea. If it were a good idea, of course, you would have come up with it. If you don't defend against bad ideas, then you won't take any action, and the new competitor will be free to launch. If the product actually is a very good idea, you just missed your opportunity.

YOU ARE A SMALL PLAYER

Here's another common reason people use as a rationale not to defend: "We're a smaller company in the market. The big, established player will defend and push back the new entrant. We should just leave it to them."

It's tempting to believe this if you are a small company—but be careful. It is very true that the big players will likely defend against a new entrant and that their efforts will push back the attacker. The problem is that during the big competitive battle, a small player can take a very substantial hit.

If a new entrant tries to enter the cheese category in the United States, for example, it is very likely that big players, such as Kraft, will defend vigorously. The new entrant will spend heavily on building distribution, awareness, and trial. Kraft will spend heavily to block the new entrant's efforts. Spending in the category will increase dramatically as the competitive battle unfolds.

In this environment, small players often take the biggest hit. In the worst case, the new entrant captures some market share, and the established big players protect their market share. The brands that get hurt are the smaller players who didn't compete as aggressively.

This is precisely what happened in the cheese category in the 1990s. ConAgra attempted to enter the category, launching a line of cheeses under the Healthy Choice brand. Kraft defended aggressively. As the battle unfolded, smaller brands such as Land o'Lakes suffered the biggest losses of market share.

When there is a competitive battle in a category, smaller players may have to defend to protect their business. In these cases, however, the focus of the defender is not on hurting the new entrant but on protecting its own share and revenue.

Some small niche businesses are indeed immune; if your segment is isolated and not likely to see any impact, then you may be fine. Otherwise, defend.

YOUR SHORT-TERM RESULTS WILL SUFFER

Short-term returns can frequently be very modest when you deploy defense strategies, especially if measured against the prior quarter or the prior year. A customer retention program aimed at defending against a new entrant, for example, might be a very effective tool for keeping customers and preventing losses to a new competitor. But the financial return on the program will be poor; you will be spending a lot of extra money to retain customers you already have. In the best case, your spending will keep the customers you otherwise would have lost, not just subsidize those who would have been loyal even without the defense plan. Either way, the returns will be small when measured against growth-oriented programs.

As a result, managers focused on short-term financial results will be inclined to limit defense spending or not to defend at all. When you defend, the financials erode, and the financial results of the business get worse.

But this is not a valid reason to abandon a defensive effort. Defensive spending delivers long-term returns; limiting the gains of a new competitor will yield benefits for many years to come. The benefit is for the long term, but the cost is incurred in the short term. A fixation on short-term results is a dangerous strategy when facing new competitors. As Harvard business professor Clay Christensen observes, "If you study the root causes of business disasters, over and over you'll find the predisposition toward endeavors that offer immediate gratification."[10]

MANY COMPANIES DEFEND TOO LITTLE AND TOO LATE

All too many companies defend too little, and when they finally start defending, it is too late. The history of business is full of stories of companies that didn't defend when they should have or didn't defend effectively.

It is important to understand why business leaders fail to respond effectively so that you don't make the same mistakes.

THEY DON'T UNDERSTAND THE THREAT

A big reason companies don't defend when they should is that they don't understand the threat. The established players think they understand the market and the competitor's idea, but they don't. They then ignore the threat or defend in a half-hearted fashion. By the time the situation is clear, the defense window has largely closed, and the damage is done. This was the case for Intel when Japanese competitors began entering its market. According to CEO Andy Grove, "By the time the data showed that the Japanese memory producers were becoming a major factor, we were in the midst of a fight for our survival."[11]

This is particularly an issue when a new entrant has a unique strategy, either a major product innovation or a new business model. The bigger the change, the more likely the established player simply won't see it, appreciate it, or understand it, and in turn won't defend as it should.

Companies can launch new products into established categories in three ways: attack the core, target a niche, or change the rules. Attacking the core involves launching a product that is similar to existing items and supporting the launch aggressively. DHL, for example, attempted to break into the domestic shipping market in the United States by offering good service and competitive prices and invested heavily in marketing and promotion. Companies aiming to target a niche go after a small part of an established market. Lululemon used this strategy to enter the sports apparel market; the company focused entirely on clothes for yoga. Strategies to change the rules occur when the new entrant introduces a new benefit, technology, or business model and tries to change the fundamental category dynamics. This is how Dyson entered the vacuum cleaner market; Dyson was the first company to highlight that vacuum cleaner bags can clog and lose suction.

Established companies generally defend effectively when competitors try to attack the core of their business. These new products are hard to miss, and they look threatening, so the defense decision is easy. For example, UPS and FedEx noticed the DHL launch and defended.

Niche strategies are a bit harder to deal with. Companies focusing on a niche often develop highly tailored products, with the business model catering to the target group exceptionally well. For the established player, it can be difficult to see these launches. Learning about a new deodorant launched in El Paso, Texas, can be a challenge for a company based in New Jersey. The defense decision is difficult because the threat seems limited. It is a just a niche, after all. Blocking niche players can be difficult, too, because the defense might require new products. It can also be difficult to establish credibility in the niche. Fortunately, since the risk from a niche launch is usually modest, the overall defensive risk is generally small.

Change-the-rules strategies are by far the most difficult launches to handle. One of the biggest problems is that companies trying to change the rules obviously aren't following existing category norms (hence the name). Very often these companies launch products that have limited customer appeal, at least until the company manages to shift how customers view the category. For a defender, it is easy to miss these threats. A diligent defending company would likely test the new product with customers, find that it has little appeal, and then decide not to defend. If the attacking company is then successful at changing the rules, however, the new product becomes appealing and begins to grow. The result? The defending company takes a huge hit as the market changes, leaving the established player behind. As legendary football coach Bill Walsh noted, "Unfortunately, too often we find comfort in what worked before—even when it stops working. We get stuck there and resist the new, the unfamiliar, the unconventional."[12]

This is likely why Hoover vacuum cleaners failed to defend against Dyson, and why Dannon yogurt didn't respond quickly to Chobani. The new entrants had ideas that appeared to be feeble to the existing player but were actually trendsetters. As Harvard professor Clayton Christensen observed, "products that do not appear to be useful to our customers today may squarely address their needs tomorrow."[13]

THEY DON'T UNDERSTAND THE COMPANY

Many defensive situations are mishandled because executives at the established company make a simple mistake: they assume the new entrants are just like them. As a result, they don't understand the full situation and then defend inappropriately.

It's incredibly tempting to believe that other people see the world the same way you do; your situation is very present and very real, so the logical thing to do is assume that the attacker is viewing things in a similar fashion. As behavioral economist Dan Ariely observes, "The great challenge lies in making the leap into someone else's mind. Psychological research affirms that we are all partial prisoners of our own preferences and have a hard time seeing the world from a different perspective."[14]

Misjudging an attacker's intent is very problematic when defending. The first issue is that you misread the threat; what looks like a small idea with little chance of success might actually be a major innovation you need to address.

The second issue is that your defense activities might actually make things worse, because you force the competition to respond to your defense, which actually makes the problem bigger.

THERE IS A BIAS TOWARD GROWTH

Defense usually involves a trade-off; in order to fund a defensive effort, executives must cut spending on something else. Usually this involves pruning back growth initiatives, which managers are often very reluctant to do.

Business leaders are hired to drive growth. Every year they invest hours and hours thinking up ways to build their business: new products that might enhance the franchise, new packaging innovations that will make the product more useful or distinctive, new advertising to reach out and connect with new customers, new loyalty programs that will resonate with existing customers and build loyalty.

As the ideas take shape, the people who have developed the plans get excited about the future; they usually deeply believe the initiative will work and build the business. It's hard not to love a commercial after you've spent a wonderful week in sunny California shooting it with a team of gifted creative people. And it's difficult to question the merits of a new product when you've devoted two years to making sure everything about it is exactly right.

When a defense situation comes along, then, there is a general reluctance to shelve the exciting growth initiative in order to respond to a competitor. As a result, the company presses forward with the growth program and elects not to defend. As former Sony executive Stephen Denny observed, "Nobody likes to be forced to compete when they've got other things on their to-do lists."[15]

The reason people emphasize growth over defense isn't hard to understand. A product manager might sum it up like this: "Let's consider the choice. On the one hand, we have this exciting growth initiative, supported by top-notch customer research. On the other hand, we see this rather ill-conceived competitive move. We know those folks are inferior marketers, and we have absolutely no data suggesting their new product will be successful. Indeed, it looks like a pretty feeble one to me. You want me to table our promising growth initiative to defend? Really?"

Confronted by a choice like this, many business executives understandably focus on their own programs, ignore the competitive threat, and suffer the consequences. But you must resist the temptation to ignore the threat facing you.

You can be confident that your initiatives will always seem more appealing, because you created them. Be careful and don't rush to judgment.

You must also remember the risk and rewards. In many cases, the risk from the competitive move far outweighs the gain from your own growth initiative. If a competitor manages to successfully break into your market, the downside risk is extraordinarily large. If you push forward with your growth initiative, you will generate incremental sales and profit if everything goes well. Generally, however, the upside will be rather modest compared to the impact of the threat.

Cutting a growth project to fund defensive efforts is a very tough decision, but it is often the right thing to do.

THEY UNDERESTIMATE THE RISK

A defense plan will be grounded in an assessment of risk. The bigger the downside risk, the more a company will need to defend. Underestimating the risk is a major reason why companies may not defend when they should or not do so as aggressively as they should.

As discussed above, companies underestimate competitive risks in part because they may not understand the competitor or the threat.

Another key reason why companies don't defend is that the executives focus on the near future. This view underestimates a competitive threat fairly dramatically. With a short-term perspective, competitive threats don't seem that scary. It would seem that a new entrant that manages to take a couple share points next year isn't really a big issue. And in that year, it isn't. But the new entrant isn't going away; once the new entrant has gained a foothold, it will continue to grow, stealing market share the following year and then the year after that. Things get very ugly over time.

Many managers focus on the short-term situation. This is in part because their goals tend to be short term; managers frequently move between positions, so focusing on the current situation makes a lot of sense. When you will only be in a business for a couple years, there is little reason to worry about the ten-year outlook. Consulting firm McKinsey did a study in 2008 of managerial decision making. Researchers asked managers how far they looked into the future to forecast the costs and benefits of a decision. Sixty-two percent of managers looked two years ahead or less, and 85 percent of managers looked four years ahead or less.[16]

With a short-term horizon, it often doesn't make sense to defend; the cost will be high, and the risk when not defending will be low. The problem, of course, is that this opens the door for competitive entries.

DEFENDING WOULD BE DIFFICULT

Many companies elect not to defend for the simple reason that a defensive initiative would be too difficult.

Some defense efforts are fairly easy. For example, if the attacker is going directly after your core business, you can fairly easily protect your business simply by doing more of what you are already doing. If a new mainstream beer attempts to break into the industry, for example, the existing brewers can simply increase spending on sales, advertising, and promotions and block the attacker. Similarly, if a new Italian restaurant opens up, the existing restaurant simply might add some loyalty programs, cut prices, increase marketing, and bolster customer service and food quality.

In other cases, however, defending is much more difficult. This is often because the attacker has a different approach to the business, perhaps a new way of distributing the product, or a new technology, or a new level of customer service. In these situations, the defense becomes much more challenging. When the only way to effectively defend is to fundamentally change your business model, you think twice before doing it.

New entrants that embrace a new distribution system can be particularly difficult to address; the entire innovation runs counter to the established company's model. A company that relies on outsourced brokers to promote its products may find it challenging to defend against a new entrant that sells directly on the Internet. Retailing giant Wal-Mart, for example, has been very slow to react to the growth of Internet retailers such as Amazon in part because defending would be difficult given Wal-Mart's infrastructure.

If a defense requires a significant change, there are three issues. First, the expense will likely be high; creating the new model will require a major investment. Second, the defense has long-term implications; by making a defensive move, the company is making a long-term bet. Third, you can damage your existing business with the defensive effort; the defense initiative creates a tension in the organization and introduces a new layer of complexity.

In the US insurance market, established players such as Allstate have struggled to defend against Internet-based competitors such Geico. The established players generally rely on a network of agents to sell policies and interact with customers. In 2010, for example, Allstate had more than 12,500 agents scattered all across the country.[17] Allstate's pricing reflected this fact. Geico, however, sold directly to consumers via the Internet or phone. By using this model, Geico could offer significantly lower rates; it didn't need to pay agents. Geico then used this point of difference to relentlessly hammer home the message that shifting to Geico could save you money.

Defending against Geico is a challenge for Allstate. Allstate can't match Geico's pricing without taking a significant financial hit. The company could sell policies directly to consumers on the web at lower rates, but this move would anger and hurt Allstate's agent network; defending in this fashion might do more damage than Geico's attack.

When defense becomes costly and difficult, there is a greater incentive not to defend; but the risk and cost of not defending can be outweighed by the risk and cost of defending.

PEOPLE ARE TOO CONFIDENT

Successful business leaders tend to be confident so they naturally assume they will do well and their competitor will do poorly. They then see no need to defend.

Confidence is an important trait in the world of business. There are many studies that highlight the general human tendency to be overly confident; most people think they are above average drivers, for example, and most people believe that they have superior talents. And it's true that any successful leader must make decisions and move forward despite criticism and second-guessing. The only way to do this is with confidence—the deep belief that one is correct. People respond to confident, decisive leaders.

In business, doubt and indecision rarely carry the day. It's hard to rally the troops with a doubting, half-hearted approach, saying, "Well, team, I think that this plan might work. Of course, a lot of things could go wrong, so it might not. And the other strategy could actually be better; I'm just not certain. It is such a pickle; we really are in trouble either way, aren't we? So, well, I hope this all works. But we really will need some luck to make it happen. Maybe we should pray."

Instead, you need confidence—the ability to get up in front of a team and proclaim, "Ladies and gentlemen, I am so excited about our plan. We have a team that is second to none, and we have a strategy that is going to work. We are going to attack our competition, and we are going to win!"

This confidence then spills over into the organization, which is great for business until the organization suddenly becomes *overly* confident. Good results lead to even more confidence. As marketer Paul Groundwater observed, when a company is doing well "you get fat, dumb, and lazy."[18]

Overconfidence can be a dangerous characteristic when it comes to a defensive scenario. A confident leader will believe in her growth plans and will be slow to recognize threats. The reasoning is quite simple: if you are very confident when you weigh the rewards of your growth plan versus the risks of the competitive attack, you will give your own plan a high probability of success while discounting the competitive attack. ("The chance my program will work? Absolutely, 90 percent. The chance the competitor will succeed? At most, 25 percent.") The result is that you favor your own initiative and discount the threat, and then the competitive move progresses, facing no defense.

Confidence is a particular problem because it tends to build over time. We all have a remarkable ability to convince ourselves that whatever we're thinking happens to be correct, and then we seek information that supports our views.

When confronted with new information, for example, people often process it in a way that reinforces what they already believe. If the new data supports our belief, then we seize it and pronounce it to be important and significant. We read it closely, noting all the details of the study and the findings. "Wow! This is a great study. This is *so true!*" we proclaim as we herald the arrival of this new and important data. We forward along the article to our friends, or we print off a copy, and we keep the information close.

If the new information runs counter to our belief, however, we are quick to discard it; we identify problems in the study or methodology or identify reasons why the study can't be applied more broadly. "Well, that certainly is a flawed study, isn't it? I really can't believe that author ignored so many significant points," we might grump. So we scan the article, then move on to the next web page, or toss the article in the trash.

This is commonly referred to as confirmation bias, and it is remarkably prevalent. As Emory University psychologist Scott Lilienfeld observed, "We're all mentally lazy. It's simply easier to focus our attention on data that supports our hypothesis, rather than to seek out evidence that might disprove it."[19]

Getting a second opinion rarely helps the situation, because people often consult with people like themselves. These people just seem smarter to us. Kellogg professor Keith Murnighan notes, "We are biased not to ask people who are different from us to evaluate our potential decisions but only to ask people who are similar to us. But different kinds of people are exactly the people we should seek out."[20]

Many academics have explored the idea of confirmation bias. Peter Wason published one of the first studies on confirmation bias in 1960. He asked study participants to identify the rule governing a series of numbers and let them ask questions to test their hypothesis. People overwhelmingly asked questions that simply confirmed their hypothesis, not questions that could potentially contradict their hypothesis.[21]

This finding was confirmed in a more recent study published in the *Quarterly Journal of Experimental Psychology*. In this study, participants attempted to determine the rules governing the movement of dots on a screen. Study participants could choose from a variety of tests to validate their hypotheses. Researchers found that when people actually chose a test that contradicted their hypothesis, they correctly used the information and changed their thinking. But people rarely chose such tests, instead favoring studies that simply confirmed the way they were thinking.[22]

Researcher Martin Tolcott and others published a particularly interesting study in 1989. They looked at how army intelligence officers evaluated battle conditions. During the study, they gave intelligence officers information about a battle scenario and asked them to determine where the enemy was most likely to attack. They also asked the intelligence officers to rate their level of confidence on a 100-point scale. The information provided was deliberately vague; it was easily possible to reach different conclusions.

The researchers later gave study participants more information, each time a balanced mix of data, with some information indicating that the enemy would attack from one direction and other data suggesting the enemy would attack from a different direction. After each set of additional information, the participants again submitted their point of view and level of confidence.

The results were striking in two ways. First, the intelligence officers were remarkably confident despite the lack of complete information; on average the officers indicated a confidence level of 77.3 out of 100. And with additional information (even contradictory information), their confidence increased significantly.[23]

All of these studies suggest that it is human nature to believe we are right and then to seek information confirming this. This insight has important implications when it comes to defense.

Most new ideas aren't completely new; it's a rare day when we come across something that makes us say, "Wow! I never imaged that was possible. That is just amazing." New products are often old concepts brought to life in new ways. Apple's innovative iPad, for example, could be considered a supremely well-executed tablet computer, an idea that had been envisioned and worked on for many years. Apple's iPhone wasn't really new, either; there were lots of smartphones in the market when the iPhone first came out.

In many cases, when a new entrant attempts to enter an established market, its executives are building on an idea that has been around in the category in some form for many years. Companies are always thinking about innovations and new products, so the established players almost certainly studied and evaluated the idea. They might even have tested the concept or the product in the market. So when a competitor shows up with a variation on the idea, the established player will be quick to dismiss the threat. Expertise and seniority can backfire. As Kellogg professor Jim Anderson observed about experience, "It can be a source of strength, but it can also be a source of myopia."[24]

This is one reason that even the savviest executives often fail to take defensive action when they should. Barry Calpino, a vice president at Kraft Foods, worked on the launch of Febreze odor eliminator early in his career. He notes that the existing players were very skeptical of the product and didn't react: "Our competitors were all looking at it. They made fun of it." Febreze is now a $1 billion business. Similarly, Microsoft CEO Steve Ballmer dismissed Apple's iPhone, stating, "There's no chance that the iPhone is going to get any significant market share."[25] And Intel's CEO misread Apple's Macintosh computer, saying, "In 1984, when Apple introduced the Macintosh, I thought it was a ridiculous toy."[26]

For this reason, ideas that established players have evaluated and rejected are often the most promising ideas for new competitors. As Harvard professor Clay Christensen wrote in his book, *The Innovator's Dilemma*, "Perhaps the most powerful protection that small entrant firms enjoy as they build the emerging markets for disruptive technologies is that they are doing something that it simply does not make sense for the established leaders to do."[27]

THE COMPANY IS TOO OPTIMISTIC

Optimism, like confidence, is an important characteristic for business leaders but a dangerous trait when evaluating a competitive threat. When a company is under attack, optimism can lead you to underestimate a competitive threat and not defend when you should.

It's hard to be against optimism. A can-do spirit is one of the characteristics of great business leaders; you have to be able to see and go after big goals and motivate your team to follow your lead.

When dealing with a growth initiative, optimism is a force multiplier. If you believe you can achieve great things, you are more likely to pursue them with vigor and energy, and they are actually more likely to happen. Energy and drive can propel projects ahead. Believing that a new product launch will go well will inspire you to work harder on the new product. Your team will be motivated by the potential success and your enthusiasm; your distributors might feel the energy and take on the product.

In some organizations, optimism is a part of the culture while negative thinking is actively discouraged. AOL CEO Tim Armstrong, for example, stated in a recent CNN interview, "Don't allow loser talk. Don't allow it in your organization. Talk about winning. Talk about how you are moving things along."[28]

The problem is that optimistic thinking is one reason established players fail to defend. An optimistic leader might proclaim, "We have the finest products in the industry. This year we're bringing to market our best new innovations, and they're going to do great things for our business. Now, you might have heard that our competition has a new product this year, too. But that isn't a big factor—they won't stop us! We will withstand the new product attack, and our business will prosper and flourish. I guarantee it."

With an optimistic perspective, the defensive threat doesn't look very scary. And thus the established company is less likely to defend. Lucy Kellaway, a columnist at the *Financial Times,* recently noted that too much optimism is a problem: "An insistence on triumphalist talk is not only naff, it is stupid and dangerous. To abstain from using the negative means half of one's vision is obscured—which is catastrophic in business. Most companies, most of the time, do not win. And when they are actually losing, it is a good idea to say so right away, so that remedial action can be taken."[29] Henry Kravis, CEO of Kohlberg Kravis Roberts, makes a similar point: "Bad news and criticism deserve more attention than compliments. We live in a world of fierce competition, and arrogance will kill you."[30]

Optimism is a particular trap because power appears to increase optimism; people who feel powerful are generally more optimistic about the future, less worried about risk, and more likely to engage in risky behaviors. In one notable study, professors Cameron Anderson and Adam Galinsky completed a series of experiments that showed how a sense of power impacts how people viewed different situations. In one experiment, for example, they asked participants to estimate their chances of experiencing different positive life events. People who felt more powerful were significantly more optimistic. In another experiment, they asked people to estimate the number of deaths from 17 different causes. People with a heightened sense of power estimated a significantly lower number of fatalities. They also found that powerful people tended to take more chances and reveal confidential information.[31]

The problem, of course, is that business leaders have power. A senior manager can shape a huge organization. Even a fairly junior product manager has considerable power; there is an entire team awaiting her direction. This means business leaders are quite likely to be optimistic, downplay risks, and take chances.

Is this a call to be pessimistic and negative? It certainly isn't. Optimism is an important characteristic in most business situations. But when faced with a question of whether to defend, it's risky to be too optimistic. A bit of caution is a very good thing.

WATCH AND WAIT

Very frequently you will encounter situations where there is a potential threat in the market, but it is simply too small to justify a full defense plan. In this case, the best approach may well be to simply monitor the threat, gauging how effective the new company is at getting started. At some point, it might become necessary to take action, so it is critical to keep an eye on the new entrant.

Defense decisions can change. What doesn't look like a threat today might appear to be a very big threat tomorrow as you learn more about it or as the market evolves. Similarly, a very scary competitive move might, upon further analysis, seem less of an issue as time goes by.

A product that seems like a very bad idea at first might start to catch on and eventually require a defensive move. This can happen quickly. As Intel CEO Andy Grove observed, "It's like sailing a boat when the wind shifts on you, but for some reason, maybe because you are down below, you don't even sense that the wind has changed until the boat suddenly heels over."[32]

In truth, when faced with a defense decision, there are really only two options: actively defend now or watch and wait.

KEY QUESTIONS

When evaluating a defensive threat, it is important to consider four important questions that can help you determine whether a defense is necessary or not.

IS THE COMPETITIVE PRODUCT A WINNER?

This question forces you to evaluate the new idea. Will customers buy it? Will the product make money? How big might it become if the launch is successful?

WHAT IS THE LONG-TERM THREAT TO US?

This is perhaps the most important question to consider. What is the potential downside? How bad could things get if the competitor succeeds? It is useful to quantify the long-term risk to fully understand the issue.

WHAT ARE THE COSTS OF DEFENDING?

How expensive would it be to defend? How difficult? Would it require a significant change in our business model? Understanding this is important because it sets up the final question.

WHICH OPTION HAS THE BEST LONG-TERM RETURN, DEFENDING OR NOT?

It is important to think about this question twice. The first time it is useful to answer it based on your honest assessment of the new product idea. The second time is it important to answer it assuming that you are wrong and that the new product will be much more successful than you anticipated.

Anyone facing a competitive threat needs to think deeply about the defense decision. It is critical to weigh both sides. It is important to remember, however, that there is a great tendency to ignore threats. Deciding to defend is often the safest approach.

Chapter 7

PLANNING THE DEFENSE

ONCE YOU'VE MADE THE IMPORTANT decision to defend, your focus needs to quickly shift to actually planning the effort. This is the stage where you figure out what precisely you will do and when you will do it. This is when you must think through all the defensive options, select the best ones, and then mobilize to execute the plan.

Planning is a critical step in the defense process for a very simple reason: there are many ways to defend. A company can use dozens of different tactics to protect its business and damage a competitor. These tactics vary widely; some are simple and basically free while others are complex initiatives that require millions in spending. There is no such thing as an essential defense tactic; figuring out how to defend is a matter of understanding the threat you face and choosing the appropriate tactics.

There are several best practices to embrace when developing a defensive plan.

GO FAST

Building a defense plan is very different from developing a growth plan because time is important; you have to move quickly.

When you're in growth mode, doing things quickly is important, but it's usually a secondary consideration. It is worth taking the time to get things right. Some organizations spend months and months developing an annual marketing plan; the process can be long, methodical, and time-consuming.

When developing the plan for an established product, companies can often afford to be slow and deliberate because things are usually moving along with no particularly urgent threats. You have to keep going, of course, because a business doesn't stand still. Executives want to see results, and the only way you can deliver results is by getting something done. But spending a month or two honing a plan is usually fine. Indeed, spending time developing a well-considered marketing plan is a best practice; it is better to spend a bit more time and get the plan right than rush to market with a half-baked effort.

Similarly, when planning for a new product launch there is generally time to review and refine it. New product teams must move with reasonable dispatch, but there is usually space for diligent planning, even if it's just while you're waiting for the technical team to work out some of the details.

The situation is much different when it comes to defense. When you are under attack, time is not on your side; you have to move fast. As Dallas Diggs, a former marketing executive at Johnson & Johnson, observed, "You've got to move quickly and you have to pick a strategy. You can't be playing around with three or four different things."[1]

Speed is important for three critical reasons. First, it's easier to get a new entrant to give up on an idea early on. When a company is just considering a concept, it has little invested in terms of resources and emotional commitment. Getting the competitor to abandon the idea isn't too hard at this point. But the longer the project moves forward, the more the situation changes: the company has invested money and time in the idea and then will be more reluctant to give up on it.

This is partly due to a flawed focus on sunk costs. In theory, we shouldn't care about the resources we've sunk into a project; that time and money are gone and in the past. The focus should only be on the future and how to best deploy the resources we now have. In reality, of course, these sunk costs feel very real. People are reluctant to give up and admit that the time and money they invested in an idea were a mistake.

Further, as time goes on, a project's financial status improves, at least on paper. Consider a project where a company planned to invest €400 million to build a factory that would generate €500 million in positive cash flows over the life of the project (in present value terms). Before the project starts, the company has a €100 million expected benefit. If the company spends €200 million on the construction in the first year, the economics of the project shift. At that point, the company only has to invest €200 million to get the €500 million in positive cash flows; the project has now become much more attractive. Even if the company has doubts about the project and decides to reduce the expected benefit to €300 million, it still looks good.

Economically, then, a defense is more likely to be successful if implemented early in project's life, before money is spent and enthusiasm for the idea grows. The best defense efforts kick in when a potential attacker is just considering the idea, because you may be able to force the competitor to have second thoughts and not launch at all.

The second reason to move fast is to maximize your options. The quicker you formulate your defense effort, the more options you'll have to work with. There are many ways to defend. You can change your pricing, launch a new product, add short-term promotions, deploy your legal team, and expand channel incentives. The list goes on and on. Indeed, the second half of this book outlines the many tactics you can employ.

But many of the options vanish as a competitor gets further into its product launch. You can't gently send a signal when the competitor has distribution and is furiously building trial; this just won't work. Similarly, you can't block distribution once a competitor has gained it; you are too late. And you can't block a competitor's efforts to build awareness when it has already been created.

The third reason to move quickly through the planning phase is that defensive efforts are more likely to work if you deploy them quickly. It's fairly easy to kill off an idea when it is just in beginning stages. Later, however, once the competitor has built awareness and trial and repeat, it is exceptionally hard, if not impossible, to get it to leave the market.

The situation changes once the new product has been in the market for a while. If initial results are good, the product builds strength. Awareness increases, and it attracts a few customers who like it. In addition, distributors see the sales building and are likely to be disposed favorably toward the product, so distribution is more secure. As the product catches on, it becomes very hard to dislodge it.

For all these reasons, quick defensive planning and execution is essential. Time is a fundamental to your success in this. You can't sit around for months debating the plan; you have to figure out the optimal course and get going.

PICK YOUR SPOT

The Battle of Gettysburg, one of the pivotal battles in the Civil War, was shaped to a large degree by location. The Union troops, under General George Gordon Meade, were able to establish a strong position on the high ground, Little Round Top and Cemetery Ridge. This played a critical role in the battle. The Confederate troops under General Robert E. Lee had to attack a strong position and suffered massive casualties as a result.

In any battle, location plays a critical role because it shapes the conflict. This is true in military battles, of course. Important battles such as D-day, Gallipoli, Waterloo, and Gettysburg weren't determined solely by location, but it was a significant factor. Location also matters in the defensive battle for a business though the question isn't geographic. The key question is this: where can you inflict the most damage on your attacker? Where is the best place to fight?

It isn't possible to do everything, even in a defensive situation with substantial budgets. Even companies with a vast marketing budget will eventually be forced to choose among the options, if only because an organization can only execute a few things well at one time. When defending, you must pick your battles.

FIVE CRITICAL STEPS

Every product category is unique, with distinct dynamics and challenges. Cars are different from industrial lubricants, and these products are quite different from a service enterprise, such as a restaurant. Regardless of the category or country, however, every new product in the world must go through the same basic steps. The process of establishing a successful business is clear and consistent regardless of the situation.

Understanding the steps in the product development process is critical because each step presents defensive opportunities; you can choose at which

Exhibit 7.1   New product launch process

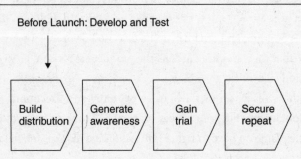

step you want to fight the defensive battle. If you can prevent a new entrant from succeeding at any of the steps, you will keep it out of the market.

STEP 1: DEVELOP AND TEST

The first step in the innovation process is product development and testing. Before people can introduce a new product or service, they have to come up with the idea, develop it, test it, and then decide to launch it. This is an obvious point, perhaps, but when it comes to defense, this stage is critical.

For many new products, this first stage can be quite long and involved; companies sometimes spend years or even decades developing and evaluating a particular new product idea. In the pharmaceutical industry, for example, it can easily take 10, 15, or even 20 years to bring a new molecule to market.

This stage very often involves a test market. A company making packaged consumer goods might launch the new product in a single market to evaluate how it sells. A retail chain might open up one or two locations to test the store concept. This information is critical to evaluate the potential of the new product.

Near the end of this first stage, an innovator has to make a critical decision: launch the product or not? Bringing the product to market is a major investment in time and money. For a big company, a new product launch can easily involve tens of millions of dollars. For an entrepreneur, the decision is enormously significant, because she will need to invest money and time, usually her own, in the new project. The question they all must consider: Is it worth it?

STEP 2: BUILD DISTRIBUTION

The second step for every new product is securing distribution. Before a new product can generate sales, it must secure a place in the sales channel.

This step is essential for every new product launch even though the way a product or service gets to the market can vary dramatically. This point is very obvious in the world of products. If a product sells through grocery stores, the company must get grocery stores to carry it. A new brand of bottled water in France, for example, has to get shelf space in key retailers such as Auchan, Leclerc, and Carrefour. Similarly, the manufacturer of a new line of baseball gloves in the United States has to get Wal-Mart and Dick's Sporting Goods to carry it.

Securing distribution is important in most business categories in some fashion or another. A new retail concept has to secure leases in key locations. A new airline has to get access to key airports. A new manufacturer of artificial knees has to sign on distributors.

In many categories, this is not an easy step. Getting a major retailer like Carrefour or Aldi to carry a product is an enormous hurdle. Eric Ryan, founder of Method, recalled how he initially approached Target about carrying his new line of products and received a quick rejection; the Target buyer reviewed the proposition and concluded, "You've got a snowball's chance in hell of ever getting into Target."[2]

STEP 3: GENERATE AWARENESS

Creating awareness and interest is the third step in the new product process. This step is obviously important; if people don't know about your product or service, or if they simply aren't interested in it, they won't buy it.

Creating awareness is the focus of many marketing efforts. This includes traditional marketing tools, such as print, television, and radio advertising, as well as newer tools, such as online advertising and social media campaigns. Public relations efforts are particularly important in generating awareness and interest since people are quick to tune out advertising messages.

Awareness-building usually follows once distribution has been established; it is most efficient to promote a product when it is available. On the surface, getting people excited about a new product before they can buy it might seem like a nifty approach, the sort of thing that might excite a new entrepreneur ("Wow! That would be fabulous!"). But it isn't very practical; there is a good chance people will look for the product, not find it, and then move on to other things, completely forgetting about the idea. By the time the product is available, they are no longer motivated to try it.

STEP 4: GAIN TRIAL

Trial is essential for every new product; if people don't try the product, they won't adopt it. Once a product has gained distribution, the focus shifts to building trial—getting folks to give it a shot.

Generating positive trial is perhaps the most important step for any new product. Customers must be convinced to try a new item, and then they must like it. If this happens, there is some hope for long-term success; the happy customer might come back and buy again. Or, even better, the customer might recommend the product to other people, or post a favorable comment on the web. If trial doesn't happen, or if the trial experience isn't positive, then the new product launch has major issues.

For this reason, trial is necessarily at the heart of any new product launch plan. Thus, a company launching a new product will hand out free samples and provide huge discounts, all in a bid to get trial. A company offering a new credit card will pay people to try it, and a new restaurant will offer huge inexpensive meals on a deal site like Groupon in order to get people in the door for the first time.

Remember AOL's "free trial" campaign in the late 1990s and early 2000s? The company gave away millions of free CDs with its software already loaded; all the customer had to do was download it and open an account. This drove trial and eventually led to repeat use and a leading market share as people responded to AOL's friendly "You've Got Mail" approach.

In most cases, the trial step follows building awareness. This is logical, of course, since it is hard to get trial for a product that people haven't heard of. The natural sequence is to first focus on building distribution, then move to awareness building, and then move on to gaining trial.

In reality, there is some overlap between these steps. Many trial-building programs also contribute to awareness. Sampling a new energy bar after a bike race is a good way to build trial, for example, but it also will likely build awareness, since some of those trying the bar may not have heard of it before.

STEP 5: SECURE REPEAT

The final step, securing repeat, is the single most important step for the long-term success of any new product. This stage of getting people who have tried the product or service to try it again is where new products ultimately succeed or fail.

A new product that gets tried out but does not get repeat is doomed: people tried the new item and decided that it wasn't good enough to warrant a subsequent purchase. This is a disaster, and it can be compounded by the fact that companies frequently lose money in the process of generating trial. A free sample doesn't create any revenue; it is just an expense. Similarly, offering 50 percent off dinner isn't a good way for a restaurant to boost profits; the meal is probably marginally profitable, if at all.

Repeat is much harder than trial for a very simple reason: people have to pay a higher price to repeat. A trial purchase is usually inexpensive. It doesn't take much of an investment on the part of a consumer to try an energy bar after a bike race. Redeeming a free coupon takes time, but there is no spending required. This trial moment is inexpensive for the customer and expensive for the company.

Repeat, however, is completely different. In most cases, repeat purchases are made at full price; the introductory offer price reductions are no longer available. Repeat purchases of the new product are more expensive for the customer but much better for the company because the company now actually generates some profits. In the best case, the customer had a very positive trial experience and is willing to pay full price for the product.

THE DEFENSIVE CHOICE

When defending a business against a new product's entry into the market, the challenge is to affect at least one of the five steps. Every new product needs to pass through all five steps, so if you can ensure that the new entrant stumbles just once, your defensive effort will succeed. A product that fails to get distribution, for example, simply can't sell; people can't buy a product if they don't have access to it. Similarly, a product that fails to generate trial will in turn miss out on repeat, since it is impossible to repeat purchasing a product if there is no trial.

While it is possible to defend at each step, it's almost impossible to defend at all stages at the same time. Partly this is a function of resources; money is always limited, even at very large companies and when the stakes are very high (which they usually are in a defensive situation). In more practical terms, however, timing dictates that you will have to choose: you can't be preventing the launch at the same moment that you are blocking repeat since these occur at different times.

Being clear on where you will defend is critical because this sets the stage for the next set of actions you must take: developing the full defense plan.

EMBRACE UNCERTAINTY

One of the biggest challenges of business is that it's always uncertain; you never know what the future holds, so the process of formulating strategy and developing plans is always difficult. In a defensive situation, however, the level of uncertainty is unusually high. As a result, anyone planning a defense has to be comfortable dealing with this high level of uncertainty.

Companies usually work hard to reduce uncertainty. Product managers conduct elaborate market research studies to understand how customers are feeling and how they will react to new ideas. When considering a new product introduction, for example, a company will often do a segmentation study to understand different consumer groups, ethnographic research to study behaviors, a pricing analysis to evaluate how different list prices will affect customer interest, a package study to evaluate shelf impact, and advertising research to gauge exactly how the creative idea will work. All of this can be combined in a full test market study, where the entire plan can be evaluated as a whole. The addition of models and simulations can reduce the uncertainty even more.

Defense requires an entirely different approach. When defending a business, the level of uncertainty is often uniquely high because despite your best efforts at competitive intelligence, there will be many things you will not know. How much is the competitor actually going to spend? What are the exact specifications of the new product? Where is the competitor sourcing a key ingredient? When precisely will it launch? Why is the competitor actually launching the product in the first place? Who is making the decisions?

The level of uncertainty is particularly high when dealing with innovative products. A totally new type of product presents an exceptional level of unknowns. As Harvard professor Clay Christensen observed, "Markets that do not exist cannot be analyzed; suppliers and customers must discover them together."[3] Apple, for example, has consistently launched highly innovative products that don't follow the established norms of a category. This makes Apple a particularly difficult company for competitors to deal with; it is hard to figure out what Apple is likely to do, and so it is difficult to get a strong defense into the market in time to have an impact.

When defending, you must force yourself to move ahead despite the unknowns. Time is of the essence, so you will probably have to start defending before you know precisely what you're defending against. Eventually the details will be clear; in time you will learn precisely what the competitor will do—the advertising, the promotion plan, the pricing, and the product. Unfortunately, by the time everything is clear, the time window in which to deploy your defense will have closed.

To defend successfully, you must operate with uncertainty and ambiguity. It can feel at times like you're defending against ghosts, a collection of rumors with a hefty dose of speculation. This shouldn't stop you from taking action.

BE FLEXIBLE

Given the level of uncertainty in defending against a new product, flexibility is critical. The only thing certain about a defensive plan is that it will never be perfect. Since you'll never have all the information you need about the attacker, the defense plan will not be optimal.

The key is to be willing and able to adjust course as new information comes in. If you learn that the launch date will be in October, not November, then the defense plan should change. If you determine that the competitor's advertising will feature a money-back guarantee, then you should adjust your defense plan accordingly, and if you learn that the competitor is hiring a huge sales organization, then your response will need to address that piece of knowledge.

Of course, having to change plans frequently can be very frustrating for an organization. Teams generally like clear direction. Plans that shift from one day to the next can make people grumpy. Your R&D manager is not going to be pleased to hear that your new product now needs to be 25 percent more effective than you originally thought or that it must come in at a cost that's 18 percent lower. Your sales team will probably tell you that changing deal terms on short notice is simply impossible to do. But you must push back; as you learn new information the defense plan must adjust accordingly.

Setting expectations is critical. If people know everything might shift, then when the changes appear, they won't be so surprised. People get most frustrated when they expect things to proceed on schedule and then everything changes. When you begin a defense effort, it is critical to remind people that the plans surely *will* change as the defense effort moves forward.

RALLY THE TEAM

Defending a business requires exceptional effort; you will need to take extraordinary organizational steps to assemble and execute the plan in a short time. As a result, rallying the team is an important step; anyone leading a defensive effort needs people on the team who understand the urgency, appreciate the importance of the plan, and embrace the challenge.

The good news is that people will frequently support a leader who is under fire. President George W. Bush received enormous public support as he rallied the United States after the World Trade Center attacks on September 11. He climbed on top of the rubble and grabbed a bullhorn: "I can hear you! I can hear you! The rest of the world hears you! And the people...who knocked these buildings down will hear all of us soon!" And everyone cheered. Winston Churchill led the British people in the fight against Hitler's Germany, proclaiming, "We shall fight in France, we shall fight on the seas and oceans, we shall fight with growing confidence and growing strength in the air, we shall defend our island, whatever the cost may be. We shall fight on the beaches, we shall fight on the landing grounds, we shall fight in the fields and in the streets, we shall fight in the hills; we shall never surrender."

Rallying the team is surprisingly easy if you work at it; a leader needs to simply step up, make the case, and then ask for help. In a defensive effort, it might go something like this:

> "Ladies and gentlemen, we are under attack. The people at Kaub Coffee are coming directly at us, and they are going to try to steal our customers. Are we going to let this happen? I can't hear you! Are we going to let this happen? What? You bet we're not going to let this happen! Anyone who thinks they can walk in and steal our customers is going to have to think again.
>
> "We're going to teach them a lesson, and I need your help more than ever. What are we going to do? What? Yes, we're going to push them back and send them packing.
>
> "I know we can do it, if we all work together and really push, and I know we will do it, because that's the kind of organization we are. When a threat comes along, what do we do? We fight, and we fight hard."

Defense can be exciting and inspiring. It is often emotional. It is okay to express frustration and anger; in fact, an expression of true emotion from a leader will often help rally the troops to the mission. As Duke basketball coach Mike Krzyzewski notes, "Anger is okay if it motivates you to do something good. Sometimes anger destroys fear."[4]

In a company that is doing well, creating a sense of urgency can be a challenge. Indeed, the better a company is doing, the more difficult it may be to get the team fired up. "Sales and profits are good," people will be inclined to say, "So what's the problem?" Two approaches often work to get a group engaged and excited about the challenge.

The first approach is to lay out the risk, in a dramatic yet credible fashion. It's essential to describe the situation and the downside potential. If people don't believe there is a problem, they'll be reluctant to take significant action to address it.

If you're in a company with a long history of success, simply proclaiming, "If this attacker gets into our market, we will go bankrupt in a year!" isn't a believable scenario. Instead, you might state, "If this launch is a success, our growth is likely to stall, and we will miss our targets and our bonuses." With this approach you will more likely get people to believe there is an issue because your statement is credible.

The other way to fire up a group is to tap into people's competitive spirit. People generally like to win; hardly anyone aspires to be a loser. If you call on people's winning instinct, you can get them excited. "Are we going to let this good-for-nothing attacker steal our business?" you might say. "Are we going to lie down without a fight? Are we going to give up and walk away? Of course not; we will stand our ground and fight."

Most important, it is critical to include the entire team; a good defense can't be executed well if only the marketing team or only the strategy team is involved. To impact the distribution channel, for example, the sales team must be part of the effort. Indeed, the salespeople are among the most important players in most defensive situations. If your defense plan includes building new products, the R&D team will need to play an important role. And to keep track of the financial risk and spending, the finance team will need to be involved.

In a defensive situation, the team leader needs to focus on the matter at hand and have a positive outlook. It's easy to complain about the long hours, the poor financial numbers, and the glorious growth initiatives you had to cancel to fund the defensive effort. But this sort of thinking doesn't lead anywhere positive. As business strategist Jim Collins writes, "Be willing to embrace loss, to endure pain, to temporarily lose freedoms, but never give up faith in the ability to prevail."[5]

A good defense requires high levels of coordination and urgency, and to achieve these your team must work together. You must lead that effort.

SET THE RIGHT OBJECTIVES

Every good marketing plan starts with objectives. Indeed, the only reason to create a plan is to achieve something. Most good business and marketing plans embrace financial objectives such as profit and profit growth. In business, financial results usually matter most. So in a typical marketing plan the goal might be to "Drive profit growth of 17 percent over the next year" or to "Reach $30 million in profits in 2014."

A defense plan is very different from a growth plan, so the objectives must be set with this in mind. In a defensive situation, the goal usually isn't to grow profits, or even to maintain profits. The goal is to protect your business from competitive attack and prevent or limit a long-term competitive problem. Indeed, it is generally best to just toss aside the typical goals of profit or profit growth. This may be unpopular, but it must be done if the defense is to succeed.

The goals you set in a defense plan should reflect the situation. Instead of "grow profits by 8 percent," you might say, "limit Philips to five share points" or "maintain market share despite the competitive entry" or "retain 90 percent of our current customers."

Setting a big profit objective when defending a business is usually a very big mistake for a simple reason: the best way to protect short-term profits is to minimize defense spending. Defensive efforts are costly; you end up spending lots of money simply to protect your existing sales. The short-term return on this spending is generally low; indeed, many defensive tactics would make little sense in a more normal situation.

Someone defending a business might ramp up advertising dramatically, in a bid to limit the impact of the competitor's launch spending. This advertising increase only makes sense due to the defense; the spending is far higher than normal. Similarly, defenders might roll out a "buy two, get one free" deal in an effort to load customers and limit trial of the competitive product. This again might be a highly effective defensive tactic, but it would rarely make sense under normal conditions, since big discounts can distort a market.

Using profit growth as a primary objective in a defensive initiative gives managers a dangerous incentive: minimize the defensive effort and protect short-term profits. By scaling back defensive activities, it is usually possible to preserve profits for a while. Cutting advertising, for example, is often a positive move in the short run in terms of profits. Similarly, reducing product quality or customer service will generate some cash. Moves like this, however, make it much easier for an attacker to steal market share and get a foothold in the industry.

Indeed, anyone attacking an established business should hope that the leadership team of the established business, the defender, has a big incentive to protect profits. In the best case, the head of the defending company is nearing the end of a three-year bonus cycle, so the stakes are huge; if the manager hits the profit target, the payout is substantial. If he misses the profit target, the payout vanishes. In a situation like this, the managers of the established business will almost certainly focus on hitting the profit number by cutting spending and investment, and this gives the new entrant a huge opportunity.

Setting the right goals is always important; if you're aiming at the wrong thing, it's highly unlikely that you will hit the right thing. When you are defending a business, the goals have to reflect that situation.

LET THE FINANCIALS FOLLOW

In most situations, especially when developing a marketing or business plan, it's best to start with the financial targets. In defense, however, this isn't the case; it is best to focus on the activities in the plan and let the financials follow.

When formulating a marketing or business plan, then, you usually start with the financial targets. To a degree, the planning process becomes a bit of a quantitative exercise: how can we deliver the profit target while building the business? Will an advertising campaign help us increase profits? Will a big sales incentive program do the job? How do we get to the number, ideally in a smart way?

In a defensive situation, however, this logic should be turned around. The financials should never lead; they should follow. When you're defending a business, the objective is to address a long-term issue. Limiting the success of an attacker's new product will yield benefits for many years to come.

The objectives of a defensive plan should focus on defensive activities and metrics that will indicate success in stopping a competitive threat. How do we address this attacker? How can we block distribution? How can we limit trial of the competitor's product? How do we retain our customers?

Once you've assembled the defense plan, you can then look at the financial impact. The financial targets, however, should be finalized only after the plan is in place. The focus should be on creating the best defense plan, not on getting to a particular predetermined financial target.

The difficult-to-swallow reality is that in a defensive situation it may be impossible to achieve the desired financial goals. A business that has been growing profits by 8 percent annually through consistent gains of market share will have virtually no chance of maintaining that profit growth trend if attacked by a competitor. A smart defensive program will hurt short-term profits, perhaps substantially, and result in a profit decline compared to the prior period. As Colgate CEO Reuben Mark observed, "We have learned from long experience that you must deal with competition immediately and forcefully, and then you emerge stronger afterward. If you are dilatory or cut back the spending to meet internal or external obligations, you are going to be in trouble."[6]

Of course, not defending will also result in a profit decline; the business is likely to lose some market share as the competitor enters, even if only temporarily. The only way to deliver good profit results would be to dramatically cut marketing spending and costs, so that profits increase even as market share declines due to the competitive launch. This is certainly the worst option of all; the business might maintain short-term profit, but with a modest defensive effort the competitor will have a very good chance of success, stealing business momentum from the established player.

When formulating a defensive plan, then, managers must realize that there will likely be a financial impact. The question shouldn't be, "How will we grow our profits again this year?" or "How do we get to our targets?" The question should be, "Well, how bad will this actually be?"

DON'T TRY TO BE PERFECT

There are times in life when perfection is clearly the goal. A bride at a wedding wants to be perfect: beautiful and elegant. An actor auditioning for the leading role in a major Broadway show wants the audition to be perfect. A presidential candidate heading into the final, critical debate wants to be perfect.

There are also times in business when you want to be perfect. A pharmaceutical company launching a new molecule will strive to get everything right; after investing years of time and hundreds of millions of dollars in development costs, the launch has to be the best it can be. A company developing a piece of advertising for the Super Bowl, the most watched show in the United States, wants to be perfect.

In a defensive situation, however, you really don't need to be perfect. Indeed, it's best to not even try. The goal is to be fast, forceful, and generally correct, and then to be flexible and nimble.

This is true for three critical reasons. First, perfection takes time. To get a perfect advertising campaign you have to spend months and months refining it. You develop the strategy and then refine it and test it. You then develop creative with your agency and submit it to rigorous testing. You might then do another round of creative development, with more testing to follow. At long last, you actually produce the ad, but then you test it again, making further revisions. This process can go on for a year or more.

In a defensive situation, there simply isn't time to do all that. Since speed is critical, every day that goes by makes the defensive effort more difficult. Spending four months debating and optimizing the perfect defense plan is a significant mistake; by the time the defense kicks in, perfect though it may be, the optimal window for affecting your competitor will likely have passed.

Second, a defense plan is always reactive by nature. This makes it basically impossible to develop a perfect plan. Defensive initiatives should always be based on the competitor's moves; you must reflect and address what the competitor is doing. The problem is that it is impossible to know precisely what the competitor is doing, and for this reason, you'll never have a perfect plan. Having more time doesn't even really help substantially. Competitive information trickles in; some of it is incomplete, some of it is conflicting. Without perfect competitive information, creating a perfect defense plan is impossible. It is best to just get on with it; you do the best you can based on what you know.

Third, defense is short term. Defensive battles usually occur over fairly defined periods of time, perhaps a quarter or six months. Companies should always be looking out for and monitoring threats. But the actual skirmishes are often brief. In the best case, a company mounts a strong defensive program, successfully pushes back the competitor, and then gets back to focusing on growth.

As a result, perfection just isn't necessary. You aren't laying the foundation for the next 15 years of the company; you generally aren't making decisions that will impact the organization for a generation (unless, of course, you fail to defend appropriately). You are simply reacting to a competitive move. Ideally, you will be done with the entire event in a few months.

LIMIT DAMAGE TO THE EXISTING BUSINESS

The goal of a defense plan is usually to protect an existing business by reacting to a competitive move. With this in mind, it's important to remember that the top priority is limiting damage to the existing business. You don't want to create a defense plan that will leave the existing business in a weak position when the dust settles.

Damaging your own brand can hurt you more than the attacker ever could. In the worst case, you defend against a product and in the process of defending you damage your brand. Then, despite your best defensive efforts, the competitor succeeds at taking a share of the market. So you spent money to defend, damaged your business, and didn't manage to push back the attacker.

To mitigate these risks, you must think about the broader impact of the defensive tactics you choose. Some tactics are for the short term and easy to reverse. Sending your CEO out to make some rather vague comments on the local business news show won't have a long-term negative impact on your brand. Similarly, increasing advertising spending or adding a sweepstakes shouldn't be problematic. Many, many defensive tactics fall into this category; they are smart moves with little long-term impact.

Other tactics, however, might have a much more substantial long-term impact. Adding a new channel of distribution, for example, can create all sorts of problems, and many of these issues will remain for years into the future. It is then necessary to balance to channels, and there is likely to be conflict between the different channels. Similarly, rolling back list prices might have a long-term impact if pricing in the industry is hard to increase later. Introducing a new brand will also create challenges in the long term even if the new brand is very positive.

A tactic that will fundamentally change your business model must be evaluated particularly carefully; the change might hurt the business in the long term, and this negates the goal of the defense plan.

THINK THROUGH THE COMPETITIVE RESPONSE

Competitive battles are never isolated events. It may seem like this to managers in the thick of it, but in most cases the skirmish of the moment is just one part of a larger, longer battle. When planning a defensive effort, then, it is important to think like a chess player and consider the broader ramifications of each move you make. In particular, it is critical to think about how your competitor will respond to your defense.

Physicists tell us that for every action there is an equal and opposite reaction. This is at least partially true where defending a business is concerned; for every action there will be a reaction. The size of the reaction, however, may be larger or smaller than the action.

The critical questions to consider are: how will my competitors react to this plan? What are they likely to do? What might they do? Is there anything they might do that would be particularly bad? If I make this particular move, what might their next move be, and how will I respond?

The goal of a defensive plan is to shape competitive behavior in a positive manner, so thinking through these questions is very important. In the best case, when faced with your defensive response, the competitor will elect to give up and discontinue the new product effort. In the worst case, the defensive action prompts the competitor to spend even more, escalating the battle, or it inspires the competitor to sharpen the launch plan in a creative and unexpected way, perhaps attacking you with more vigor and enthusiasm, thereby increasing the overall threat. This is not a positive step forward for your business.

Competitive battles get more complicated when there are multiple players involved; with several companies the level of uncertainty goes up, because the interplay between the different entities is now harder to predict. For example, assume you're running a business with one main competitor. A new player launches a new product into your market, and in response you dramatically increase discounts to limit trial and protect your business. Your competitor, seeing this move, is likely to also dramatically increase discounts. The combined effort knocks out the new entrant, but now it isn't clear how you can reestablish the higher prices. If you increase your prices, will your competitor follow? Or will it stick with the new, lower price levels?

FOCUS ON ACTION

As is usually the case in the world of marketing, analysis is important in defense, but by itself it doesn't help you. The focus should always be on action: what precisely are we going to go do? Marketing plans that focus too much on analysis, research, and strategy aren't very helpful, because they never make the connection to action.

In a defensive situation, the team leader must step forward and mobilize the group. This is not the time to sit around a conference room debating this and that. It's a time to make quick decisions based on what is known and then move forward with all due dispatch.

Beware of confusing internal discussions with meaningful action. Talking about doing something doesn't help you; you have to actually do it. Similarly, organizing for action is of no help if it doesn't quickly result in something happening. Strategist Jim Collins, in his book *How the Mighty Fall*, notes that many executives confuse reorganization with meaningful action. Collins writes, "Reorganizations and restructurings can create a false sense that you're actually doing something productive."[7]

TO ARMS

When fighting a defensive battle, the focus has to be on picking your spot and moving quickly. There is usually no time to waste; every day that goes by, your competitor makes progress, and your window for effective defense closes a little bit. Fortunately, you don't have to be perfect, just good enough to make life difficult for the new entrant.

Chapter 8

STOPPING THE LAUNCH

A RUMOR COMES IN: A new entrant is thinking about entering your market. Often it is just a whisper; perhaps one of your customers mentions it to a sales person in passing. "So I hear Siemens is developing a new product to enter your category next year," or "Isn't Samsung getting into this market later this year? Someone told me that at the trade show last week." What do you do?

Developing a new product is a long process. In many companies there is an elaborate chain of events for turning a concept into a fully developed new product, often with a series of stages and gates. The first stage might be ideation, with the next gate being concept validation based on a quantitative test of the concept. The next stage might be product development, followed by a more elaborate test of the product and concept to verify both the concept and the product delivery.

In most cases, you won't hear about a threat until it is well into the development cycle. Or if you do hear about it, the threat will be so vague that it makes no sense to take it seriously, so you will decide not to defend at this point. Learning that GE is looking at entering a particular category isn't very significant; it's likely that GE looks at thousands of business opportunities each year.

However, what about the rumor that appears to be a real initiative? If you have adequate reason to believe a competitor is planning to launch an attack on your product or company, the best place to stop it is right at the start, by preventing the launch.

PREVENT THE LAUNCH

When you defend very early in the development process, the goal is quite simple: prevent, prevent, prevent. In the best case, the attacker will decide that the idea isn't promising enough to justify significant investment or that the hurdles are simply too big to surmount. So the competitor decides to focus on other, more compelling opportunities. "Subjecting the enemy's army without fighting is the true pinnacle of excellence," observed Sun-Tzu; "the highest realization of warfare is to attack the enemy's plans."[1]

Simply creating doubt about the new product idea among executives inside the attacker's company is an accomplishment. If executives begin to question their own launch, they may be reluctant to invest heavily in the idea and create more interim hurdles to ensure that the product is on track. Both of these factors can work to your advantage; as a defender, you don't want to face a passionate, committed, and optimistic attacker. When a product is in development, the basic defensive strategy is simple: convince the attacker that the new product launch is a bad idea—that it just won't work.

As you know, every new product is based on a set of financial projections. Smart businesspeople rarely do things they believe will lose money and fail. If you can convince your competitors that attacking you would be a bad idea, then you've accomplished the goal: you've prevented their launch, and they may give up the idea entirely.

There are many moves a defender can make at this "prevention" stage. All have a similar objective: convincing the attacker to abandon the cause.

COMMUNICATE YOUR COMMITMENT TO DEFEND

Perhaps the simplest way to prevent the launch is to let the attacker know that you will defend. You want the attacker to understand in no uncertain terms that if they launch their product, you will take extreme actions to defend your business. You will launch a ferocious defense.

This is a powerful approach. If the new entrant understands and believes that you will defend aggressively, it will have to take your position into account when considering the launch and cannot simply ignore you and your intentions. This forces the attacker to factor the probable defense into the launch plan, and, most important, into the financial projections for the launch. Simply put, the attacker will need to plan on spending more to overcome the probable defense or reduce sales forecasts in light of the defensive activities. Either of these moves will make the new product less attractive financially and increase the chances that it won't be launched at all.

Consider a hypothetical company planning to launch a new line of stoves called Koblenz Classics. The company has developed some initial financial projections, perhaps assuming 10 percent market share with about €15 million in marketing spending. The company has a variable margin of 40 percent and €10 million in overhead. This leaves a profit of €11 million. Presumably this is sufficient to move forward.

The existing category leader hears about the new launch and is concerned. The established player makes it clear that it will spend very aggressively to protect its market share and invest an additional €30 million in advertising and promotional spending to support the business.

This leaves Koblenz Classics in a difficult position. The defensive efforts by the category leader will certainly have an impact on the launch, which means the new entrant must do one of two things. First, the entrant could increase spending to perhaps €25 million in a bid to hit the 10 percent market share. Second, the new entrant could reduce its share forecast, perhaps to just 7 percent, since it will now be harder to gain any market share. Either move has a substantial negative impact on the new entrant's financials. In the first case, profits fall to just €1 million. In the second scenario, there are no profits at all (see exhibit 8.1).

The new financial outlook raises an important but difficult question for the new entrant. Is the product launch really worth doing? Are the returns high enough to justify the necessary investment?

Exhibit 8.1 Koblenz Classics Stoves financials

	Initial Plan	Revised Plan A	Revised Plan B
Category size (million €)	900	900	900
Market share (%)	10%	10%	7%
Revenue (million €)	$90	$90	$63
Cost of goods sold	54	54	38
Variable profit	36	36	25
Marketing	15	25	15
Overhead	10	10	10
Operating profit	11	1	–

In many cases the decision would be that it doesn't make sense. So the new entrant scraps the launch, and the established player retains its business. The defensive mission has been accomplished with just a simple declaration of war.

Signaling a commitment to defend is surprisingly easy to do; you simply fire up your public relations team and engage the business press. Your CEO, for example, might give an interview to an industry publication where she makes the point quite clearly. She might say, "Our top priority this year is protecting our market share, and we will be spending an additional €25 million in advertising and promotions to support this goal."

When a CEO makes a statement to the media, chances are very good that competitors will hear it. Anyone preparing to enter a new market will watch the existing players closely, so you can be fairly confident that your message will get through.

Jamie Dimon, CEO of banking giant JPMorganChase, provides a classic example of this strategy. Earlier in his career, Dimon was CEO of Bank One, at the time the largest bank in Chicago. In 2003 Washington Mutual, an innovative and aggressive regional bank, announced plans to enter the Chicago market. Jamie Dimon sent a very clear message to Washington Mutual CEO Kerry Killinger. Dimon told a reporter from *The Wall Street Journal*, "Maybe Chicago will be one of those markets where everyone here will lose money for a while. So be it."[2] This comment was of course widely picked up. Dimon made it clear that he would fight to defend the Chicago market. But he was even more specific and said that he would spend so much on the defense that his business would lose money.

Dimon's statement didn't persuade Washington Mutual to abandon the launch, but it should have. Bank One defended heavily, and by 2006 Washington Mutual had captured only a 0.3 percent share of bank deposits in Chicago and was closing many of its branches.[3]

Most important, signaling is best accomplished in a public forum; this reduces the chance that you will get into legal trouble. Sending a letter to your competitor is not a good approach, especially if the letter suggests it shouldn't enter your market. It is also not wise to deliver the message while passing your competitor on the way to the men's room at a conference: "So, Peter, we're going to kill you if you come anywhere near our market. You better back off." To avoid legal complications, always communicate openly and publicly.

The brewing industry provides yet another example of proper signaling. In one small African country, the established brewer had a market share of almost 100 percent; there was basically no competition in the mainstream beer category. There were a few imported beers, but they were expensive and had a very small market share. Several years ago, a new entrant announced that it would be entering the market with a massive new product launch. The existing brewer knew the threat was serious, because the new entrant promptly began building a brewery with enough capacity to support a major share position in the country.

The decision to defend was fairly easy; this was a direct attack on a very profitable and important business. The defense effort was multifaceted, but one important tactic was sending a clear signal to the attacker. So the established brewer went to the town where the new entrant was building its factory and bought up all the billboards and put up advertising for its brand. The established player painted buildings, painted cars, and advertised on bus shelters. It was a massive, overwhelming marketing move. The message, which was surely delivered, was essentially this: "We know about this, we don't like it, we have a lot of money, and we will knock you out."

The commitment to defend must be communicated with a great deal of sensitivity. Defensive activities are often subject to scrutiny, and if taken too far, comments can rub regulators the wrong way. You should generally avoid being too specific or threatening. You shouldn't announce directly and with fanfare that you are "going to kill anyone who even thinks about entering" our market, or "I don't care what it costs, we'll ensure that anyone who attacks us will fail," or "We own this market, and there isn't anyone who is getting even a piece of it."

What might seem like old-fashioned bluster and trash talk can easily be misconstrued as anticompetitive behavior in the hands of a gifted and eloquent attorney. Indeed, a capable lawyer can make hay with any of the statements above. If someone from a large company made the first comment, for example, a lawyer in court might simply ask, "So, Mr. CEO, when you said...now what was it again? Oh yes, here it is...when you said, 'We are going to kill anyone who even thinks about entering our market,' what precisely did you mean?"

"Well, I just meant that we'd fight to protect our business," the CEO might calmly reply.

The lawyer might then logically ask, "So you're saying you try to kill off your competitors, correct? I think that is precisely what you said. You said you would engage in anticompetitive activities, in other words. Is that right?"

"Well, of course not," the CEO might stammer. "We were just saying that, well, we'd do *something*."

"And that something, well, that would be attempting to kill off your competition, correct, sir?" presses the attorney. "I'm just trying to understand what you meant by the phrase 'kill anyone who even thinks about entering our market.'"

"But I didn't mean that," explains the CEO. "I was just making a comment."

"So it was a lie, then, is that right?" The attorney's tone becomes a bit more challenging. "Do you routinely lie in the course of your business, sir? Is this a normal business practice?"

And it gets worse from there.

When signaling a commitment to defend, it is best to rely on broad, general phrases, the meaning of which is ambiguous except to the person considering attacking your business. For them it would be quite pointed and clear. Phrases such as the following should be fine: "We are in an increasingly competitive market, so we will be investing much more in supporting our core businesses this year," and "Investing in and protecting our vitally important industrial lubricants business is our main focus this year. We are going to do everything we need to do in order to build this important area for the company."

Brewing giant SABMiller recently used gentle but clear language when discussing the South African beer market. Managing director Norman Adami stated that it was "sacred ground" and noted, "We hate to lose."[4] Gopal Vittal, executive director at Hindustan Unilever, was more direct when discussing emerging competitors in the Indian market. He stated, "This is a market that we own, and we are not going to cede anything. If it comes at the cost of short-term profitability, we will find ways of recouping that. We've been here 75 years, and we are not going away."[5]

The commitment to defend must be communicated carefully, in public, and with extreme care and sensitivity. But when executed well, this easy approach can block a new product before it even gets out the door.

DESTROY THE TEST

Many new product decisions rely heavily on market research results. Before investing millions in a new idea, most companies will conduct various studies evaluating its appeal. A retailer might open one or two stores to see how well a concept resonates with consumers before opening hundreds of locations. A toothpaste company might launch a new product in just one city or retail chain to see how it does before launching the product broadly.

Destroying your competitor's market research efforts can be an effective way to slow a launch. If you can ensure that the test results are negative, then the company is less likely to proceed with a bigger launch. Simply ensuring that the test results are not usable also reduces the likelihood of a launch; you take away a key piece of support for the investment.

If you're able to blow up a competitor's market research study, there are two likely outcomes, and both are favorable for you as defender. First, the attacker might conclude that the idea just isn't a good one. Given the poor test results, the team might decide that it doesn't make sense to proceed further with the product development and launch. Second, the attacker might actually recognize that the test results were skewed by the defender and conclude that the product might have performed well in the absence of competitive meddling. Counterintuitively, this outcome is good for the defender as well; it clearly sends the message that the defender knows about the launch and will take action. This will in turn wreak havoc with the attacker's game plan.

So how do you destroy a competitor's market research?

The first step is to find the market research study. This can be quite difficult because many market research studies are successfully hidden, especially small-scale studies such as focus groups and online concept tests. On occasion, however, you find out about a competitor's test. If you're in the retail industry, it's difficult to hide a new store. It's also hard to hide a new product in a grocery store.

Good competitive intelligence is essential to finding products in test. Your sales force can play a particularly valuable role here; your field representatives should constantly be looking for new, unexpected items. If anything new shows up, your sales reps should be asking questions and then let you know what they've found.

Once you've identified the research test, then you set out to muck it up it by taking actions of your own. The easiest approach is to do things that make the test unreadable. If you do something dramatic and unusual in the test area, then the results of the test will not be usable; the data is a jumble. Adding a huge promotion aimed directly at the new product, for example, will shift the market. Launching several of your own new products will confuse things further.

Increasing advertising spending dramatically will add another variable. For example, chip maker Frito-Lay routinely revs up promotions in a market where a competitor is testing a new product.[6] Similarly, McDonald's significantly increased promotional spending when competitor Wendy's started testing a new breakfast line in the western part of the United States.

A more malicious approach is to make it difficult for a competitor to simply execute the test at all. If you believe your competitor has a limited supply of product, for example, you can buy up all you can find. If you buy the product, then the competitor has nothing left to test it with customers.

Attacking a competitor's test is a common form of defense, and it can have quite a powerful impact. In retailing, for example, when a major chain tests a new store format, other chains react. If the competitor opens a store in a particular mall, competitors often begin doing things to impact the test in that particular mall, sometimes opening additional outlets, discounting heavily, and promoting aggressively. All this activity decreases traffic at the test store, so it is less likely to seem like a success.

A leading US salad dressing company took this approach several years ago. Salad dressing is a large and profitable category. One of the leading players in the industry heard that Procter & Gamble was testing a line of salad dressings in Denver. The location wasn't a surprise; Denver is a fairly reasonable market to test an idea like this because it is a smaller city, far from other towns. The grocery chains in Denver at the time were local, so it was easy to limit distribution of the new product. The TV market was isolated, so buying advertising time was easy and fairly efficient.

Now, this was not good news for the leading salad dressing company; P&G is a skilled competitor with deep pockets. If P&G decided to enter the category, it would create a massive competitive fight and force the category leader to spend millions to protect its market share.

Defending was an easy decision; the established player couldn't sit back and do nothing while P&G captured a significant share of an important market. Executives at the established company eventually decided that the best approach to minimize the chance of a launch from P&G was to attack the test. P&G is a fairly rational, data-driven company. If the test market failed, it would significantly decrease the chance that P&G would invest in the new product and roll it out nationally.

To destroy the test, the established player ordered its sales representative in Denver to visit all the grocery stores in town and simply buy all the salad dressing—*all* of it. The sales representatives were supposed to buy the Wishbone product, the Seven Seas product, the Kraft product, and the P&G product, *all of them*. After doing this, the sales representatives just threw away the product and returned to the store the following day and, again, bought all the salad dressing on the shelves. This went on for some period of time.

This action accomplished two things, both of which were very positive for the defending company. First, it destroyed the test. With all the purchases, the sales data for the salad dressing category in Denver showed very unusual trends compared to the previous year. Sales appeared to be soaring, and the market share figures for the different brands were moving quickly in all directions, driven simply by what products were on the shelf each day. Of course, the sales information simply reflected the efforts of defending company. For P&G, the test was now useless. The fact that the P&G products might have gotten 5 percent of the market indicated nothing at all. As a result, P&G couldn't use the test information. The test didn't provide any data that would support the launch.

Second, the established player sent a rather clear signal to P&G. When the test data showed strange trends, the P&G team clearly understood that a competitor was reacting and understood the message: "We know about this test; we will defend our business if you try to encroach on it, and we will take exceptional actions. We are also just a little bit crazy."

All this put P&G in a very difficult spot. The test market didn't show that the product would succeed. It was clear that the existing competitors would defend, and there was reason to believe they would do exceptional and somewhat outlandish things. Presumably, the odds of success were low from the beginning; that's why the company had been test marketing in the first place. With this new information, the chances were even lower.

Not surprisingly, P&G didn't launch the product in a large geography.

This defensive effort was certainly expensive; it took sales focus and resources to implement the defense plan. But these costs were tiny compared to the potential risk. By destroying the test, the defender forced the attacker to reconsider and protected its market share.

MAKE SOME THREATS

A good way to stop others from doing something is to threaten them by simply explaining that if they proceed there will be swift and negative consequences. This forces them to think twice about whether they really want to move forward and take the risk of the negative outcome.

This technique can be very effective with children; I use it quite frequently with my son, Charlie. I'll simply state: "Charlie, if you continue to hit your sister, then you aren't getting dessert tonight," or "Charlie, if you don't stop asking if you can eat that piece of candy before lunch, I will throw it out the window." Charlie has learned that I am not afraid to follow through with my threats so he tends to listen and act in the desired fashion.

When defending a business, threats work exactly the same way. If you threaten a competitor, they will have to think twice about carrying out their plans.

With kids, missing out on dessert or losing a piece of candy are fairly significant and important matters, so these tend to work well as threats. In the world of business, the most powerful threats are usually financial. Your goal is to illustrate to the attackers that if they proceed with the launch, something financially undesirable will happen. Ideally, the financial impact of the threatened action is enough to destroy the financials of the new product launch, making the entire proposition not worth pursuing.

Threatening is a highly effective means of defense; it can certainly force competitors to think twice before proceeding with the launch of a competitive product by changing its economics. Indeed, a strong, well-crafted threat is often the very best way of defending. The message should be very clear; the goal is to communicate, as one marketer, who wished to remain anonymous, put it: "If you touch me, I'll hit you."

The intensely competitive laundry category provides a perfect example of this dynamic. In the United States, Clorox and P&G are two major players in the category. P&G is the leader in the laundry detergent category, and Clorox is the leader in the bleach category. Several years ago, Clorox was preparing to launch a new line of detergents in a bid to drive growth. In response, P&G spread the word that it would be launching a line of bleach. Clorox eventually thought better of the move and elected not to launch the detergent line, and P&G never launched its bleach line. P&G's move was effective despite the fact that, as one executive recalled, "It was all a ruse. We didn't have any plans to enter."[7]

P&G was involved in another, more subtle battle in the salty snacks category. In January 2004 a very odd article appeared in *Advertising Age* stating that P&G was considering reviving the Eagle brand of snacks.[8] This was a peculiar bit of news, since the Eagle brand, created by Anheuser-Busch in a bid to break into the salty snacks category, had failed in a rather spectacular manner some time before. Why would P&G bring that brand back to life?

As with most strange stories, however, things were more complicated than they seemed. At the time, P&G was a small player in the world of potato chips; the company had introduced the Pringles brand in 1971 and had a market share of about 10 percent.

In late 2001, about two years before the *Advertising Age* article appeared, P&G had launched a new brand of tortilla chips called Torengos and invested heavily in building the new product line. Like Pringles, Torengos came stacked in a can. The can was triangular instead of round, since many tortilla chips are that shape.

The people running PepsiCo's Frito-Lay business were not pleased with P&G's bid to expand in the salty snacks category. Frito-Lay dominates this category, with very strong brands such as Lays, Fritos, Doritos, Cheetos, and Ruffles. For PepsiCo, this was an exceptionally important business, and an aggressive move by P&G was not good news.

The Frito-Lay team responded to the P&G move by spending heavily on its existing businesses. They also created and launched Lay's Stax, a product that featured chips stacked in a can, very much like Pringles. Frito-Lay supported Stax very heavily, with lots of advertising, in-store promotions, and high-value coupons. The Frito-Lay team certainly knew that by attacking Pringles, P&G's strong business, it would send a clear message to P&G to back off and stop promoting Torengos. At the same time, the launch would put financial pressure on the Pringles line, making it hard for the P&G team to invest more money in Torengos.

For P&G, the launch of Stax was very bad news, because P&G now had to defend the Pringles business against this rather big counterattack.

While this competitive battle was unfolding, the article appeared in *Advertising Age* that P&G planned to revive the Eagle brand. Finally, things made complete sense; P&G was going to protect its Pringles line by threatening a massive, direct attack on Frito-Lay. For Frito-Lay, this was a very serious threat.

Would P&G actually have launched the Eagle snacks line? Probably not; it was simply a bad idea. But it wasn't inconceivable, so Frito-Lay had to take it seriously.

The result of all this threatened activity was fairly predictable. P&G eventually killed Torengos and didn't launch the Eagle snacks line. Frito-Lay cut back support for Lay's Stax and stopped directly attacking Pringles. After an intense skirmish, order and profits returned to the category.

A clearly delivered, credible threat is a very powerful defensive weapon. If the attacker believes the threat is large and believable, it must consider the threat when weighing whether to proceed with the launch at all.

PREEMPT THE LAUNCH WITH YOUR OWN PRODUCT

If you hear that your competitor is thinking about launching a dynamic new product, one way to stop the launch is to simply introduce the idea first. This maneuver will almost certainly force your competitor to reconsider the entire launch.

New businesses thrive on buzz and excitement. Bringing something new to the market is thrilling, and this can generate news and create attention. For a new entrant, there's nothing like this free media coverage, particularly when it highlights all the product features. Conversely, it's difficult to generate excitement around a "me-too" new product. Bloggers have little incentive to talk about the second, third, or fifth new tech device. CNBC usually doesn't spend a lot of time on things that aren't innovative and different; who wants to hear about another strategy consulting firm? Financially, launching an innovative new product is very different from launching a product that is second or third to market. The innovative product will likely require less marketing spending and get a quicker start because it will generate lots of free press and trial from innovation seekers. The late mover must plan for much higher marketing spending and a slower buildup of sales volume, with a smaller market share.

For a defender, this presents a compelling opportunity. If you learn that a new competitor is considering launching a particular type of product, just launch the idea first. By occupying the first mover position, you become the innovator and can then change and perhaps destroy your competitor's proposition.

More important, when you execute this strategy in defending, you don't have to launch the perfect product. The goal is simply to fill the space in the market. So developing a product that is adequate is likely to be sufficient. The most important thing is speed.

The fastest approach is simply to publicly announce the intention to launch the idea. By claiming to be developing the idea, you immediately force your competitor to reconsider and reevaluate the entire enterprise.

If the attacker has strong patents and trademarks, then it might not be possible to launch the competitor's idea. But creating and enforcing the protection of intellectual property is difficult. As Ohio State professor Oded Shenkar observed in a recent article, "patents provide only limited protection, since they're costly—and in many cases impossible—to enforce. They can be 'invented around' or may require disclosure that actually makes imitation easier. The truth is most products, processes, practices, and ideas are not protected by patents."[9]

Unilever recently employed this approach in Turkey. The company learned that a new competitor was preparing to launch a new dishwashing liquid, so Unilever quickly moved to launch the idea first. CEO Paul Polman explained the move: "In 25 days, we launched our dishwashing liquid, and we're still waiting for our competitor to come."[10]

Nike recently preempted a competitor in the sports apparel market. Under Armour is a fast-growing company; revenues have risen from $725 million in 2008 to almost $1.1 billion in 2011. The company got its start producing tight, form-fitting clothes that wick away sweat and water. Under Armour called it compression apparel. The launch was very successful as people from various sports adopted the clothes. Buoyed by the success, Under Armour quickly expanded into other segments of the athletic apparel and equipment market, including footwear.

Nike viewed Under Armour's progress with obvious concern; Under Armour publicly stated that it was directly attacking Nike, and the company's launch into footwear put it in direct competition with Nike's core business.

Executives at Nike knew that Under Armour was planning to expand globally; a European launch, for example, was almost an inevitable move. In 2011 Under Armour claimed to have 87 percent of the compression apparel market in the United States, but it had only a tiny foothold in Europe.

To address the Under Armour threat, Nike launched a line of compression apparel in Europe, calling it the Nike Pro Baselayer. The Nike product line was very similar to Under Armour's. For example, Nike's line of products included

Hypercool, for warm-weather use, and Hyperwarm, for cold-weather use, paralleling Under Armour's ColdGear and HeatGear.

This move by Nike had two rather good results. First, it gave Nike a growth opportunity; the product might actually turn into a profitable business in Europe. Second, and perhaps more important, it blocked Under Armour on that continent. Launching a "me-too" product line wouldn't be impossible for Under Armour, but it would be a huge, daunting challenge.

By moving fast, Nike blunted the impact of its competitor's innovation and protected the Nike business in the long term.

German airline Lufthansa used the same approach to hold back the growth of discount airlines in Germany. Lufthansa created a subsidiary called Germanwings, a low-cost airline that was distinct from Lufthansa in branding, pricing, positioning, and operations. On its own, the new airline presumably made little sense; there was no reason for Lufthansa to cannibalize its own business, especially with a lower-margin brand like Germanwings. However, given the competitive situation, Germanwings made perfect strategic sense; with Germanwings established in the market it was much more difficult for other low-cost carriers such as Ryan Air to enter.

TAKE IT TO COURT

The legal system provides many opportunities for defending a business. Indeed, one of the most common defensive approaches is to sue your potential competitor. Talk to your lawyers to identify potential claims; it could be a patent suit or a trademark suit. You could sue based on trade secrets. The important thing is to involve the legal system.

There are several benefits to filing a suit. In the best case, you will win the suit. In the case of a patent suit, you might receive a favorable judgment, which might saddle your competitor with a large fine and block it from the market. This makes it difficult or impossible for your competitor to proceed with the new launch and sends a rather dramatic message.

Starwood Hotels, for example, killed Denizen, Hilton's new brand of lifestyle hotel, by filing suit; Starwood accused Hilton of stealing trade secrets. The companies eventually settled the matter, with Hilton agreeing to kill the Denizen brand and not pursue that segment of the market.

You don't have to win the case to benefit; the process of suing a company can be very positive for a defender regardless of the outcome. Suing the new entrant forces it to react; the courts do not appreciate it when a company ignores a legal filing. So a suit takes time and attention. It also takes money; hiring lawyers, especially good ones, is an expensive proposition. As Harvard professor Michael Porter observed, "Suits force the weaker firm to bear extremely high legal costs over a long period of time and also divert its attention from competing in the market."[11]

Taking an attacker to court is particularly effective with small start-up companies. Most new companies are short on two things: time and money. Securing the funds needed to grow is a challenging task, so most new companies have limited resources and only a relatively short period of time before the money runs out. By suing a small company and taking it to court, you force it to spend time and money fighting a legal battle. This substantially reduces the company's odds of success.

A legal battle also creates uncertainty; you can never be certain how things will turn out. This uncertainty makes life difficult for an attacker, particularly a small company trying to raise funds. Many investors steer clear of ventures with major legal issues; with all the challenges in the launch of a new venture, a legal risk is simply too much. This makes filing suit particularly effective when defending against a start-up that needs to raise additional funds.

CREATE OPERATIONAL BARRIERS

Anything you can do to make life difficult for your competitors increases the chance they will give up and go away. Everything that slows down the attacker will work to your advantage.

One way to make life difficult for your attacker is to hire your competitor's key people. This might be the general manager leading the venture, for example. If you learn that the new product launch is being led by Martha Simpson, you can approach Martha and offer her an exciting new job at your company. Or you can use a recruiting firm to approach Martha in a less direct way; probably it wouldn't be wise to just call her directly.

Hiring Martha will likely benefit your company; she might be a dynamic leader with new ideas. This is a win-win situation; you add a great person to your team and damage your attacker. In the worst case, however, Martha doesn't work out at your company and leaves after a year or so. Whether Martha stays with your company or not, the loss to the attacking company is a definite setback.

You can also hire people supporting the launch, such as key sales leaders or scientists. Each move on its own isn't likely to cripple the attacker, but taken together the losses will reduce the impact of the competitor's launch.

You should be aware of employment agreements that may include non-compete clauses and confidentiality provisions.

Another way to make life difficult for your attacker is to lock up key suppliers and partners, so the attacker has a hard time getting the assets needed to launch the new product. If you know your competitor needs a certain component for its product, for example, you can contact the suppliers and try to buy up all the supply. If capacity is tight, this approach can make life very difficult for the attacker.

For example, in the telecommunications industry a global leader in pagers at one point learned that a competitor was testing a new product and considering entering the category. The existing player learned that the competitor's product relied on a battery of a particular size and that the global supply of this battery was very limited. So the established player arranged to buy up all the batteries in the world. This meant that the attacker had no batteries; the company couldn't even create enough products to do a customer test and as a result couldn't launch the product.

In the brewing industry, one established player learned that a new entrant was considering building a brewery in its market. So the established player funded a community group concerned about the impact of the new brewery on the local water supply; this local group fought the brewery and claimed it would lower the water levels. This approach worked out very well; it made life very difficult for the new entrant and delayed the launch substantially.

Every obstacle you can put up in the way of your competitor will cause it trouble and help you to protect your market.

IF ALL ELSE FAILS, STRIKE AN AGREEMENT

There's an old saying: "If you can't beat 'em, join 'em." In a defensive scenario, if it isn't possible to stop a competitive launch, the best move might be to strike an agreement. This could take many forms: an acquisition, a partnership, or some other sort of arrangement. The core insight is that the competitor may well cause more damage to you by launching than it stands to gain, so the optimal solution is some sort of an arrangement.

The simplest approach is an acquisition; buying a potential competitor is an easy way to prevent it from becoming a bigger threat. The cost of buying a new start-up company is often very modest, making this the optimal solution. If you wait until the product succeeds, the price goes up dramatically.

Agreements are likely to be scrutinized by regulatory bodies, however, so proceed with caution. Some pharmaceutical companies, for example, have gotten into trouble for agreements they struck with generic drug companies to delay the launch of unbranded products.[12]

THE BEST DEFENSE

The best defensive efforts prevent larger battles. It's important to remember that the fastest, easiest, and most efficient way to defend against a new product launch into your category is to stop the product launch. If you're successful at this stage, you've saved yourself a lot of time and money before things get much, much worse.

Chapter 9

BLOCKING DISTRIBUTION

EVERY NEW PRODUCT MUST REACH customers; it has to get distribution. This is true in every industry. If you can ensure that your competitor can't break into the sales channel, you block its access to the market and protect your business. It is very simple: no distribution means no sales and no competitor.

Blocking distribution is one of the most powerful techniques in defensive strategy because it is exceptionally effective. Indeed, this is an area where many of the most intense battles take place.

Anyone who has launched a new product knows that gaining distribution is a core part of the launch plan. If you can't get your product in front of customers, it simply won't sell, even if it is the finest product in the world. For example, if you get only 25 percent of stores to carry your item, you will miss out on most of your potential sales. As marketer Paul Groundwater notes, "Shelf space is critical."[1]

THE POWER OF BLOCKING DISTRIBUTION

If you can keep a competitor's new product out of the market, you will kill it. Even reducing your competitor's distribution by just a small amount can have a big financial impact. Marketing spending is frequently fixed, so a smaller distribution base will result in lower sales and substantially lower profits. It might cost £20 million to build awareness of a new product in Great Britain. This figure will be the same whether every store in the country carries the product or just a few. The financial situation, however, changes dramatically.

Exhibit 9.1   Super Shine year 1 financial proposition

	Original Plan
Total stores	50,000
Distribution achieved	80%
Stores carrying the product	40,000
Unit sales per store per week	15
Price per unit	$4
Retailer margin	35%
Manufacturer revenue (million)	$81.1
Manufacturer variable margin (%)	60%
Manufacturer variable profit (million)	$48.7
Marketing expense (million)	$20
Fixed overhead (million)	$18
Operating profit (million)	$10.7

Consider this simple example: a new shampoo called Super Shine is coming to market. The new product team assumes that 80 percent of stores will carry the shampoo, so out of the 50,000 stores in the market, 40,000 will carry Super Shine. Based on market research studies, the team believes that each store that carries the item will sell 15 bottles per week, at a price of $4.00. With a retailer margin of 35 percent and gross margin of 60 percent, variable profits will be $48.7 million. With $20 million in marketing spending behind the launch and fixed overhead of $18 million, the business will make $10.7 million in profits in year one. This a good return for a new product; many new products lose money during the initial phase. The financial picture will improve in future years, of course, since the business won't require such high levels of support after the first year (see exhibit 9.1).

If the established players can limit the new product's distribution, however, the financial proposition quickly changes for the worse. If distribution only reaches 50 percent of the stores, Super Shine will lose more than $7 million in the first year (see exhibit 9.2, scenario B). If the defenders can limit distribution to 20 percent of stores, the numbers look very grim for Super Shine, with a loss of over $25 million (see exhibit 9.2, scenario C).

Distribution is a promising place to defend. If you can limit the distribution of a competitor's new product, you can have a substantial impact on its financial prospects.

Exhibit 9.2 Super Shine year 1 financial proposition: updated

	Original Plan	Scenario B	Scenario C
Total stores	50,000	50,000	50,000
Distribution achieved	80%	50%	20%
Stores carrying the product	40,000	25,000	10,000
Unit sales per store per week	15	15	15
Price per unit	$4	$4	$4
Retailer margin	35%	35%	35%
Manufacturer revenue (million)	$81.1	$50.7	$20.3
Manufacturer variable margin (%)	60%	60%	60%
Manufacturer variable profit (million)	$48.7	$30.4	$12.2
Marketing expense (million)	$20	$20	$20
Fixed overhead (million)	$18	$18	$18
Operating profit (million)	$10.7	($7.6)	($25.8)

Distribution is a particularly promising place to defend, because new entrants often have a only small window to establish distribution before the new product advertising and promotion support begins. Simply delaying distribution can create enormous problems for the new entrant. In the case of a consumer product, for example, some retailers will quickly pick up the new item, and these firms will want to see sales start to increase. If the product just sits on the shelves, retailers might decide the product just isn't working and discontinue it to make room for other, more promising new items. To prevent this, the new entrant must quickly begin spending on advertising and promotions to create some initial sales.

But if a number of retailers wait to pick up the new item, the initial spending will be highly inefficient. The marketing effort might be successful at creating awareness and interest, but customers won't be able to find the item in the stores. And if people can't find a product, they can't buy it.

The new entrant is then in a very difficult spot. Spreading out the marketing spending is a logical solution, but it will reduce support levels, so there will be less investment in promoting the product each week. This will result in slower sales. It will also increase the chance that the spending won't be sufficient to break through the clutter and get attention. A substantial increase in marketing spending would be required to provide strong support over a long period of time. This would have a substantial (and negative) impact on the overall financial proposition.

Defensive strategies in the area of distribution can succeed in three ways. First, it might be possible to keep the competitor from the market entirely. This is an optimal outcome. Second, you can limit or slow your competitor's buildup of distribution. This is helpful and might be sufficient. Third, even if you can't block the new entrant, you might be able to at least maintain your presence in the sales channel, ensuring that the new entrant steals space from other players in the industry and not from you.

APPROACHES TO BLOCKING DISTRIBUTION

There are a number of ways to block distribution. Perhaps the most common is to work with channel partners and encourage them to support your products instead of those sold by the new entrant. If you can prevent distributors and retailers from taking on your competitor's items, you will damage or knock out your competitor.

Blocking distribution by working with channel partners can occur at many different points; the precise focus will vary depending on your category and geography. In many industries, products flow through a rather elaborate chain between the manufacturer and the customer. For a product selling in a grocery store, the first step is often a distributor, who takes the product and sells it to its customers, individual retailers. The second step is usually the grocery chain, such as Safeway, Tesco, or Carrefour. The third step is then each individual store location in the chain. It's possible to block distribution at all of these points: a defender can make it difficult for the new entrant to sign up distributors, to get into major chains, or to get the product on the shelf at each store.

In crafting a defensive effort at this stage, it is essential to consider each of the players and identify points of relative strength. The goal is to find a place where you have an advantage over your attacker.

Another way to block distribution is to create regulatory barriers that stop your competitor from launching at all. If your country's government passes a law that prevents a new competitor from entering your category, the threat vanishes, at least in the short run. Alternatively, if your government creates regulations that are impossible for a new entrant to comply with, then again you've eliminated the threat.

There are many ways to make gaining distribution difficult for your competitors. Some of these moves are particularly nasty, and they are ethically and legally questionable as well. So be sure you get legal input before proceeding with any of the tactics discussed below.

ACQUIRE THE DISTRIBUTORS

A very effective approach to blocking the competition from distribution is simply to buy the distributors. This can be expensive and complicated, but if you own and control the distributors in your market, you make it exceptionally difficult for a competitor. You simply decide not to carry the competing product.

Without access to distributors, a new competitor is in a very difficult position. The firm can try to build its own distribution network, but this is complex and enormously costly. Creating a new one is exceptionally challenging, and very frequently it is simply impossible.

Your company doesn't have to own *all* the distributors for this approach to work. In a category with several big players, each company can acquire its own distributors. In this scenario, all the major distributors are owned by the established companies. This makes it virtually impossible for a completely new entrant to get into the category. It locks in the status quo. This situation isn't as favorable as owning all the distributors in a market, since your established competitors can still launch new products and make life difficult for you, but it reduces the chances that a new entrant will pop up one day.

In the US soda industry, for example, Coca-Cola and Pepsi now own most of their bottlers. In 2009 and 2010, both companies acquired their large bottlers and distributors. This move limits the risk of a competitive attack; Coke and Pepsi's bottlers simply won't carry a threatening competing brand. Anyone hoping to attack the market would need to figure out a way around this challenge, perhaps by creating an entirely new distribution system, with new factories, trucks, billing processes, and salespeople. The cost of this would be exceptionally high and virtually prohibitive. And there would be no guarantee of success, since the Coke and Pepsi distributors would aggressively defend against the new entrant.

Not surprisingly, Coke and Pepsi both acquired their distributors when the US market became more competitive, with a number of new companies entering the category. Defending against each new entrant would have been a challenge, since there were so many. Locking up the distribution system reduced the competitive risk dramatically; the move addressed multiple competitive threats at one time.

In Ontario, Canada, 80 percent of beer sales are handled by the Beer Store, a retail network that is owned by the big established players: Anheuser-Busch, Molson-Coors, and Sapporo. By owning the key retailer, the big players make it difficult for new entrants to enter the market and generate sales. Greg Taylor, cofounder of Steam While Brewing, a small Canadian brewer, found it challenging to get sales in the Beer Store, which isn't particularly surprising. He explained, "there's an imbalance of opportunity to market your products within those stores."[2]

SABMiller provides another example. SAB is one of the world largest brewers, with annual sales of over $19 billion. The company is the industry leader in many countries. South Africa is one of its core markets; SAB has a market share of well over 90 percent in that country.[3] Several years ago, SAB received word that Anheuser-Busch, another of the world's largest brewers, was considering entering the South African market. SAB responded quickly to the threat and created a network of fourteen distributors that carried only SAB products. By locking up all the key wholesalers, SAB made it very difficult for competitors to enter the market; you can't sell beer without a strong distributor.

Controlling the distribution system is a highly effective form of defense; it creates enormous barriers that an attacker has to surmount. In most cases, the attacker (wisely) won't even try.

CREATE INCENTIVES FOR KEY CHANNEL PARTNERS

Acquiring a distribution system is effective but often impossible; the cost might be too high, government regulators might prevent a purchase, or, given the fragmentation in the channel, it might be impractical to get a controlling position.

An alternative approach is to give channel players very substantial financial incentives to act in a positive fashion. When facing competitive attack, this usually means giving distributors and other key channel players an incentive to expand distribution of your products and not pick up the new entrant's products. Distributors are generally motivated by the same thing that motivates most business executives: making money and being successful. If you can give the distributor a strong financial incentive to support your product line instead of the new entrant's product line, you can ensure that the distributor supports you. As Carter Cast, former head of Walmart.com, observed, "If you keep the channel happy, you block the competition."[4]

For this approach to work, the distributor needs to see a greater advantage in supporting you than in supporting the new entrant. This means the incentives have to be substantial to be effective. Virtually all new product launches include programs for distributors—perhaps a certain amount of free product, help with resetting store shelves, or money to be used for promotions to support the new product line. A defender must overcome these incentives and shift the equation for distributors. If a new entrant is planning to give a distributor $100,000 to promote the new line, your defensive offer needs to be larger, perhaps $200,000, and include more attractive options.

There are many ways to structure these sorts of arrangements. One approach is to simply offer channel partners an incentive payment based on certain performance metrics. For example, a company selling yogurt might offer a retailer a large financial payment if the chain simply maintains distribution of its items. So if a retailer carrying 12 varieties of yogurt still is carrying 12 varieties in nine months, despite the new product entry, it receives a large cash payment. A more attractive goal would be to reward a retailer for adding items, for example, for expanding the product assortment from 12 items to 14.

A more direct and controversial approach is to make the incentive based on *not* picking up the competitive product. So a defender might offer a large payment if the channel partner elects not to support the new entrant. Payment in return for category exclusivity is highly effective.

A less direct approach is to reward overall performance. For example, you might offer a channel partner additional funds for increasing shipments over the prior year's number; this motivates the distributor to support your product instead of the competing item. This might be a $2-per-case incentive if a particular distributor orders 15 percent more cases than during the same period of the prior year.

Kraft Foods is a leader in the retail cheese category in the United States. Several years ago, ConAgra, another major food company, announced plans to extend its then-successful Healthy Choice brand into the cheese category. This was a major threat to Kraft's business. Healthy Choice wasn't likely to increase overall cheese consumption; it would simply steal share from established players, with a lot of it coming from industry leader Kraft.

A major part of the defense plan was a distribution initiative. One of the big challenges in selling a refrigerated product is getting space in stores, since there is only so much room in a store's refrigerator case. To capitalize on this, Kraft went to retailers and offered an accrual program; if retailers maintained distribution of Kraft cheese over the following nine months, they would earn a substantial incentive payment.

This program was very effective at protecting Kraft's distribution and, in turn, market share. It didn't keep the Healthy Choice products out of distribution entirely, but it ensured that Kraft wouldn't lose its place in the stores.

Intel employed this technique to defend its microprocessor chip business. Executives at Intel, worried about the growth of competitor AMD, offered computer manufacturers funds for remaining loyal to Intel. The payments were startlingly large; Dell alone received about $6 billion in rebates between 2002 and 2007.[5] This technique was very effective at building loyalty, but it crossed the legal line. Intel was eventually hit with a substantial fine for using its dominant market power to block competition.

BUNDLE YOUR PORTFOLIO

A particularly powerful tool to motivate distributors is bundling or linking together a range of products. This approach works particularly well for companies with a broad product line. The concept is simple: leverage your total portfolio to provide a compelling incentive for your distributors that's very difficult for new entrants to match.

Consider a company that sells four different medical product lines. For the purpose of this example, let's call it Quandry Medical. Sales of each product in Quandry's portfolio are about 250,000 units a year. Quandry relies on a

Exhibit 9.3   Quandry Medical financials

	Product 1 Catheters	Product 2 Needles	Product 3 Valves	Product 4 Cords
Sales (thousand units)	250	250	250	250
Price per unit	$10	$15	$10	$5
Sales (thousand)	$2,500	$3,750	$2,500	$1,250
Quandry margin	20%	10%	15%	20%
Quandry variable profits (thousand)	$500	$375	$375	$250
Distributor margin	10%	10%	10%	10%
Distributor profits (thousand $)	$250	$375	$250	$125

distributor to promote its products, who makes a 10 percent margin on each product and carries just one line of catheters.

A new competitor, Lincoln Medical, suddenly announces plans to enter the catheter market. Lincoln Medical plans to launch a high-quality product at a competitive price. To encourage distributors to carry the new product, the company will offer distributors a payment of $250,000 (in theory to cover the cost of adding the product to the warehouse and computer system) and a promotional bonus of $300,000 for achieving first-year sales targets. All this is in addition to the standard 10 percent distributor margin.

This sort of offer would not be unusual; the new entrant will have to work hard to secure distribution. Lincoln would lose money in the first year, but the business would become profitable as the introductory offers are scaled back in the second and third years.

Lincoln's offer would presumably be quite a compelling proposition for the channel. The distributor stands to make $550,000 plus the typical margin. Considering the distributor currently makes only $250,000 on the catheter line, this offer would be hard to resist.

For Quandry Medical, this situation is a substantial problem; the company is at risk of losing a major portion of its business to this new and very aggressive competitor.

To keep the new competitor out of distribution, Quandry must create a more compelling proposition for the distributor. The simplest option is to offer a large payment to distributors in return for category exclusivity. The payment would presumably have to be more than the $550,000 offered by the new entrant, perhaps $600,000. This approach is fairly problematic, however. Quandry's catheter business only makes $500,000 per year, so a payment of $600,000 would wipe out all the profits. This is a huge hit. It also might raise questions about anticompetitive behavior, since Quandry is now running the business at a loss while defending.

For Quandry, bundling is a much more promising approach. Quandry could offer distributors a special short-term 7.5 percent promotional credit off total sales of all its products in return for maintaining distribution of Quandry products, including catheters. This offer would be lucrative; a total of $750,000, so it would certainly get the distributor's attention. Each of Quandry's businesses could absorb this payment; every business would remain profitable on a variable basis. The payment would be a promotional credit, so distributors might actually use it to drive Quandry's business, making this a win-win proposition. Most important, Quandry's offer would be much bigger than the new entrant's offer.

The new entrant would be hard-pressed to match this offer; loading this type of spending onto the new product proposition would likely make the entire venture much more unprofitable. Increasing the distributor incentives wouldn't necessarily address the issue, either, because Quandry might respond with even greater incentives.

FIGHT THE BATTLE IN-STORE

Most consumer products are bought at a store; someone walks up to the shelf, picks up an item, and decides to buy it. A. G. Lafley, CEO at Procter & Gamble, called this "a moment of truth."[6] As Lafley pointed out, this is the moment where everything comes together; the packaging, the pricing, the look and feel of the product, and the in-store promotion. This is true for bananas, DVD players, detergents, socks, and any other product bought in a retail location.

If an established player can dominate the in-store environment, it will be impossible for a new entrant to get any sales; the best advertising in the world won't work if the consumer can't find the product in the store.

More important, the in-store battle is fought store by store, location by location. Securing retail distribution is usually a two-step process: the first is a central chain-level decision made at headquarters, which is usually rational and driven by numbers; the second is store-level execution, when the item is actually placed on the shelf. This second step is driven by superior execution, actually moving products around in each individual store and ensuring that the guidelines from headquarters are executed consistently. The shelf battle can occur in thousands of different locations; for a mass-market product there could be 10,000 or 20,000 individual points of distribution, or even more in a country like Mexico, which is dominated by small retail locations.

An in-store battle usually plays to the strengths of the established players, since they often have a big sales force in place. An established company with a direct store delivery model is in a particularly strong position; it is very difficult for an attacker to replicate this in short order.

There are many ways to get a product off a shelf or minimize its presence even if the chain has agreed to carry the item. The easiest way is to influence the shelving plan. Many retailers use what is called a planogram to organize shelving. The planogram shows each product and where it should be located.

Individual stores are then supposed to follow the planogram. If a new product is placed far from eye level, with a very small presence, its impact on the shelf will be minimal, and it will be hard for customers to find it.

Influencing the planogram is often easier than you might suspect, because at many retailers the large established player actually creates and manages the planogram. The established company also organizes shelf resets when the shelving configuration in a particular store is updated.

If the large player responsible for the category planogram is worried about a particular new product, it simply needs to ensure that the new item is put in an inconspicuous location. The large player can also delay shelf resets, making the changes slowly, over time, to slow up the distribution build of the new product.

A smaller established player can also influence the planogram, making suggestions for category shelving. Producing a new study showing the optimal shelving arrangement will often work in favor of the established players, since it would presumably be based on actual sales results, when the new product wasn't yet in distribution.

Even when the shelf has been reset, opportunities remain for battling the new entrant. One approach is to add in-store promotions that draw attention to your product and obscure the competing new product. In-store display units can be very effective at attracting attention, for example, as can in-store signage.

Chip giant Frito-Lay used this approach when dealing the entry of Nabisco's SnackWell's brand. The company added extensive in-store promotions in advance of the Nabisco launch, including a new rack program that essentially duplicated a rack that Nabisco was planning to use. This defensive approach was very effective. One executive involved in the launch noted, "They won't get the shelf space they thought they'd get because we had it one month before."[7]

Another even more devastating approach is to simply remove your competitor's product from the shelf entirely and put it in the back room of the store. This action is highly effective, because the competitor's product is now essentially out of distribution. In one Caribbean country, for example, a brand of frozen hamburgers pursued this approach. The brand, a major player in the category, was concerned about a new competitive entrant that was offering a quality product at a very reasonable price. The established player was not successful at persuading the retail chains to reject the new item. So the defender took the fight directly to the stores. The primary tactic was engaging the grocery store staff; the established player paid store employees to take the competitive product off the shelf and move it to the back room. This rather aggressive (and legally and ethically questionable) approach was highly effective; sales of the new entrant quickly dropped. One industry insider watched the situation unfold. He summarized what happened to the new products: "They just died."[8]

CREATE OPERATIONAL BARRIERS

If a company cannot build a factory or open a store, it can't enter a market. Thus, creating operational barriers can effectively keep a competitor out of a market. There are many different ways to do this.

One approach is to leverage community groups to oppose the construction of new stores or factories; an active, energetic group of citizens can inspire a local government to block permits, and without permits, construction can't move forward.

This is how grocery giants Safeway, Supervalu, and Ahold tried to slow the growth of Wal-Mart. The companies hired a consulting firm that led a series of campaigns opposing the construction of new Wal-Mart stores. Safeway alone hired Saint Consulting Group more than 30 times. As a result, virtually every new Wal-Mart location faced local opposition, much of it funded and coordinated by the established players. In Bakersfield, California, for example, a group called Bakersfield Citizens for Local Control fought against two new Wal-Mart locations, citing environmental and competition concerns.[9] Michael Saint, founder of Saint Consulting Group, explained, "our goal is always to kill Wal-Mart."[10]

Backus, at the time the leading beer company in Peru, created enormous operational barriers to block the entry of AmBev in the early 2000s. Backus was the dominant player in the market with Cristal, the top brand, and a market share of more than 90 percent. AmBev planned to enter the market and build its Brahma brand. AmBev planned to use a recyclable 620 ml glass bottle, the industry standard. Backus, however, was able to convince government regulators that it owned all the 620 ml glass bottles in Peru. Jose Antonio Payet, the chief legal strategist at Backus, explained the logic in an interview: "The bottles here belong to Backus, and Backus does not want to contract with AmBev. Backus has placed an enormous amount of 620 ml brown bottles in the market.

These bottles are Backus's assets; Backus has bought them, has put them in the market to sell its beer. Backus does not want its label to be taken off and allow them to be filled with some other beer. This would affect its property and is legally inadmissible."[11] This made the new product launch much more difficult for AmBev.

By creating operational barriers you can often put enough roadblocks in the way that a competitor may have a very difficult time entering your market. It might not completely block a determined competitor, but it will make competing with you much more expensive.

SECURE GOVERNMENT SUPPORT

Government regulations can be an enormous help when attempting to block a competitor. This approach can work particularly well when battling a foreign company.

In every country the government creates rules and regulations that impact commerce. In some countries the regulations are strict and tightly enforced, and in other countries the oversight is more relaxed. But there are always at least some regulations that companies must follow.

A simple way to prevent a foreign competitor from entering your market is to secure import barriers or tariffs. A high tariff can deny a competitor access to the market; it can destroy a new entrant's value proposition, pushing up prices and making the new product uncompetitive. In turn, this will damage the attacker's overall financial picture, since sales will be lower than anticipated, making it more difficult to justify the cost of the investment at all.

Government rules and regulations can prevent competition or make life very difficult for new entrants. Both of which are positive for the established players. In the airline industry, for example, both Germany and Canada have sharply limited Emirates Airline's access to the market. Germany permits Emirates to fly to only four cities.[12] This slows the growth of Emirates and protects Lufthansa.

A different German industry, education, recently employed a similar approach; local universities influenced government officials to deny a foreign school the necessary zoning permits to build a new campus. The effectively kept the new entrant out of the market.

In the United States, government regulations require that domestic airlines are owned by US companies; there is a limit on foreign ownership. This effectively reduces foreign competition. Similarly, Korea recently passed a law requiring new supermarkets opening within one kilometer of traditional stores to secure approval from local authorities and small business associations, a significant hurdle indeed.[13]

Even dentists can embrace this opportunity. Recently dental associations in several states in the United States have moved to defend the lucrative teeth-whitening business by securing government rules requiring that only licensed dentists provide the service. For example, the Connecticut State Dental Commission (a group made up largely of dentists) passed such a ruling. This move effectively eliminated the threat posed by new entrants such as salons. As one lawyer observed, the dentists are "using government power to stifle honest competition."[14] And effectively so; after the dental board imposed the rule, many of the new providers closed down.

China is particularly aggressive at protecting its domestic companies from foreign competition. While many industries are technically open for free commerce, China has a series of regulations that effectively limit new entrants. For example, China requires that all tires be imprinted with Chinese characters. This means that international manufacturers must create new molds, increasing the cost of entering the market. China requires that gas appliances have burners that can withstand temperatures of over 700°C. This effectively prevents manufacturers that rely on aluminum burners from getting into the market.[15] China also has rules on government procurement, limiting purchases to certain approved products. This hurts foreign competitors, since their products rarely make the list. As John Frisbie, president of the US-China Business Council, observed, "These rules in essence will keep out not just American companies over here but also American companies operating in China."[16]

The launch of Italian pasta Barilla in the United States provides a powerful example of how government support can be used to protect a business. In the mid-1990s, the US pasta industry was dominated by several huge companies, including CPC, Borden, and Nestle. The industry was big, stable, and slow moving. Companies were profitable, though not enormously so, since the products were essentially commodities and consumers bought largely based on price. As a result, companies focused relentlessly on reducing costs in a bid to increase margins and profits. So the companies substituted cheaper types of wheat, thus gradually eroding product quality.

Barilla, the number-one pasta company in Italy, studied the US market to find opportunities to enter. The United States was the largest pasta market in the world, so Barilla was particularly interested in finding a way to establish a presence. The executives at Barilla noticed two odd things about the US pasta business. First, product quality was poor and getting worse. With the big players focused on cost reduction, the pasta simply wasn't very good. One way this quality reduction showed up was in cooking time. Cheaper pasta has to be cooked for just the right amount of time; if the pasta boils too long, it quickly turns into a pile of mush. Second, pricing in the category was odd. While product cost was the same for all the items, the established players priced using a two-tier system, with spaghetti at 99 cents and specialty cuts, such as rigatoni and rotini, at a higher price, about $1.49.

Barilla entered the US market in 1994. Initially, Barilla focused on selling a high-quality imported product at a price of $1.29 per box, consistent across all types. This was higher than the price of most spaghetti items, but lower than the price of competitive specialty cuts.

Initial results for Barilla were quite good; the brand picked up about 6 percent market share, with the biggest gains in areas with a large Italian population. Thus, Barilla grew particularly quickly in cities such as Boston and New York. Unfortunately, growth then slowed, and the promising initial momentum fizzled out.

The team at Barilla looked at the situation and determined that the primary problem was the pricing of spaghetti. People were not willing to pay $1.29 for a box of Barilla spaghetti when competing brands were available at a price of 99 cents. A pricing study confirmed this fact; while price elasticity in the pasta category was high, the key threshold price was 99 cents. When the price of spaghetti went above 99 cents, sales fell dramatically.

To address the situation, Barilla decided to cut the price of the entire line to 99 cents a box. By doing this, Barilla brought its prices in line with the category. This gave consumers a very strong value proposition; Barilla was a well-regarded brand with an excellent product selling spaghetti at a competitive price and specialty cuts at a lower price than other manufacturers.

The established players were now very concerned; Barilla was clearly becoming a threat. The initial launch at the higher price point was a problem, but the defenders could make a case that Barilla would be a small niche player selling premium imported pasta at a high price. This would be a small business and a small threat. Barilla's big pricing move, however, transformed the situation. Now Barilla was taking aim at the heart of the existing players' business; it was very clear that Barilla wasn't planning to be a small player in the category. Barilla wanted massive growth. With the 99-cent price, the only way Barilla could be profitable would be to take substantial market share from the existing brands.

For the established players, Barilla was a threat in two ways. First, Barilla might take their market share. People were not likely to eat more pasta now that Barilla was available in the market; Barilla's growth would come from stealing market share from the existing players. Second, Barilla's flat pricing scheme would make it difficult to keep the two-tier pricing structure in the category. If established players had to follow Barilla in the pricing, profits would fall even more.

To defend the business, the established players worked together in the National Pasta Association, an industry trade group. The association went to the US government and made the case that Barilla was dumping—selling product below cost. The US government frowns on dumping. As a result, in 1995 the United States Commerce Department imposed a duty on imported pasta, saying any company importing pasta had to pay a certain amount on each pound imported.

This tactic was successful—to a degree. It did precisely what the established players wanted; it destroyed Barilla's economics. Barilla could no longer import pasta from Italy and sell it at 99 cents per box; the duty ensured that this would be a money-losing proposition. The executives at Barilla quickly realized this fact; the message was clear.

Unfortunately for the established players in the pasta industry, Barilla did not throw in the towel and abandon the effort. Instead of simply raising prices and resigning themselves to be a niche player in the US pasta business, the Barilla executives decided to counteract the duty on imported pasta by investing $115 million to build one of the largest pasta plants in the world in Ames, Iowa. The plant was virtually identical to a Barilla factory in Foggia, Italy.[17]

With that move, Barilla avoided the duty since it was no longer selling imported pasta. This also meant that Barilla was more committed than ever to the US market; after having invested millions in a plant, Barilla was not about to simply exit the market.

Since that time, Barilla has grown substantially. In 2001 it became the largest branded pasta in the US market. In 2002 market share reached 15 percent, and by 2010 share climbed to about 25 percent.[18]

In the end, government support provided protection for the established US pasta companies, but it was short-lived.

INTRODUCE NEW PRODUCTS

Every channel of distribution has only so much space for new items. In a retail store, the physical space on a shelf is limited; not every product will fit. In a warehouse, the space to hold inventory of products is finite. Online retailers face fewer constraints, since they are not wrestling with a physical store presence, but there is still a limit on warehouse space. In virtually any category, there is only so much room for new products at any one time.

One way to make it difficult for a new competitor to get distribution is to launch new products that occupy the available space. If there is only one new product in a category in the first quarter, then it will have no competition for space; distributors will likely pick it up. There is usually a natural churn in a category; some items don't sell well or fade away, and they need to be dropped. This opens up space. With only one new product coming out, there's a good chance it will occupy this newly opened space in the category. By launching new products, however, an established player can force a new entrant to fight for distribution. Channel partners can't pick up all the items, so they now have to choose. And this can help the established player.

There are two different approaches to this strategy. One option is to launch an identical or roughly similar product. If Spicy Mexican shows up in the refried bean category, an established player introduces Super Spicy. And if ReNu appears—a new toothpaste with a claim of being made from recycled newspaper—the established player might launch Second Life, with a very similar proposition. A distributor might then reason, "Well, this recycled newspaper toothpaste idea seems fairly intriguing. Young people are buying some strange stuff these days. I better add one of those items to the mix." The distributor then has several similar items to choose from, instead of just the one new product from your competitor.

The other option is to launch different new products into the category; not copying the attacker's idea directly, but creating clutter and confusion. In this case, the established player might respond to the launch of Spicy Mexican by introducing a line of organic products or a line of products in a squeeze bottle.

Launching different products puts pressure on the distribution channel, too, because now distributors have to choose which items to carry. It is unlikely that a distributor can devote meaningful space to Spicy Mexican, the organic line, and the squeeze line all at once.

Minute Rice, the largest brand of instant rice in the United States, used this technique when defending against the launch of a similar product from its competitor Uncle Ben's. The Minute Rice team quickly launched a flurry of new items, bringing ten different items to market at the same time as the Uncle Ben's product. By launching items such as an instant brown rice and a convenient "bag and boil" pack, the Minute brand made it more difficult for Uncle Ben's to gain shelf space. As one executive explained, "We weren't going to keep them out, but we wanted to minimize their exposure."[19]

It is important to keep in mind that when blocking distribution it isn't essential to get 100 percent success. The goal is simply to limit the distribution, preventing the new entrant from reaching significant distribution levels.

A WORD OF CAUTION

Blocking distribution is a very effective form of defense. Indeed, in some respects it is the most powerful approach. If an established player can dominate a channel, there is little chance that a new player will succeed. Simply put, no distribution means no sales and no company.

For this reason, government regulators scrutinize efforts to block distribution with particular vigor. The best advice is quite simple: tread carefully.

Chapter 10

LIMITING AWARENESS

HERE IS A FAIRLY BASIC point on launching new products: If people aren't aware of a product, they won't buy it. This fundamental principle explains why companies launching new items spend so much money attracting attention.

For this reason, limiting a competitor's attempts to gain product awareness is a core defensive tactic. Low levels of awareness will result in low levels of trial and, in turn, low levels of repeat. Ultimately, this leads to a small or unsuccessful business. So, if you can slow a new entrant's building of awareness, you can significantly reduce the competitive threat.

NEW PRODUCT? WHAT NEW PRODUCT?

The goal in limiting awareness is quite simple: ensure that customers don't hear about the competitor's new product. It's difficult to completely stop a company's efforts at building awareness; when a new market entrant invests millions in advertising and promotions, you can't stop everyone from noticing it. But even partial success in this area can be very helpful for the established player. In many cases, all you need to do is ensure that awareness is lower than planned. This will lead to lower sales and force the attacker to reevaluate the launch.

Small reductions in awareness can create major problems for new entrants, because trial and repeat are always subsets of awareness. A portion of customers will be aware of a new product. And then a smaller portion of that group will try the new item, and an even smaller portion of that group will become a repeat buyer.

Lower-than-planned awareness results in fewer initial sales, and then, in the best case, the company gives up, or distributors decide to discontinue the product due to slow sales. Losing support from partners such as distributors and retailers isn't an unusual problem; they have limited space for products and are constantly looking for items that sell quickly. Pruning products that sell slowly and swapping them for products with better sales is a common way for retailers to improve financial results. Thus, even a small decrease in awareness can ultimately result in a new product line failing entirely.

Consider a new outdoor energy bar company. Let's name it for the highest mountain in Colorado (and in the continental United States), Mt. Elbert. We'll call the company Elbert Alpine Energy Bars. The marketing team at Elbert Alpine Energy Bars has created a plan to create awareness among 60 percent among the target group of consumers. Based on market research, Elbert believes that half the people who are aware of the new product will try it. So if 60 percent of people are aware, 30 percent will try it. Elbert also believes that two-thirds of people who try the product will become repeat purchasers. This means that ongoing market penetration would be 20 percent. Elbert expects

Exhibit 10.1 Elbert Alpine Energy outlook

	Forecast
Population	3 million
Awareness	60%
Trial (of those aware)	50%
Repeat (of triers)	66%
Ongoing penetration	20%
Customers	600,000
Bars per week per customer	0.5
Weekly sales (bars)	300,000
Price per bar	$2
Weekly sales	$600,000
Total stores	1,000
Sales per store	$600
Sales per store target	$500

customers to buy the product at a rate of one bar every other week, or 0.5 bars per week. With a population of 3 million people in the launch geography, a price of $2 per bar, and 1,000 stores, this leads to average weekly sales per store of $600. If retailers need to see sales per item per store of $500 to maintain distribution, Elbert should be OK. It is comfortably above this benchmark, certainly high enough to hold its space (see exhibit 10.1).

Now let's say that one of the existing players in this category is able to cut awareness of Elbert's product modestly. The weekly sales projections quickly fall. This is true even if other elements of the plan don't change, and the ratios of awareness to trial and trial to repeat remain the same. If awareness only reaches 45 percent, weekly sales per store fall to $450, below the retailers' target to maintain distribution. And if awareness reaches just 30 percent, weekly sales fall to only $300. Now the product is in trouble (see exhibit 10.2).

By limiting awareness, defending companies create major problems for Elbert; retailers will quickly drop the item as sales fail to hit the sales target. Elbert could invest more in marketing efforts to try to overcome the impact of the defensive campaign, but this would also put pressure on the financial projections.

Exhibit 10.2 Elbert Alpine Energy outlook: updated

	Forecast	Scenario 1	Scenario 2
Population	3 million	3 million	3 million
Awareness	60%	45%	30%
Trial (of those aware)	50%	50%	50%
Repeat (of triers)	66%	66%	66%
Ongoing penetration	20%	15%	10%
Customers	600,000	450,000	300,000
Bars per week per customer	0.5	0.5	0.5
Weekly sales (bars)	300,000	225,000	150,000
Price per bar	$2	$2	$2
Weekly sales	$600,000	$450,000	$300,000
Total stores	1,000	1,000	1,000
Sales per store	$600	$450	$300
Sales per store target	$500	$500	$500

BLOCK AND LIMIT

There are two basic ways to interrupt a competitor's building of awareness. The first is to block a competitor entirely, so it can't reach customers. The second is to limit the impact of a competitor's communication efforts.

Blocking a competitor is a wonderful thing: if a new entrant simply can't reach customers, then it has no opportunity to build awareness and can't succeed. The problem is that blocking awareness of a competitor isn't easy to do. Great entrepreneurs usually make for great press—it's difficult to keep a creative person with a great new idea from getting some attention. It is also hard to stop new entrants from running an advertising campaign if they have the money to pay for it.

Limiting the impact is a more common approach, and it can be highly effective. The goal is to ensure that customers don't focus on the competitor's message. The new entrant might get in front of customers, but the message doesn't motivate action; customers stick with the brand they know.

Limiting impact is in some ways even better than blocking a competitor entirely. When effectively done, the new entrant invests in a marketing campaign to build awareness, but it simply doesn't work. The result is that the new entrant is weakened financially; the money is gone with little to show for it. The attacker then exits the market, bloodied and battered from the experience.

There are many ways to limit awareness of a competitor's new product. More important, some of these techniques are essentially free; they can be implemented with very little investment.

LOCK UP KEY MARKETING VEHICLES

Perhaps the simplest way to block a competitor's awareness-building efforts is to lock up key marketing vehicles. If you buy all the advertising space, then there isn't any available for your competitors, and you've made their job much harder indeed.

Many marketing vehicles promise category exclusivity. So if one type of company is promoting its product at a particular time, another company can't step in and do the same thing. Media companies promise exclusivity to ensure that the marketing vehicle is effective. The companies that distribute coupons in the Sunday newspaper, for example, work on guaranteed exclusivity, so you don't generally see two salad dressing companies running ads in the same sale flyer on the same day. Similarly, many sponsorship programs also promise sole ownership of a property, though they may charge a premium for it. Anheuser-Busch, for example, has secured advertising exclusivity for the beer category during the Super Bowl, perhaps the biggest single marketing event in the world (of course, the company pays dearly for this privilege).

When a competitor appears, then, a logical move is to invest more in marketing efforts, quickly acquiring exclusivity wherever possible. There are two benefits in doing this. First, you strengthen your business. Second, you ensure that your competitor can't purchase the space.

Financially, this means that many marketing opportunities that might not have made sense before now look better. Investing in an in-store promotion might help your business to a certain degree, but perhaps not enough to warrant the spending in ordinary times. But when you combine the incremental sales impact with the defensive impact, the financial calculation might change significantly.

There is an obvious problem with this approach, which is that you can't buy everything. The world is full of marketing opportunities; there are hundreds of television networks, millions of websites, and thousands upon thousands of sponsorship opportunities. It simply isn't possible to buy them all, even for a company with vast resources.

So this technique works best when there are a few critical marketing vehicles and a small window of time. Companies that sell Easter egg decorating kits, for example, are well positioned to use this sort of approach; a defending company can buy all of the coupon slots in the three weeks leading up to Easter and guarantee that an attacker can't deliver a coupon. At the same time, a company can buy all the in-store advertising vehicles and retailer promotion windows, and lock up the store. If a new company can't deliver a coupon and can't get some in-store activity, it won't be able to build much awareness and will likely fail.

Locking up marketing vehicles is a common defensive approach in many categories. When Cialis and Levitra were entering the erectile dysfunction market in 2005, for example, established player Viagra purchased the advertising for an entire year on Epocrates, an important handheld computer system used by physicians. This ensured that Cialis and Levitra could not advertise on that vehicle at all during the first 12 months of launch.[1]

In Russia, electronics retailer Eldorado responded to the entry of German retail giant Media Markt by purchasing all the billboards near Media Markt's new stores. Eldorado also changed colors, moving from its traditional blue and yellow brand design to red and black, very similar to Media Markt.

Similarly, as Washington Mutual was entering the Chicago banking market, established player Bank One signed a sponsorship deal with the Chicago Bears professional football team. The timing wasn't a coincidence; Bank One might have had no great interest in being a Chicago Bears sponsor but didn't want Washington Mutual to capitalize on the opportunity. A Bank One spokesperson stated at the time that the move "reaffirms in our hometown that we're Chicago's leading bank, and we intend to stay that way."[2]

In the world of soccer, Adidas has invested millions to slow the growth of Nike. One of the key strategies Adidas uses is to lock up the World Cup. In 2010, for example, Adidas sponsored a third of the teams and the entire event. As Adidas CEO Herbert Hainer observed, "We have protected our ground fairly well."[3]

OUTSPEND THE NEW ENTRANT

The simplest way to ensure that a competitor cannot build awareness is to simply outspend that market entrant. If the new entrant is outspent by five times— say, the established player meets the new competitor's $2 million in advertising with an advertising campaign of $10 million—it will be a challenge for the new competitor to gain much awareness. There will simply be too much spending in the market.

This approach doesn't necessarily require a new strategy or new creative development. The established business can simply invest more funds in the current campaign. As marketing veteran Gary Rawlings explained, "Whatever the brand has been doing, just do more of it."[4]

This strategy can work across all media types. With television and radio advertising, the established player can simply buy more time on important shows. In the world of online search, the defender can pay more to buy clicks and strong online placement. At a trade show, the established player can secure the most prominent location and put up the fanciest display, so that people spend more time at the established player's booth and less time wandering around looking at the competition. In-store, the established player can invest more in displays and promotional materials to create clutter and ensure the new entrant doesn't stand out.

Heavy spending may not be sufficient on its own to block awareness-building; however, so it's not wise to rely on this approach alone. The competitor's advertising might be particularly impactful, for example, so that even with relatively limited spending people notice it and pay attention. A more disconcerting risk is that the new entrant has a particularly exciting new idea, which will make people pay attention. If media outlets pick up the idea and profile it in articles, the new entrant can generate buzz and awareness with very little spending indeed.

The changing media world makes it particularly risky to rely only on heavy spending to block awareness. Years ago, when it was difficult for an individual company to have a broad reach in the media market, defending companies could more easily have an impact on awareness-building; with heavy spending all the key vehicles could be controlled. Today, with the rise of the Internet, online forums, and social networking, individual efforts have a bigger impact, and free media in the form of formal or informal endorsements are more powerful. This means that small new entrants have an opportunity to generate buzz even if established players control all the traditional advertising venues such as print, television, and radio.

INTRODUCE SIMILAR NEWS

One of the most effective approaches to blocking awareness is to introduce similar news. This fragments attention in the market, ensuring that one company doesn't stand out as unique and different.

Introducing similar news can be easy to do; you simply follow the new entrant's lead. If the new entrant is talking about environmental friendliness, then you talk about environmental friendliness. If the new entrant is discussing social media, then you talk about social media. If the topic is a new technology, then you talk about a similar new technology.

Politicians routinely use this technique to block opponents. In 2011, for example, Sarah Palin scheduled a news conference at the same time that Mitt Romney was announcing his candidacy for president. The goal was quite simple: deny Romney sole media attention. As one political strategist explained, "There are only so many minutes in the nightly news. There is only so much space."[5] Similarly, Texas governor Rick Perry announced his candidacy on the day of the Republican straw poll in Iowa. As the *Financial Times* observed, "Instantly, Mr. Perry reduced that event to a sideshow and diminished the rivals who had chosen to take part."[6]

Timing is critical. For this approach to work, your news must hit the market at the same time as the attacker's news, or, even better, just before. Being late is a disaster; you miss the story window, and the effectiveness of your efforts diminishes dramatically. News cycles are short, so being a day or two late will never work; the story comes and goes, and the damage is done.

Most important, all your plans don't need to be finalized in order to use this strategy; it is possible to announce something before you have it finished. Or you can simply announce that you *plan* to do something or that you are excited about new study results. The goal is to make it seem like you have similar news. As marketing strategist Jack Trout observed, "Perception is reality. Don't get confused by facts."[7]

Intel used this strategy to blunt the launch of a new chip from AMD, its key competitor. In September 2003, AMD announced with great fanfare that it had a new 64-bit microprocessor for the desktop computer market. This was big news, since the existing microprocessors from both Intel and AMD were just 32-bit ones. To blunt this news, several days before AMD's big announcement, Intel announced that it had a new version of its 32-bit processor that was just as fast as AMD's new chip, if not faster, and would sell for a similar price. Media outlets covered the news, of course, reporting on the two new products. The interesting twist in the story is that Intel apparently had no plans to actually sell the new version of its 32-bit microprocessor. It was technically possible to make it, but the company didn't plan to move forward with it.

By the time this point came to light, however, the story had come and gone; people were discussing other things. Intel effectively blocked AMD's moment in the sun with a bit of showmanship. As *Wall Street Journal* reporter Lee Gomes observed, "Intel did its best to summon rain clouds for the AMD parade."[8]

Hewlett-Packard used the same approach when defending against Kodak in digital printing. Kodak attacked the printer market by focusing on the high price of ink. Kodak set the price of its printers at a fairly high level and then significantly cut the price of ink. The theory, presumably, was that HP would not want to cut the price of its ink, leaving a potentially large segment of the market open for Kodak.

HP quickly responded to Kodak's launch by adopting an economy message. HP began running ads featuring a low-price message. One ad stated, "Introducing the HP Printing Payback Guarantee. We'll cut your printing costs or we'll cut you a check."[9] HP didn't actually cut its prices, but it shifted its message. By mimicking Kodak's economy message, HP muddied the waters and blocked trial on the Kodak items.

There is nothing wrong with copying someone else's idea, provided that there is no legal limitation in the form intellectual property law. However, this tactic can be utilized even if it runs counter to intellectual property law. There are two broad ways to do this.

First, it is possible to announce something without necessarily following through. If a new competitor announces that it has a great new technology for environmental friendliness with a strong patent, it is still possible for an established player to announce that it is working on a different technology with similar functionality. Moving in this fashion will blunt the impact of a competitor's move without running at all counter to legal restrictions.

Second, an established player can decide to take on the risk of a court battle and do something that might be found in violation of laws if prosecuted. Many legal judgments are not black and white. As one attorney I worked with at Kraft Foods advised me repeatedly, "The question isn't whether you can do it or not. The question is how much risk do you want?" Sometimes it makes sense to take some risk in order to blunt awareness of a competitor's products.

The problem with introducing similar news is that this might give momentum to the new idea. Your goal in introducing the news is to split the attention. The challenge is that the total amount of attention to the idea might then increase, so what began as new start-up's somewhat crazy idea starts to look like an important industry-wide trend. An eager business reporter might then write a story about the emerging trend and all the reasons why it is catching on at this particular moment. And then, before you know it, the idea is gaining momentum, and your competitor has suddenly gained a foothold.

FILE A COMPLAINT

Attacking your competitor's marketing materials can be a promising approach. If you can convince a regulating body to force your competitor to take its advertising off the air, you may be able to do irreparable harm to the competitor. By the time the competitor is able to retool the marketing efforts to resolve the dispute, the key window for promoting the product may well have passed.

For example, PepsiCo, owner of Gatorade, used this approach in a bid to slow the growth of Coca-Cola's Powerade. In 2009, PepsiCo sued Coca-Cola for making false advertising claims and asked the judge in the case for a preliminary injunction, barring Coca-Cola from running the advertising.[10] This took the wind out of Powerade's sails and limited awareness of the product. Mission accomplished for PepsiCo and Gatorade.

SECURE GOVERNMENT REGULATIONS

If a competitor cannot legally promote its product, it will not be able to build awareness, get trial, and secure repeat. Without the ability to market and promote, it is exceptionally difficult to launch a new product.

A fairly unusual tactic for defending a market is to secure government regulations blocking the promotion of the category. If successful, this approach ensures that competition cannot take action, and it locks in relative market shares.

The U.S. tobacco industry is an example of what happens when the government outlaws the promotion of a category. In 1971 the United States blocked advertising in the tobacco category. The result of this was quite predictable: market shares were essentially locked in place, since it was now incredibly difficult for a new brand to enter the market.

For this strategy to be successful there must be a reason why the government would pass such regulations. In the case of the tobacco industry, there were clear health issues related to smoking that warranted the regulations.

As a result, the strategy is only relevant for certain categories in certain circumstances. Even when it is a feasible approach, this strategy should be deployed with care; a block on promotional activities will increase the barriers to entry, but it also makes it harder to support the category overall or to introduce innovations. A category such as smoking remains, because smoking is addictive. Many other categories, however, will decline, potentially dramatically, in the absence of continual support.

HEIGHTEN THE CHALLENGE

There are many tactics for limiting a competitor's attempts to gain product awareness. If you are able to successfully slow a competitor's efforts at building awareness, you can hurt its entry into the market, reduce initial trial and repeat sales, and significantly reduce the long-term competitive threat.

Chapter 11

PREVENTING TRIAL

IF CONSUMERS DON'T TRY A product, they won't buy it again. This is why limiting trial is at the heart of defensive strategy, with many of the most intense battles playing out in this realm. If you can reduce the number of people who try your competitor's product, you can be quite confident it will fail to develop into a successful, established business.

The Chicago air transportation market provides a vivid example of this. In May 2011, British entrepreneur Richard Branson's new airline, Virgin America, began service from Chicago to Los Angeles and San Francisco. Simply entering the market was a challenge because the established players, United Airlines and American Airlines, fought hard to block access. When Delta Airlines reduced service in Chicago, for example, releasing gates at capacity-constrained O'Hare airport, American Airlines quickly leased them, making it more difficult for new airlines, such as Virgin America, to gain access. Nonetheless, Virgin America managed to secure space after a long battle and finally began service in 2011. Richard Branson proclaimed at the time, "We've had to fight our way into Chicago. This year, we gave them a really good left hand, and we're here to stay."[1]

As Virgin began service, American and United quickly moved to defend their business by blocking Virgin's trial. American and United made some classic defensive moves. First, the airlines matched Virgin's fares in the challenged markets (Los Angeles and San Francisco). Second, both American and United Airlines added flights on the route, giving customers more choice and more flexibility than Virgin. The established players also had flights leave at exactly the same times as the Virgin flights. Third, the established players offered customers promotions such as double frequent flyer miles. The promotions were targeted precisely at the most at-risk customers, those who lived in Chicago, San Francisco, or Los Angeles. As United spokesman Rahsaan Johnson stated, "Our strategy is squarely focused on giving customers the most convenient schedule and access to the broadest network. We have competed with multiple carriers in these two Chicago–West Coast markets for years. We will continue to do so and will continue to win."[2] The situation was quite clear in January 2012. From Chicago to San Francisco, American had six flights a day and United had ten. Virgin America had just three flights. Every flight was $258 round trip, exactly the same price.

American's and United's efforts to limit Virgin's growth appear to have been successful; there is little reason for people to try the new airline. If they sustain the defensive effort, they might eventually push Virgin out of the market.

IF YOU KILL TRIAL, YOU KILL THE PRODUCT

One of the most basic challenges in launching a new product is getting people to try it. People are busy, seemingly more so every year. Convincing them to take the time and the risk to try something new is one of the reasons launching a new product is difficult. As a result, if you find yourself defending against a new product in your category, you'll want make gaining trial as challenging for your competitor as possible.

Limiting trial is particularly important because trial is the critical step in a new product launch. With many new products, getting trial is the focus of the entire launch plan. This is the moment when all the work of building distribution and awareness pays off: the customer actually tries the new product or service.

If a defending company can suppress trial on a new product, the long-term risk will be limited. Repeat rates are based on trial rates; people can't repeat purchasing a new product unless they try it. A company might plan on getting 50 percent of people in a market to try a product, with 40 percent of this group becoming repeat buyers, yielding an ongoing market penetration rate of 20 percent. If a defender can limit trial to just 20 percent, then the ongoing penetration rate will fall to 8 percent, even if the rate of conversion from trial to repeat remains the same.

Just like other strategies we've discussed, the defender doesn't have to completely stop trial; in many cases simply *delaying* trial is sufficient. If trial develops slowly, sales of the new product will develop slowly as well, bogging down the new entrant's momentum and straining its resources. In the best case for the defender, the new product is dead before customers get around to a repeat purchase.

To understand why blocking trial is so important, it is useful to consider a typical new product launch plan. In year one, the company begins selling the item but in a limited geographical market with modest support. The goal is to verify the product's appeal. In year two, the company expands the launch, spending heavily as the new product achieves broad distribution. There might be a strong advertising campaign, a series of discounts and promotions, a sampling program, and a social media push. With all the support, sales begin to grow as people try the new offering, but the product loses money: spending is high and sales are modest.

In year three the investment continues, but perhaps at a slightly reduced level. Sales continue to build as more people try the product, and those who were happy with the initial experience repeat their purchase. The financial situation improves; sales are rising and spending is a bit more modest.

Things get better in years four and five, assuming all is going well. Spending falls once the initial launch period has passed. Trial rates decline, too, but more people have become loyal customers and repeatedly buy the product. Meaningful profits begin to appear.

Consider the introduction of a hypothetical new vacation home rental company called GTHR (Good Times Home Rentals). The company charges $5,000 per year to manage the rental of a family's vacation home. GTHR has a cost per house of $2,500, resulting in a profit of $2,500 per house. From market research studies, the company has learned that it will have to offer a $2,000 discount to secure a new customer, but initial repeat rates are an encouraging 60 percent, with retention after that of 90 percent. GTHR's leaders develop a launch plan that includes a limited launch in year one, with a significant expansion in year two. So in year two the company will invest $450,000 in advertising and public relations, another $450,000 in year three, and then $75,000 in years four, five, and six. It expects to get 100 new customers to try the product in year one and 1,000 new customers in year two, with additional customers in years three, four, and five. The company's fixed costs increase from $500,000 in year one to $900,000 in year two and then remain at that level.

With this set of numbers, the company will lose money in year one and lose even more in year two with the broader expansion. The business will become profitable in year three and then make significant profit by year four. The company will have cumulative profits of about $5 million through the first six years (see exhibit 11.1).

If an existing player defends and limits trial, however, the situation changes quite dramatically. Reducing GTHR's trial in years two and three by 50 percent has a huge impact on the financial picture. In year three, for example, GTHR now loses significant money instead of making a little. And the cumulative profit through the first five years of operation drops to a loss of about $15,000.

The situation never really improves for the attacker; lower trial rates lead to lower repeat rates and fewer loyal customers. Trial won't substantially increase in later years, since spending needs to fall to make the business profitable. Depressing initial rates has a long-term impact on the business.

Blocking trial is a critically important task for a defender: if you limit trial, you kill the new product.

Exhibit 11.1   GTHR financial forecast: initial

	Year 1	Year 2	Year 3	Year 4	Year 5	Year 6
Trial (customers)	100	1,000	800	200	200	200
Repeat rate	60%	60%	60%	60%	60%	60%
Retention rate	90%	90%	90%	90%	90%	90%
Total customers	100	1,060	1,454	1,269	1,282	1,294
Revenue (000s)	$500	$5,300	$7,270	$6,343	$6,409	$6,468
New customer discount (000s)	$200	$2,000	$1,600	$400	$400	$400
Costs (000s)	$250	$2,650	$3,635	$3,172	$3,204	$3,234
Marketing spending (000s)	$50	$450	$450	$75	$75	$75
Fixed costs (000s)	$500	$900	$900	$900	$900	$900
Profit (000s)	($500)	($700)	$685	$1,797	$1,829	$1,859
Cumulative (000s)						$4,970

WAYS TO LIMIT TRIAL

To drive trial, new entrants generally do two critical things. First, they promote the benefits of their product. They will proclaim that it is new, different, and special in a bid to generate interest from potential customers. Second, they offer incentives to reduce the barriers and get customers to take action.

Exhibit 11.2   GTHR financial forecast: updated

	Year 1	Year 2	Year 3	Year 4	Year 5	Year 6
Trial (customers)	100	500	400	200	200	200
Repeat rate	60%	60%	60%	60%	60%	60%
Retention rate	90%	90%	90%	90%	90%	90%
Total customers	100	560	754	710	779	841
Revenue (000s)	$500	$2,800	$3,770	$3,550	$3,895	$4,206
New customer discount (000s)	$200	$1,000	$800	$400	$400	$400
Costs (000s)	$250	$1,400	$1,885	$1,775	$1,948	$2,103
Marketing spending (000s)	$50	$450	$450	$75	$75	$75
Fixed costs (000s)	$500	$900	$900	$900	$900	$900
Profit (000s)	($500)	($950)	($265)	$400	$573	$728
Cumulative (000s)						($15)

Exhibit 11.3   GTHR profits

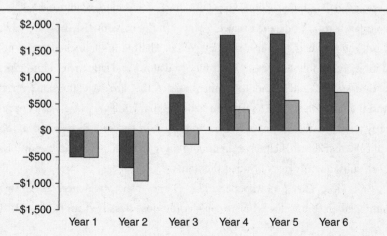

Defenders can take steps to blunt both of these efforts, reducing the appeal of the competitor's new product or limiting the attractiveness of the incentives. If the defender is successful at either task, trial rates will fall, and the new product will be in trouble.

When blocking trial, timing is critical; the defensive effort must occur at the right moment. In most cases, this will be as the new entrant ramps up the launch plan in a bid to drive trial; the defensive effort needs to meet the new entrant's spending.

There are many ways to limit trial; this is a very fruitful area for defensive thinking and many competitive battles unfold here.

LAUNCH A SIMILAR PRODUCT

The simplest way to block a competitor's efforts to build trial is to launch the same thing. If you introduce a new product that delivers the same benefits as the new entrant's product and back it with strong support, you will have a major impact on your competitor's results. You might not keep everyone from trying the new competing product, but you will ensure that you capture much of that trial and that your competitor doesn't. This technique might also help you block distribution, as discussed in the preceding chapter.

This isn't a complicated strategy. If a new company launches a paper towel that is twice as long as the typical paper towel, the established player launches a long paper towel too. If a software company introduces a program in the educational market that helps students collaborate with video chat, the established player in the market also introduces video chat. In the 1990s, Unilever's Hellmann's brand of mayonnaise developed and launched a line of new products called "Hellmann's One-Step Dressings," for potato salad, tuna salad, and coleslaw. Kraft Foods, the other big player in the mayonnaise category, saw the Unilever products in a test market. When Hellmann's launched the product nationally the following year, Kraft followed along and launched a similar product under the Kraft brand: the same product, the same size, the same varieties and the same price. The Kraft team believed that Unilever's idea wasn't particularly good but didn't want to risk having Unilever succeed. By responding, Kraft split the market with Unilever, reducing sales on each item. Unilever and Kraft both subsequently discontinued the items.

Salt Lake City's newspaper, *The Desert News*, watched as Craigslist launched an online site where people could post classified ads for free. Unlike most other newspapers at the time, *The Desert News* regarded this as a clear threat and took action. The company defended by quickly launching its own site, www.ksl.com. This move ensured that Craigslist wouldn't be able to gain significant trial in Salt Lake City. By 2011, Salt Lake City was the only major city in the United States where Craigslist was not the dominant player in classified ads.[3]

There are two important things to remember when working with this strategy. The first thing is that timing is everything; the established player's defensive product should hit the market at the same time as the new entrant or before. In the best case, the defensive product hits the market slightly in advance of the competing product; this makes it particularly difficult for the new competitor to get trial, because customers will likely try the defending product from the established company first. People who like the defending product will probably stick with it. People who don't like the defending product will likely sour on the entire category, perhaps concluding, "Those long paper towels? Oh, I tried one of them. They really aren't too good; they're hard to handle."

Launching a defending product simultaneously with a new entrant will still be effective; if the new items hit the market at the same time, then trial rates will most likely split. Customers will try one or the other, but with two to choose from, the trial rates for the new product will fall substantially.

A late launch, however, is a problem. Launching the defensive product after the new entrant has already gotten to market just won't work as well because many people will try the first new product and then see no need to try another one. As a result, the defensive product will have little impact on trial rates for the new entrant.

The second thing to remember about this strategy is that the product doesn't have to be particularly good. Of course, ideally the defensive product is better than the new entrant; if people try both, they end up choosing the defensive product. However, the defending product can be substantially inferior to the new product. Trial isn't driven by product quality; it is driven by awareness and interest in the basic idea. A defensive product that is quite weak can still get awareness and interest.

The Chicago newspaper market provides a classic example. Chicago has two strong daily newspapers, the *Chicago Tribune* and the *Chicago Sun-Times*. In 2002 the *Chicago Tribune* launched a new publication called *Red Eye* aimed at young adults, especially those commuting to work. The newspaper, which came in a tabloid format, featured short articles with a heavy dose of sports and entertainment news. The *Chicago Sun-Times* was not pleased with this move since the *Sun-Times* reached a similar audience with the same sort of tabloid format.

To address the threat posed by *Red Eye*, the *Sun-Times* quickly created a new publication called *Red Streak*. The product was very similar to *Red Eye*. The key difference was that executives at the *Tribune* had spent years developing *Red Eye* while the *Sun-Times* developed *Red Streak* in just a few days. John Barron, the *Sun-Times* editor, explained in an interview, "The *Tribune* was going after our demographics, and we weren't going to let them do that without a fight." He continued, "The plot line for *Red Streak* from the start was to confuse the marketplace and not allow the *Tribune* to set up a successful paid-circulation tabloid."[4]

Both publications hit the market on the same day. The result was quite predictable: *Red Eye* fell far short of expectations as the defensive product reduced overall trial levels. The *Sun-Times* never charged for *Red Streak*, which essentially meant that the *Chicago Tribune* couldn't charge for *Red Eye*. This substantially damaged the financial prospects of *Red Eye*.

If given the choice between launching a good product on a timely basis and launching an inferior product quickly, it is far better to launch the inferior product when defending a business since speed is everything.

This dynamic is not the case when thinking about growth initiatives; a new product launched with growth in mind needs to secure repeat, and the only way to get repeat is to delight customers when they try the product.

The plastic trash bag category provides another good example of this strategy in action. In the United States, there are two strong brands of trash bags: Glad and Hefty. In 2004 Glad introduced a completely new line of trash bags. It featured an innovative new technology that dramatically improved the performance of the trash bag: a bag that stretched as it filled. The bag retained its basic integrity instead of puncturing when it encountered a hard, sharp object or shape. This new product addressed a significant consumer issue—bags that tore when you used them.

Glad introduced the new line of bags with a subbrand, calling the new items Glad Force-Flex. The packaging highlighted the new technology with an innovative graphic showing how the bags prevented punctures and using the line "Stretchable Strength."

As one might imagine, the people at Hefty were not pleased with the new Glad launch; Glad had a clearly superior technology that addressed a major consumer issue. Unfortunately, Hefty could not quickly copy Glad's technology. This put Hefty at risk of losing significant market share.

The team at Hefty decided to copy the idea anyway, so Hefty developed a new product called Hefty Ultra-Flex and launched it just after the Glad product. The box featured a diagram explaining that the bag prevented punctures, much like the claim on the Glad box. Hefty's box carried the line, "Thick, strong, and stretchable." The product itself, however, was similar to the old Hefty product, not a dynamic new technology.

The result was predictable. Glad consumers largely tried the Glad product. Hefty consumers largely tried the Hefty product. Even with an inferior product, Hefty prevented the loss of major market share to Glad. Both products survived and still remain in the market several years later. By moving quickly, Hefty both blocked Glad and capitalized on Glad's idea.

There are times when it might make sense to launch a completely inferior or unsustainable product simply to knock out a competitive product: a pure suicide mission. This is the approach Coca-Cola took when dealing with the launch of Crystal Pepsi in 1992. Pepsi's new product was a clear, noncaffeinated cola, designed to bring interest and new life to the cola category. Coke set out to torpedo the Pepsi launch by confusing people into thinking of Crystal Pepsi as a diet drink. Of course, Crystal Pepsi had a lot of calories and wasn't a diet drink at all.

Sergio Zyman, chief marketing officer of Coca-Cola at the time, later explained what happened: "We said we would launch a Tab Clear product and position it right next to Crystal Pepsi, and we'd kill off both in the process. We basically repositioned the competition." The launch worked well from a defensive perspective, according to Zyman. "Within three or five months, Tab Clear was dead. And so was Crystal Pepsi. It was a suicidal mission from day one. Pepsi spent an enormous amount of money on the brand and, regardless, we killed it."[5]

When launching a defensive product, pricing is an important thing to consider. Defenders have much more freedom with pricing than new entrants; defenders can set very low prices and undercut a new entrant, because a defensive product doesn't necessarily have to be profitable. In fact, a defensive product that loses millions might be a very good idea if it protects a profitable existing business. The entrant must price for profit; the defender can price for loss.

However, there are two important things to remember when considering price. First, defending with a low price might actually create a bigger problem; if a defender cuts price, the attacker might respond by cutting price, creating a price war in the market and increasing the competition. Second, if the idea is likely to survive in one form or another, setting a low price will limit the long-term opportunity. It might be much more profitable to keep pricing high and capitalize on the profit potential of the idea.

There are a variety of legal issues related to intellectual property to consider when launching a similar product. One of the biggest issues is that the new entrant might have a patent on the new idea or technology. This is something to consider, since the price of a patent violation can be high. Another issue is that the new entrant might have established a trademark that prevents the defender from copying the name or the descriptor.

Many companies don't let intellectual property laws slow down a defense, for three reasons. First, most legal questions are gray; it isn't entirely clear what is allowed and what isn't. If a situation is debatable, some people argue, it is fine to proceed and let the chips fall where they may. Second, intellectual property disputes often drag on for an extended period of time. If a suit takes six months to resolve, a defending company will have had plenty of time to block the new entrant's trial. Third, suits require somebody to file them, and often a new entrant won't have the resources to do this.

Launching a similar product raises all sorts of ethical questions. Most of us grew up thinking that it was wrong to copy someone else's work; getting caught looking at another student's answers to a math test would generally lead to a trip to the principal's office with a call to the parents and a school suspension to follow. So isn't it wrong to just copy another company's work?

The rules in business are quite clear: copying is fine as long as you aren't violating a competitor's intellectual property such as patents and trademarks. Remember that school isn't life. Lucy Kellaway, a columnist at the *Financial Times*, observed that copying someone's idea is perfectly acceptable behavior. She noted, "There is nothing to be ashamed of in this. It is good to copy—we would have died out as a race if we didn't do it. Copying gives me access to an infinitely richer and more varied menu of ideas than if I had to limit myself to my own meager store."[6]

CONSIDER THE BRANDING

Branding becomes a big question when launching defensive new products. The question to consider is whether it is better to leverage your existing brand or to create an entirely new brand. It is important to think this issue through carefully.

Every time a company launches a new product in an existing business and product line, it faces a branding question. There are several different approaches. The simplest way to introduce a new product is to rely entirely on the existing brand and launch the new product with just a descriptor. For example, Coca-Cola frequently uses this approach, launching new items with the Coke brand and a descriptor. This model was used for Vanilla Coke and Cherry Coke. Tire brands like Bridgestone might use this approach when introducing a new tire with a deeper tread, calling it Bridgestone Deep Tread.

A slightly different approach is creating a new subbrand, which involves keeping the existing brand and adding a new secondary brand. The existing brand is more prominent than the new subbrand. In the Bridgestone example, a new product might be called Bridgestone Double Black tires. The primary brand here is still Bridgestone, with the deeper tread tires being a feature of the new subbrand, Double Black.

Introducing a new brand is a more complex approach. There are two ways to do this. One is to launch a completely new brand. In the tire example, Bridgestone would create a new brand called simply Double Black. Bridgestone would then have two completely distinct brands, Bridgestone and Double Black, with no connection between them. The other way to launch a new brand is to connect it to the existing brand through an endorsement, such as "Double Black from Bridgestone."

When launching defensive new products in order to limit trial, the branding question is an important one. The decision should ultimately be driven by the strategy. If you have a strong brand that resonates with customers, and your goal is to protect this brand by ensuring your existing customers don't try the new entrant's product, then it makes sense to leverage your existing brand. It will be difficult for the new entrant to pull your customers away if you provide a similar proposition under the brand that they already love. For example, people who love Starbucks will presumably go to Starbucks for a hot chocolate rather than stop at an entirely new store offering a new specialty hot chocolate.

However, if your goal is primarily to hurt the attacker or capitalize on the new idea, then you may want to launch a new brand. This is particularly important if the new entrant is going after a different target market than you are. For example, if your brand sells to middle-class families, and the new entrant targets the older wealthy elite, then you'll need to think seriously about creating a new brand or at least a new brand endorsed by the old brand. In this case your existing brand isn't likely to be an effective platform for a defensive effort.

LAUNCH A DIFFERENT PRODUCT

Creating a different, new product is another way to block trial of a competitor. The concept here is that people can only try a certain number of products at one time, so providing an alternative and cluttering a market will reduce trial rates on each one.

For example, several years ago, Kraft Foods responded to the launch of Hellmann's salad dressing by introducing two new product lines, Kraft Special Collections and Kraft Light Done Right. The new products created clutter in the category and blocked Hellmann's trial.

The logic of this strategy is quite simple: if there is only one new product coming to market, then it will get all of the trial in the category; there is no competition for the "latest, greatest" position. Anyone looking for something new will immediately head to the new entrant. If there are three or four or even eight new products launching all at once, the position of "latest, greatest" is up for grabs.

This dynamic is important in view of customer segmentation. In many categories, there is a group of customers wanting to purchase the newest products; these are the innovation seekers, people who fundamentally like trying and experiencing new things. With no competition, a new entrant will capture this group and get a fairly substantial boost.

In many categories there is also a group of people who are dissatisfied with the existing products and are looking for new options. Again, with no competition, a new entrant will get this group to try its product.

When applying this strategy of blocking trial, the goal is to launch innovative, appealing products. For the strategy to work, the new products should be exciting and attractive. The products should also target the same group of customers as the new entrant's product. If a new product comes to market targeting teenagers, the established player seeking to defend should launch a product aimed at teenagers. Launching a product targeting another group isn't likely to impact the new entrant's trial rates substantially.

This common strategy tends to be effective, and it avoids issues related to intellectual property since the defending company is launching a new idea. However, this can be a challenging to execute because it depends on creating an appealing new product. In many categories, creating a good new product is a huge challenge and takes a lot of time and effort.

LOAD UP CUSTOMERS

Loading up customers is a simple defensive tactic and one of the most common. The goal is to encourage customers to buy large amounts of existing product before the competitive product hits the market. When the new entrant appears, customers will be reluctant to buy the new product since they are already long on inventory. Someone with 50 rolls of paper towels in the pantry will be a little hesitant to buy another roll of paper towels, even one of good quality and a favorable price.

Clorox used this approach to defend against Procter & Gamble in the bleach category. P&G's CEO A. G. Lafley described the situation in a recent interview: "In the 1980s P&G tried to get into the bleach business. We had a differentiated and superior product—a color-safe, low-temperature bleach called Vibrant." P&G went to a test market in Portland, Maine, and created a robust plan to support the launch, including a distribution drive, strong promotions, and solid advertising. But things didn't work out too well. Lafley explained, "Do you know what Clorox did? They gave every household in Portland, Maine, a free gallon of Clorox bleach—delivered to the front door. Game, set, match to Clorox. We'd already bought all the advertising. We'd spent most of the launch money on sampling and couponing. And nobody in Portland, Maine, was going to need bleach for several months. I think they even gave consumers a $1 off coupon for the next gallon. They basically sent us a message that said, 'Don't ever think about entering the bleach category.'"[7]

Loading is a very effective defensive approach because you are asking customers to do what they would do anyway: purchase your product. Essentially, you want your most loyal customers to capitalize on the offer. And they will often respond; you are simply rewarding them for loading up on your product.

Companies rarely offer loading incentives in the course of day-to-day business. Loading up consumers usually makes no sense; giving big incentives to existing customers to shift around volume is not an efficient way to drive profitable growth. Consumers temporarily load up their pantries, then draw down the inventory over time. The company sees sales jump but then quickly decline again as consumers reduce inventories. For this reason, companies usually work very hard to ensure that loyal customers can't take advantage of big discounts.

A defensive situation is unique, however, and tactics that make no sense as offensive tools become very valuable as defensive tools. Loading is such a tool, and as a result the offers often attract quite a bit of attention. They deliver big savings on products that are rarely discounted so aggressively, and consumers eagerly participate in these programs.

Loading up can work with customers, both individual consumers and businesses, and with channel partners, such as distributors and retailers. The theory is the same: people will be reluctant to buy a new product if they are long on inventory.

An easy way to load consumers is through promotional incentives. Distributing coupons promising $1 for purchasing multiple items is an easy way to encourage loading. Similarly, an in-store discount that delivers a big incentive for a multiple purchase will encourage loading up the pantry.

There are two things to keep in mind when considering consumer incentives. First, the incentive must be based on purchase of multiple units. Giving consumers a coupon saving 50 cents on one item will not drive loading up; this will just drive the purchase of one item. A better coupon offer would be savings of $2 on four items. Similarly, the best in-store offers will be based on multiples.

Second, the incentive must be big enough to motivate the desired behavior. A very modest discount might be efficient, but it won't prompt exceptional loading. The best offers need to be big enough to attract consumers' attention.

Channel partners can also be loaded up through incentives. Giving distributors a big, short-term discount will encourage them to increase inventory levels because they can purchase the product at a discount and later sell it at full price, thereby increasing their margins and profits. Similarly, offering distributors a discounted price contingent on purchasing a certain amount will give distributors an incentive to buy heavily.

Loading is startlingly easy in most categories; big discounts tied to heavy purchases will prompt loyal customers to take action. This elevates the barriers for a new entrant and substantially increases the challenge. For this reason, loading up should also be at the top of the list when evaluating possible defensive tactics.

SIGN EXCLUSIVITY AGREEMENTS

A simple way to block trial is to sign an exclusivity agreement with your customers to ensure that they remain loyal. If customers agree to an exclusive arrangement, then it will be exceptionally difficult for a new entrant to get trial. One of these deals creates a very substantial switching cost: customers suffer a considerable loss if they try a new item.

W. L. Gore & Associates, the maker of Gore-Tex, the well known waterproofing material, uses tough exclusivity agreements to block competitive products. Gore-Tex is the clear leader in the waterproof sports apparel industry, with an estimated market share of 70 to 90 percent. Gore requires its apparel maker customers to only use Gore-Tex or lose access to the product. This makes it hard for competitors to even get trial. One competitor lamented, "We were really naïve at the beginning. We weren't expecting such an unfair and really frustrating situation."[8]

Concert ticket seller Live Nation relies on five-year contracts to protect its business. The company locks venues into long-term deals with staggered terms. By doing this, only a small portion of the contracts come up for renewal each year, and this ensures that a new competitor will have to work very hard to build even a small amount of trial in its critical first year.[9]

Most important, an exclusivity agreement does not need to continue in perpetuity; the agreement is only important during the phase when the new entrant is attempting to secure trial. If the new product has heavy marketing support running from July to September, for example, an exclusivity agreement only needs to cover this time. After September, the new entrant's marketing spending will decrease, so the risk of trial will decrease, and the exclusivity agreement can end.

In addition, it isn't essential to have exclusivity agreements with everyone in an industry; a few well-placed deals will reduce sales of the new product substantially and ideally ensure that the new entrant never hits critical mass.

To be effective, an exclusivity agreement must be generous. New entrants will work very hard to overcome the agreement, so the financial incentive for your existing partner has to be very significant. Exclusivity agreements work best in certain types of categories. They are most effective when there are a small number of important customers; setting up a few exclusivity deals can have a significant impact in a market like this.

In a category like dishwasher detergent, for example, exclusivity agreements are not likely to be particularly effective: there are millions of consumers, and each consumer isn't particularly valuable. Logistically, getting consumers to sign an exclusivity agreement isn't feasible. It is also difficult to verify behavior; there is no way to be sure that a given consumer has remained loyal.

Computer chips, however, is a category where exclusivity agreements are exceptionally powerful as a defensive tool; there are just a few big customers, and each one is important. It is also easy to monitor whether the company is complying with the agreement.

EXPAND TRIAL-BUILDING PROGRAMS

Newer categories pose a unique challenge when it comes to blocking trial, because with an emerging category the overall trial rates are usually low due to the lack of initial awareness of the category. In this case, a new entrant can substantially help the category gain awareness through the marketing investment it makes in its new product. This will in turn increase overall category penetration and trial simply by reaching and convincing new people to give the category a try.

This is a complex situation for an established player. On the one hand, the new entrant isn't directly targeting the existing business, so in a sense this is less of a threat; if the new entrant is successful, the bulk of the trial will come from people outside the category. On the other hand, the new entrant is directly targeting the potential growth opportunity in the category. If the new player scoops up all the remaining trial moments, then the opportunity cost for the established player is enormous.

In this situation, a promising defensive strategy consists of the existing player dramatically increasing spending on trial-building programs. The goal is to build overall trial rates in the category to make sure that people who try the category sample the established player's product and not the new entrant's product.

The established player can invest in all of the core trial-building tactics when pursuing this approach: sampling, events, advertising, promotional offers, trial packs, and more.

The financial calculations behind the spending are quite different in this situation. Most new companies strive to invest in the most efficient and effective trial-building programs, focusing on those tactics with a positive return on investment. When a new entrant is on the horizon, however, the economics change substantially, and ideas that might not have made financial sense initially now make very good sense.

In terms of timing, this strategy is best executed in advance of the new entrant's launch, when there is less trial spending in the category. If the established player can increase overall trial rates from 40 percent to 70 percent in the month leading up to a new entrant's launch, the game changes dramatically; the new entrant now must get people who have tried the known player's products to switch, and this is a substantial challenge.

Groupon provides a classic example of this strategy. Groupon began operation in 2007, offering daily discounts to people in Chicago. The company then expanded to other cities in the United States and beyond. As the idea took off, Groupon accelerated its expansion. In part this was due to the opportunity; as the appeal of Groupon became clear, the opportunity was obvious. In part, however, this was due to the threat of competing entries. Groupon has fairly little in terms of intellectual property, so it was easy for competitors to copy the idea. The best way for Groupon to defend was to move quickly to expand trial, in both existing and new markets, and that is what the company did. Obviously, once a consumer had established a relationship with Groupon, it was substantially more difficult for an attacker to make headway since consumers had no desire to add a second daily deals site to their already overflowing inboxes.

CRITICIZE THE COMPETITIVE PRODUCT

A fairly simple form of defense in the area of limiting trial is to attack and criticize a competing product; by highlighting all the problems of a competing entry, an established player can decrease trial rates for the new entry.

There are two effective approaches to this strategy: attack the benefits and highlight the risks. In questioning the benefit, a defending company seeks to reduce the appeal of a new product by eroding its support. If an established company can challenge the claims of a new entrant, then the new product's overall proposition erodes, and the likely trial declines. Apple CEO Steve Jobs used this approach frequently to defend his products; he would highlight the flaws in competing products and dismiss the threat. In March 2011, for example, Jobs attacked competitors in an analyst presentation, stating, "Everybody's got a tablet. Is 2011 going to be the year of the copycat? ... Most of these tablets aren't even catching up with the first iPad. But we haven't been resting on our laurels." He continued with his basic approach later in his presentation, saying,

"Sixty-five thousand apps specifically tailored for the iPad. Now that compares to our competitors who are trying to launch these days with at most 100 apps. And I think we are being a little generous here."[10]

Procter & Gamble employed the same strategy with Pampers to defend against the launch of a new diaper from Huggies, the brand owned by rival Kimberly-Clark. In the United States, P&G and Kimberly-Clark dominate the diapers category. In 2002 Huggies introduced a new version of its popular Pull-Ups product. It was targeted at moms of toddlers, as the primary benefit of the new diaper was that it was easier to change, since it featured an easy-to-use tab on the side. This was of course quite a benefit when dealing with toddlers who squirm and wriggle when they're being changed. Unlike infants, toddlers are on the move, so changing a diaper can be a challenge.

P&G could not easily copy Huggies' new diaper design on its Easy-Ups line, so P&G responded by attacking the new Pull-Ups diaper. P&G ran a commercial featuring a toddler running though a fancy dinner party naked; the little guy had removed his diaper on his own, presumably using the easy-to-use tabs. He was gleefully waving it over his head as he ran, and the elegant guests were, as might be expected, mortified. Mom was mortified, too.

P&G's goal was quite clear: turn Huggies' unique point of difference from a positive into a negative, effectively proclaiming, "The new feature not only is not much of a benefit; it is a significant problem." The implication is that parents are far better off with a diaper that is more difficult to get off since it reduces the chance that kids will remove it on their own.

Kimberly-Clark responded by suing P&G for the advertisement, and eventually Kimberly-Clark won the suit. By the time that occurred, however, P&G had blunted Huggies' advance.

Highlighting the risks associated with a new product is another promising defensive angle. This strategy is most effective when there is a basis for the defense—when the established company can identify a problem with the new entrant. However, there doesn't need to be an actual problem for the strategy to be effective; the established company can simply run spots with a warning to customers: "Don't be fooled by new entrants."

The osteoporosis drug Actonel responded to the launch of Boniva by directly attacking the new product. Actonel took out full-page ads announcing, "What about that new osteoporosis medicine, Boniva? Boniva is not proven to prevent fractures beyond the spine. Get the proven fracture protection of Actonel." The ad featured a pleasant-looking lady stating, "I asked for one good reason to stick with Actonel. My doctor gave me seven." The ad then highlighted seven common locations of fractures.

The Actonel team managed to pull off a defensive coup on January 11, 2006, when its full-page ad attacking Boniva ran in *The New York Times* on page A11, just in front of Boniva's ad on page A13.

GlaxoSmithKline used this approach in the HIV market to limit trial of competitive products. One Glaxo ad featured shark-infested waters and stated, "Don't take a chance—stick with the HIV medicine that's working for you." Another ad recommended that patients ask their physician, "Will the HIV medicine make my skin or eyes turn yellow?" This was a common side effect of competing items.[11]

One of the more remarkable examples of a company disparaging a competitor's product comes from Argentina. In 1997 Procter & Gamble was preparing to introduce its Ariel brand of detergent to that market. Unilever was the category leader—with a market share of about 80 percent—and the company was logically concerned about P&G's entry. Shortly before P&G's launch, Unilever apparently began running advertisements for a small toilet-seat maker, Ariel del Plata. The ads featured rear ends and toilet seats, repeating again and again "Ariel, Ariel, Ariel." The campaign effectively connected the name Ariel with toilets, wiping out any chance that Procter & Gamble would be able to make consumers associate the name with detergent.[12]

DELIVER OUTSTANDING CUSTOMER SERVICE

Providing good service to customers is almost always a wise idea: good service leads to happy customers, and happy customers lead to repeat purchases and positive word of mouth. When under attack from a competitor, however, the need to deliver great service grows substantially. Perhaps the most important thing a company under attack can do is simply deliver an outstanding customer experience.

There is always a basic tension in business. Customers always want better service and products. All people taking a trip would love to travel on an airline that provided free meals and drinks, big seats, wonderful in-flight entertainment, a shower at the arrival airport, and a limo to shuttle them to their final destination. Companies, however, need to make money, so they simply can't give most customers everything they want—it just costs too much and erodes their profits. People who are willing to spend a ton of money can get lovely service, but most everyday customers are usually left with a fairly unsatisfying experience.

This is the case in virtually every industry. Business school students would love personal, one-on-one sessions with top faculty, but it is impossible to deliver this. Technology customers would love to have their calls answered on the first ring by eloquent and smart people, but delivering this service experience is just not possible economically most of the time.

The balance companies need to consider is this: just how much product quality and service will our customers pay for? Where can we trim back in a bid to maintain margins and make some money? In most industries where products have similar price points, the established players provide similar service propositions; over time competitors watch each other and end up in about the same place.

In a defensive situation, however, the balance shifts rather dramatically; when there is a new entrant trying to break into the market, one promising defensive move is to dramatically improve the customer experience to build customer loyalty before your competitor arrives. Sergio Pereira, chief marketing officer at office-products company Quill.com, observes, "You have to insulate your best customers. It's like a vaccine."[13]

One simple approach is to substantially increase inventory levels in order to avoid running out of stock. One of the easiest ways for a new entrant to get trial is to simply be available when an established player's product isn't. Being out of stock drives trial to the competition, and in many cases the winner will be the new entrant, since the new entrant is presumably spending heavily on the launch.

One large insurance company had a major issue with its customer service following the financial crisis in 2009 and 2010. Due to changing capital requirements, the established player had to limit the number of policies it could sell. This forced the independent agents who relied on the company to start working with competitors; the agents didn't have a choice. And this dynamic led to the established player losing the lead in its critical segment.

Spending heavily on customer service and loyalty programs also makes sense in a defensive situation. This might include expanding the call center or encouraging customer service representatives to be more proactive and aggressive at addressing complaints. The logic here is fairly obvious. In a defensive situation, you want to minimize trial of the new entrant. If you provide out-standing service, you make it less likely that the new entrant will get trial. Weak customer service, however, can lead to unhappy customers, and unhappy customers are more likely to head out in search of new alternatives in the market.

When considering customer service improvements, it is essential to realize that the economics are very different in a defensive situation. For an established business, the value of a customer is fairly easy to calculate, and you spend on the customer consistent with this value. In a defensive situation, however, the economics change because customers become much more valuable; if they leave, it hurts you and helps your new competitor. Investing in customer retention efforts is particularly important in the six months leading up to a competitive launch; you don't want to give your customers a reason to defect.

THE PRIMARY BATTLE

Limiting trial is often the primary battle when it comes to defense. An effective defensive program aimed at blunting a new entrant's trial can significantly decrease the risk that the new product will succeed. It's always difficult for a new entrant to build trial, and when met with a strong defensive effort, the task can be almost impossible.

Chapter 12

FIGHTING REPEAT

IF YOU MISS THE CHANCE to eliminate a new entrant in the early stages of its launch, you have to focus on preventing a repeat. By this point the new entrant has secured distribution, gained brand awareness, and generated trial. You can't limit awareness once people are aware; it is just too late. Similarly, you can't block trial when people have already tried a product or service. All that is left—the only remaining opportunity for an established player—is diminishing the new entrant's repeat rate. If a new entrant manages to get people to try its product and if customers have a good experience, there is a good chance people will buy it again or repeat. You have to focus on stopping this process.

This is a difficult task, but there are still many things an established player can do at this point in the battle.

BLOCK REPEAT!

By the time a competitive battle shifts to defending against repeat, the new product's launch is well underway; the product is in the market and selling. People are trying it, and many are presumably enjoying it and will purchase it again. To successfully defend in this stage, the established player has to find a way to stop the repeat process, to ensure that customers who tried the new product don't purchase it again.

If the established player can pull this off, blocking repeat is a very effective way to have an impact on a new product. Without repeat, sales of a new product cannot be sustained. More important, perhaps, profit will be limited; it is usually expensive to get trial, so initial purchases are often unprofitable transactions. For many products, profit only appears when customers begin to repeat and purchase without the introductory support and discounts.

Conversion rates matter enormously in the economics of a new product. For example, what percentage of people who are aware of a new product actually try it? And what proportion of the people who try a product buy it again? This figure is particularly significant, because a small shift in the repeat percentages can have a huge impact on the overall economics of a new product.

One advantage of defending at this stage is that the threat is now clear. It is possible to see your competitor's product, evaluate it, and talk about it with customers. Defenders can do wonderful market research studies at this point and identify precisely how well the new product is doing and why. A company that decided not to defend initially due to a lack of information might be in a very different position by the time repeat begins.

It is far easier to prevent trial than to prevent repeat, just as generating trial is more difficult and expensive for the new entrant than getting a repeat purchase.

Timing makes defending at the repeat stage particularly difficult. Trial usually occurs at a particular time, when the new product's introductory marketing support is in the market. Defending during the trial period is a bit simpler because the battle is fought at a certain point in time. Repeat is often a longer process, one that can stretch out over months or years. So the defensive battle is longer and thus more costly.

Can you stop customers from buying a product they like? The answer is yes, but it is easier in some cases than others. To a large degree, the repeat challenge depends on how good the new product actually is. If customers have a very positive trial experience, it will be harder to block repeat. Conversely, if the trial experience was mediocre, it will be easier.

Companies forced to defend at the repeat stage have several different options to consider. Many of these are familiar; they could have been used earlier in the battle at much lower cost. They may well be effective at this point, but the cost will have gone up significantly.

ACQUIRE THE NEW ENTRANT

The most effective way to stop repeat for a competitive product is very simple: buy the company. This takes care of the issue; the new entrant is now part of your organization. An acquisition is also a way to prevent the launch entirely. The difference is that by waiting you confirm the threat, and the cost goes up dramatically.

Drug store giant Walgreen's used this approach when confronted with the fast growth of online drug chains. In 2011 Walgreen's put down $409 million to acquire Drugstore.com. This was a steep price to pay for a young company that had lost money the previous year. But Walgreen's executives presumably knew that Drugstore.com was a growing threat; in 2010 it had achieved revenues of $456 million and three million repeat customers.[1] The best way to neutralize the Drugstore.com threat was simple: buy it.

Internet finance giant Intuit used the same technique when dealing with Mint.com, an up-and-coming Internet financial company. Intuit, founded in 1983, was a leader in the world of personal finance with its Quicken brand. Mint entered the market in 2007, offering consumers a free online personal finance system. Mint's price was right: free. With a strong proposition, Mint quickly grew, attracting 1.5 million customers by 2009. For Intuit, Mint was a major competitive threat; the company had a strong proposition and a dangerous price, especially when compared to Quicken's offering. To deal with the issue Intuit bought Mint in September 2009. Mint's founder and CEO Aaron Patzer summarized the situation perfectly in the merger announcement: "This acquisition makes sense to me because, first and foremost, Mint.com and Intuit share a common vision."[2] Intuit paid $170 million and took care of the threat.

Coca-Cola recently also used this approach in Brazil. When a new local entrant called Jesus became the number two soft drink in the state of Maranhao, Coke went ahead and bought the company. With Jesus securing repeat purchases, an acquisition was one of the few alternatives Coke had to protect its business.[3]

An acquisition is particularly attractive in certain situations. If the competitor has strong intellectual property protection in place, an acquisition makes good sense because you can gain control of the idea. Without strong intellectual property protection, you can probably copy the new product idea, which is a much less expensive approach. But if the new entrant has patents and copyrights that are difficult to attack and break, an acquisition may be the only option to effectively deal with it.

An acquisition is also a good option if the new entrant is quickly gaining repeat. Any new venture that builds repeat is a very real threat, because repeat suggests the business is fundamentally appealing to customers. It also indicates that the previous defensive efforts were not successful; despite all the defensive work, the new product survived and is gaining traction in the market. At this point, an acquisition may be one of the few options to stop the growing problem.

Competitive dynamics also may make an acquisition the best option. If there are several large players in a category, gaining access to the new idea takes on more urgency; you can potentially gain market share from your competitors and prevent one of your competitors from owning the new product idea.

Finally, if the new entrant is able to create network effects, it could be very difficult to stop it, making acquisition a promising approach. Recreating a web of connections is very tough to do, even with all the spending in the world. Duplicating an auction site such as eBay is simply not feasible even with all the money you can muster; eBay attracts both sellers and buyers, and this network of connections is impossible to replicate. Similarly, Facebook has an incredible web of connections.

Acquiring a new entrant gives the established player a number of positive options. One approach is to run the company as a distinct business, retaining the existing management team if possible, providing capital, and working to support the new venture's growth. This can be a very appealing option; the new venture might generate significant growth, especially when the risk of a major defense goes away.

Anheuser-Busch used this approach with its acquisition of Goose Island, a Chicago-based brewer. Executives at Anheuser-Busch were concerned with the fast growth of small, premium craft brewers. To address the issue, they purchased Goose Island for $38.8 million in 2011. After completing the deal, however, they let Goose Island operate independently.

The downside of this approach is that it creates substantial complexity; the acquiring company now must manage multiple brands. In addition, there may be few synergies between the organizations, which limits efficiency.

To keep things simple and maximize efficiency, the established company can fold the acquired firm into its existing business; the management teams come together and the businesses are integrated. In most cases, the established company will become the dominant player. Over time, the new entrant may fade away.

There are problems with this approach. The established business may not be able to run the new entrant successfully; a start-up with a fast-moving and unique corporate culture might not thrive when combined with the culture of a big, established corporation. Branding can also be a problem; combining the brands means that the unique associations—the brand meaning—will fade.

The simplest approach is also the most brutal: kill off the new company. This seems like a counterintuitive move: why buy a company just to kill it? But in the world of defense, eliminating a threat can be a major benefit. In some cases, the new company is worth more dead than alive.

IBM employed this technique to deal with a new challenger in the mainframe computer business. Platform Solutions created software that let inexpensive servers act like high-cost mainframes. This was a significant risk to IBM's business. To deal with the threat, IBM acquired Platform Solutions in 2008 for $150 million and then simply killed the product, effectively eliminating the threat.[4]

For a company with a healthy core business, acquisitions are perhaps the ideal form of defense: if a threat appears, buy it. In this fashion, the established player is able to capture innovations in the market and reduce the risk that a new entrant will grow into a major threat.

The biggest issue with an acquisition is the high cost. The new company may sell, but only at a premium price. This forces the established player to think very hard about the costs and benefits: is it really worth investing in a big acquisition just to eliminate the threat? Has the situation really gotten to this point?

There are two important points to remember when it comes to the economics of defensive acquisitions. The first is that the price is usually lowest early on. When a company is new to the market, with modest levels of trial and repeat and a growing number of repeat buyers, the price is usually modest. Most companies focus on multiples when pricing an acquisition, such as price relative to revenue or price relative to profit or some other metric. New ventures, with modest revenues and profits, are inherently cheaper; acquiring a company as it begins to secure repeat may well be financially feasible. Once the company grows, however, the situation changes; with higher revenues and profits comes a higher price.

Timing is critical, then, when looking at a defensive acquisition. Moving quickly keeps the prices lower. Waiting can be a problem. In the worst case, the new venture grows quickly, and the price rises accordingly. By the time the established player is ready to move forward with an acquisition, the price is out of reach. It is simply too late. Marketing veteran Carter Cast has some simple advice: "Buy them before they can scale."[5]

The second important point is that managers should evaluate a defensive acquisition with a distinct perspective; it is a fundamentally different from an offensive acquisition. Many and perhaps most acquisitions are undertaken to drive profit growth. A company might acquire another firm in a new, fast-growing industry or buy a competitor in order to reduce costs and increase profits. With an offensive acquisition, the financial calculations are quite clear: the upside is compared to the cost. An acquiring firm will typically develop a financial model that looks at the future cash flows of the target company, discounts the figures using an appropriate rate, and then compares the resulting figure to the price. If the value of the company—the present value of the discounted cash flows—is higher than the purchase price, it makes financial sense to proceed. But if the value of the company is smaller than the price, the acquisition doesn't make sense financially.

A defensive acquisition requires a different set of calculations. In many cases the primary benefit isn't the upside potential; instead, it is the reduced defensive risk. There is enormous value in buying a competitor that is about to take 30 percent of your profit—you avoid losing a huge sum of money. The new company might be marginally profitable with little value on its own. But to an established player, eliminating the threat could be a huge benefit. So when evaluating a defensive acquisition, the purchase price should be considered relative to the value of the acquired firm plus the reduced risk.

The financial markets don't necessarily appreciate this line of thinking. Investors want to see growth in profits and cash flow. The idea that a company would invest primarily to eliminate a threat isn't appealing; the investment produces nothing in incremental profits and cash flow versus the current state. Still, making that acquisition is incredibly important.

An acquisition won't work in every case because sometimes the owners of the new company simply won't sell; they may love building a company or they may profoundly dislike the established player. In this case, a partnership arrangement of some sort might be most productive.

Still, most people have a price, and the established company can usually pay it, at least before the new entrant has grown substantially. If there is enough money at stake, the owners of the new firm can use that money to fund a different company. Any company with outside investors will find a high sale price difficult to resist. Kevin Plank, the CEO of athletic apparel company Under Armour, explained things quite clearly in a recent interview: "If I ever was offered an amount of money that was larger than what I believed I could get the company to, I would be obligated to sell."[6] This means that Nike could eliminate the Under Armour threat at any point just by offering the right price.

One issue that often arises in the world of acquisitions is securing government approval. In most countries, government agencies need to review proposed business combinations, and these defensive acquisitions get particular scrutiny. This is another reason to move early. Buying a company with a 1 percent market share isn't likely to cause much concern; it is a tiny venture so it won't significantly impact the overall competitive dynamics in the industry. Government regulators may well approve it. Buying a company with a 20 percent market share, however, is an entirely different proposition.

Companies are often reluctant to pay a high price for an acquisition because doing so seems like an admission of failure—it looks like the new entrant succeeded in the market and now you're giving it a ton of money. It looks like your competitor won, and you lost. Marketing executive Carter Cast notes that this is a dangerous line of thinking. His advice is clear: "Swallow your pride. Buy them, and if they won't sell, partner with them."[7]

INTRODUCE A SIMILAR PRODUCT

This strategy can be employed to prevent a launch, limit distribution, and block trial. It can also be used to limit repeat, though the competitive dynamics are now quite different; your defensive product is now late to the game.

By matching the competitor's offering, the established player can fragment the market and diminish the uniqueness of the new entrant's proposition. Customers who like the new product now can choose from several similar offerings. This puts pressure on the new entrant. And people who haven't yet tried the new product will probably divide their loyalty between the different products in the market.

Copying a competitive product during the repeat phase is an efficient approach because by this stage it is fairly clear whether the new product will be a success. Using the same strategy with a totally new product is sometimes inefficient because it isn't yet clear whether the new entrant actually has a good idea. All the resources devoted to developing the proposition might be wasted. Waiting until the new entrant is building repeat increases the chance that the defensive product is really needed and that there is an opportunity in the market. Amazon CEO Jeff Bezos explains how this works: "The strategic value of close following is in not having to go down all the blind alleys. You let smaller competitors check those out, and when they find something good, you just quadruple down. If you're following close enough, and the arena is slow-moving enough, the fact that you're not first down that path doesn't hurt you much." [8]

Entering later can be successful. Oded Shenkar, a global management professor at Ohio State's Fisher College of Business, notes that "nearly 98 percent of the value generated by innovations is captured not by the innovators but by the often overlooked, despised copycats."[9]

This approach works particularly well if the industry is somewhat slow moving, since copying a product generating repeat means that you are already significantly behind the new entrant in terms of timing. In fast-moving industries, simply copying a new entrant at this stage may not be sufficient; the new entrant might be on to the next thing. This is a problem in an industry where the dynamics are changing quickly; it can be difficult to catch up.

It is important to remember that launching a similar product during the trial phase is quite different from launching a similar product during the repeat phase. In the trial phase the new product simply needs to attract a portion of people interested in the new concept. The goal is to reduce trial rates on the other product. That is, the product can be almost identical.

In the repeat phase, the defensive new product must attract people who have already tried the competitor's item. This makes things much more difficult. If people liked the new entrant's item, they will be inclined to buy it again after their positive experience. It will be difficult to get them to shift to a different item, even one launched by a well-known name in the category. For example, if someone tried and liked new Kobe Delight Oyster and Clam salad dressing, it will be difficult to get them to try Wishbone Oyster and Clam salad dressing. Why would they change to another brand?

If people don't like the new product, they will be reluctant to pursue the concept: if they try a Kobe Delight Oyster and Clam salad dressing and don't like it, they won't be that interested in Wishbone Oyster and Clam salad dressing. The implication is that a defensive product launched in the repeat stage must be *notably superior* to the competitor's product. There must be a point of difference—the defensive product either must be dramatically superior in some fashion or notably cheaper. Launching a similar item works in the trial phase but usually not in the repeat phase. The challenge is bigger, and the product must be different and better.

PepsiCo's Tropicana brand of orange juice encountered this issue as it battled Coca-Cola's Simply brand of orange juice. Tropicana was the category leader for many years. It came packaged in a cardboard container, similar to a milk carton. Coke entered the category in 2001 with the launch of Simply. Coke used a clear, plastic carafe for Simply, a unique packaging in the category. Despite the apparently long odds, Simply gained about 14 percent of the market, largely at the expense of Tropicana. The new brand built trial and repeat followed in turn. Tropicana eventually decided to copy the clear, plastic carafe after consumer research revealed that packaging was a key driver of their purchase. As a Tropicana spokesperson explained, "The biggest insight was that consumers like to see the juice."[10] The move helped Tropicana slow Simply's growth, but it didn't push back the new entrant. Tropicana's move simply matched the competitor. If Tropicana had used the same new product to block Simply's trial, it would likely have fared much better.

REDUCE PRICES

One way to blunt a competitor's repeat business is to reduce prices of your products. Lower prices create a stronger value proposition; it is hard to compete with the low-price, high-quality combination. A customer who tried and liked a new entrant might buy it again, becoming a repeat buyer. But if the established player offers an exceptionally good deal, it is harder for a customer to justify buying the new product again.

Cutting prices is not a great way to build a business in most situations. When a differentiated player cuts prices in a bid to drive growth, a series of bad things happens: quality perceptions can shift, margins shrink, competition may respond, and the business in total may weaken.

A defensive situation is unique, however, and the trade-offs are quite different. Stopping the new entrant becomes the top priority; if your competitor can secure broad repeat for its product and become a viable player in the category, it turns into a long-term threat. If a price cut can slow down the new entrant, that move may make sense.

This approach works best when the products are similar. Simply cutting prices will be effective against comparable products, but much less effective if the new entrant has a particularly unique or special item. Indeed, cutting price could be the worst response when faced with an innovative new entrant; it might simply increase the perception that you have an inferior offering at a low price.

Cutting prices to block repeat is a risky strategy. The challenge is that it can be difficult to restore prices in a category after the competitive battle has passed. If a leading player aggressively reduces prices, other players in the category will have to respond, and in many cases they will do this by reducing prices in turn. For example, if the leading company in the industrial drill bit industry cuts prices by 25 percent, other drill bit manufacturers may cut prices, too. This, of course, is the intent of the move; to erode profits in the category in a bid to drive out the new entrant.

The problem is that once the new entrant gives up, it can be difficult to get prices back up, so your business may suffer in the long term. In part this is because competitors might not follow the price increase; they may be reluctant to risk losing market share in order to improve margins. The bigger issue is that customers might grow accustomed to the lower price levels, and the defensive price then begins to seem like the "correct" price. Customers may stop buying when prices return to their previous levels.

This problem is most pronounced when using price cuts in a bid to block repeat. Using low prices to limit trial is a less of a risk. In a repeat situation, the battle will occur over months or even years and is rarely just a onetime event. As a result, price cuts to battle repeat are particularly dangerous because they may permanently shift pricing expectations in a category.

If a defensive price cut introduces a level of price competition in a category, it can destroy profits for a very long time. Sometimes this continues for many years, so the financial hit from the defensive move outweighs the potential loss to the new entrant. Proceed with caution!

One way to reduce prices while minimizing the risk to the core business is to launch a new, low-price brand. This lets the established player introduce a price competitor to the new entrant while protecting the existing business. Airlines employ this strategy frequently, launching low-cost carriers to deal with new low-price entrants without damaging the core business.

Food giant General Mills used this approach very effectively to deal with a new product launch from Kraft Foods in the boxed dinner category. At the time, General Mills was the clear leader in the category with its Hamburger Helper brand. Hamburger Helper was essentially dinner in a box; consumers just had to brown some meat and then add Hamburger Helper to create a tasty meal that included noodles and sauce. Hamburger Helper had a market share of more than 80 percent in that category with excellent margins; it was a profitable and stable business.

Kraft Food entered the category in 1999, launching a new Stove Top stuffing product called Stove Top Oven Classics. The new line of products was similar to Hamburger Helper in that consumers just had to add meat to have a complete dinner. The product line was different because it used stuffing instead of noodles and because it focused on chicken, not hamburger. Consumers also prepared it in the oven, not on the stove. Kraft supported the launch with heavy promotional support and more than $15 million in advertising.

The Hamburger Helper team viewed Kraft's move as a major threat. It responded first by introducing Chicken Helper, a version of Hamburger Helper that used chicken instead of hamburger. This was a successful introduction, but it didn't stop Oven Classics; the business grew, gaining trial and repeat.

General Mills then responded by launching Chicken Helper Oven Favorites. This product was almost identical to Stove Top Oven Classics; it was for use with chicken in the oven. It also used stuffing. And it came in a big red box, just like Oven Favorites. The key difference was that General Mills' Oven Favorites was priced a dollar lower than Kraft's Oven Classics.

The launch of Oven Favorites created a problem for Kraft. If Kraft cut its price to match the price of Chicken Helper Oven Favorites, the financials for Stove Top Oven Classics would take a terrible hit; a one-dollar drop in margin would mean Oven Classics would make essentially no profit at all. If Kraft didn't cut its price, sales of Stove Top Oven Classics would fall as consumers shifted to the similar but less expensive Chicken Helper Oven Favorites.

Confronted with two unpleasant options, Kraft decided to exit the category, losing more than $50 million on the launch in total. Group vice president Mary Kay Haben explained that the category "became crowded quickly with low-priced competition."[11]

General Mills then repositioned Chicken Helper Oven Favorites, changing the packaging to be consistent with the rest of the Hamburger Helper line and increasing the price. When the dust settled, the Hamburger Helper team had eliminated the competitive threat and ended up with a new, successful addition to its product line.

SECURE GOVERNMENT SUPPORT

One clear way to slow the growth of a new international competitor is to get government support. Legislation and tariffs can eliminate even the toughest competitor.

Some countries are particularly aggressive when it comes to using legislation to protect established businesses from competitive attack. France, for example, has a number of laws designed to support small retailers. One law blocks the sale of books for less than 5 percent below the cover price. This protects small, independent bookstores because large retailers can't leverage their scale to compete on price.[12]

This technique isn't just for blocking distribution and trial; it can also be used to ensure that new entrants can't gain repeat. Indeed, it is often easiest to make the case for government support when the new entrant is growing; at this point the threat is very clear and might prompt action. For example, in 2011 appliance giant Whirlpool asked the US government to impose duties on appliances imported by Samsung and LG Electronics. Whirlpool took this step only after imported brands had gained significant market share. It was quite clear that without government support it would be very difficult to slow down growth of the imported products.[13] Years earlier, Harley-Davidson finally fought back against Japanese motorcycle companies with the help of a steep tariff on imported motorcycles put in place under President Ronald Reagan.

FILE SUIT

Filing suit against a new company is an expensive task. In many cases it only makes sense to pursue this option when the threat clearly is a major one and the new entrant has started growing sales and building repeat purchases.

Suing a company as it builds repeat accomplishes two positive things for the established player. First, it might force the new company to refocus its approach, to change a name to avoid a trademark issue, or to change technology to deal with a patent dispute. This helps the established player, because the new entrant must make a major change at a critical time in the life of the company. In the best case, a suit will force a new entrant to exit the market entirely.

Second, filing suit creates a distraction; the new company now must focus time, money, and energy on figuring out how to respond. It also creates uncertainty. All of this slows down the new entrant.

Entrepreneur Ric Trader launched a lawn-care company in Florida in 1998. He called the company Yard Doctor Landscaping and successfully grew the new venture. Revenues reached more than $1 million per year by 2002 as he generated awareness and trial, and then converted this trial into repeat business.

At this point, Lawn Doctor, an established national lawn-care company, became concerned about Yard Doctor's growth. Lawn Doctor's attorneys sent a cease and desist letter and, after Mr. Trader didn't respond, filed suit. The legal battle went on for three years. Eventually, Mr. Trader agreed to a settlement and gave up rights to the name Yard Doctor. After all the legal battles, however, he threw in the towel, selling the business and exiting the market.[14]

Toy giant Mattel used the legal system as part of its response to MGA Entertainment's Bratz line of dolls. MGA introduced the Bratz brand in 2001. Bratz dolls were somewhat sultry and sexy, very different from Mattel's Barbie line of dolls. After a slow start, Bratz quickly caught on, with sales in 2005 exceeding $2 billion.

In 2005, Mattel filed suit. The company made multiple allegations against MGA. One of the key charges was that the Bratz idea was developed by Carter Bryant when he was an employee at Mattel. Mattel CEO Bob Eckert explained the move by saying, "We have an obligation to defend ourselves against competitors who choose to engage in fraudulent activities against us."[15]

Mattel won major legal victories in 2008: a $100 million judgment and ownership of the Bratz products. The legal battle continued through the appeals process, however, and eventually decisions were reversed. The legal skirmish continues even now. But sales of the Bratz line faded and the legal battle created uncertainty around the future of the brand.

Frito-Lay employed the same strategy when battling Princeton Vanguard's Pretzel Crisps brand of pretzels. When Princeton Vanguard tried to file for a trademark on the Pretzel Crisps name, Frito-Lay contested the application. This sparked a fierce and protracted legal battle that forced Princeton Vanguard to spend more than $1 million on legal fees. Company founder Warren Wilson expressed his frustration in an interview, complaining, "This fight is about a big company that wants to dominate the snack food category by crushing a little company like ours rather than by competing with us."[16]

AVOID THE SITUATION

Clearly defending at the repeat stage isn't hopeless; there are many things a defender can do to neutralize a threat. But it isn't easy; the new product may well be gaining momentum, winning over customers and generating better financial results. In most cases, you do not want to get to this point. The best approach is to find a way to neutralize the competitor before the battle becomes about repeat.

If you are fighting at this stage, it is critical to get on with the task; this is not the time to wait. A company generating repeat is a substantial threat; the new entrant gets stronger and becomes of an issue every day that goes by.

Chapter 13

DEFENSE NEVER ENDS

IT IS TEMPTING TO THINK of defense as episodic. A competitor attacks your business, you react and take action, and then things settle down and get back to normal. So sometimes defense is important, and sometimes it isn't.

This is a dangerous line of thought. It is very true that defensive battles flare up at certain times depending on competitive actions. But companies that want to protect their business need to think about defense all the time. Defense never ends.

There are two particular things companies should always focus on: preventing attacks and preparing for battle.

PREVENTING ATTACKS

Fighting a new competitor is exciting and dynamic; in the world of business, there is nothing quite like a good competitive tussle. But in an ideal world, companies never have to enter into these battles. Defending a business takes time and money. It is an enormous distraction. Preventing attacks is the optimal approach. As Harvard professor Michael Porter observed, "the most effective defense is to prevent the battle altogether."[1]

It is impossible to completely prevent competitive attacks. People think in different ways, and even the strongest company can find itself on the receiving end of a major new competitive move. But there are things companies can do to reduce the chance of an attack.

FILL THE GAPS

People launch products when there are opportunities in the market or when there are gaps. Indeed, unmet customer needs are the basis for most new product development. If there are no compelling opportunities in a particular category, there will likely be few new entrants. Ultimately, the numbers have to work; it can be difficult to justify a new product launch if there isn't a significant space for a new player.

One important way to prevent attacks is to fill gaps in the market, introducing products and services that meet various needs. So if a group of customers wants an environmentally friendly product, then launch an environmentally friendly product. If another group of customers wants a cheap, low-performance item, introduce that. The logic is simple: if you don't do it, someone else might, and then you will have a very big problem. Moving first reduces the risk. As marketer Carter Cast observed, "If you are responding, you are already a step behind."[2]

Many companies aggressively work to identify and fill gaps in their market to limit competitive moves. Consumer products giant Unilever used this technique to protect its important laundry franchise in Brazil. Executives at Unilever recognized that there was a space in the market; there was no detergent with a low price but high perceived quality. In part to prevent a competitive entry from a local player, Unilever created a new brand to fill this gap in the market. In 2009 Procter & Gamble acquired the high-end shaving brand called Art of Shaving, thereby heading off a potential attack on its important Gillette franchise. The same year, Coca-Cola and PepsiCo both acquired brands in the coconut water business, addressing a potential competitive threat.

Filling gaps requires a mind-set change when evaluating new product introductions. In general, companies launch new products and services when there is a compelling financial proposition. At many companies, the new products team explores an idea and ultimately creates and defends a set of financial projections, with the key question being whether or not the new product idea delivers enough incremental sales and profit to justify the investment. The core issue: does the growth opportunity justify the spending and the risk? Is the financial upside sufficient to support the investment?

This approach works fine for new products aimed primarily at growth, when the investment is optional. It clearly doesn't make sense to launch a new product if the projections suggest that it doesn't make sense financially.

But this mind-set doesn't work well for new products created to fill gaps in a market and to prevent attacks from competitors. In this case, the benefit of the new product is the prevention of a competitive move, not incremental growth. Thus, a product that provides very little financial upside in the short term might actually be a very good idea if it prevents a competitor from occupying the space in the long term.

As a result, gap-filling new products require a different set of financial calculations. The analysis has to consider the venture's financial outlook and also evaluate the chance that a competitor would go after the opportunity and the risk such a move would pose. When all of the inputs are factored in and adjusted for the risk, the answer will be clear, at least in theory.

The problem is that actually completing these calculations is exceptionally difficult. Indeed, in more than 20 years in the world of business, I've never seen a company complete the calculations with any degree of confidence.

Two general rules are useful when considering gap-filling new products. First, if the idea is compelling, it probably makes sense to launch it regardless of the financial returns. The world is full of innovative people looking for opportunities. If there is an exciting opportunity in your category, odds are pretty good that someone will eventually see it and go after it. So moving first is a very good policy.

Second, don't worry too much about cannibalization. Many managers, especially those with financial integrity, will focus on cannibalization when evaluating a new product; there is no reason to launch a new item if the main result is that it will just draw customers from your existing products. In that case, you have the expense and complexity of a new product introduction and get little real growth in return. So when considering a new product launch, these managers will quantify the cannibalization and factor it into the calculations; if a new product has a revenue of $10 million, but only $5 million of that is in addition to what existing items generate, then the new product should only receive credit for $5 million in the financial calculations.

The problem with this logic, however, is that this calculation is based on the assumption that the business would retain the existing sales volume without the new product. This is a flawed assumption; in many cases, the company would lose the volume regardless. Focusing too much on cannibalization increases the risk of competitive attack. A company that is focused on protecting its own margins so much that it won't introduce a good product that customers want primarily because this would damage the existing business is at great risk indeed.

The idea of filling gaps also applies to acquisitions; there are times when it may make sense to pursue an acquisition for defensive reasons in order to block another company. Perhaps the easiest way to enter an existing category is with an acquisition; launching a new product is difficult, especially when confronted with a company committed to and skilled at defensive strategy. It may make sense, then, to acquire a company as a blocking tactic, preventing another competitor from carrying out the acquisition and using this to gain a position in the market.

Food giant Nestlé purchased Kraft Foods' frozen pizza business in 2010. This was a major financial investment, but it made perfect sense; it helped Nestlé's important frozen foods division and, perhaps more important, ensured that a different competitor wouldn't acquire the business and use it as a platform for future growth in frozen foods. This would have been a big issue for Nestlé, the industry leader.

Similarly, retail giant Toys"R"Us acquired legendary toy brand FAO Schwarz in 2009. This was a smart defensive move because it prevented FAO Schwarz, a well-known brand with a long history, from falling into the hands of a more aggressive retailer determined to rebuild the brand. As Toy R Us CEO Jerry Storch explained, "The FAO Schwarz name is one of the premier names in toys."[3]

Defensive strategy is probably a key reason why luxury giant LVMH quietly purchased a 17 percent stake in Hermes. LVMH CEO Bernard Arnault is an aggressive, tough competitor, well aware that it would be a big problem if family-owned Hermes ever sold to one of LVMH's competitors. By owning a portion of Hermes, Arnault reduces the chances of this happening. Luxury analyst Marc Willaume noted, "If one day things change—if, for example, family members a few generations from now decide that they want to sell—Mr. Arnault will have positioned himself to be the referee."[4]

DON'T GET GREEDY

Business leaders are generally rewarded for delivering exceptional results. And in many cases this is defined as delivering very high short-term profits. A manager who manages to increase profits of a business by 25 percent will frequently earn a large bonus, a nice stock option grant, a prize or two, and in many cases a promotion to a bigger job with the potential for even greater incentives for delivering more positive results.

The problem is that many of the moves that build short-term profits increase the risk that a business will come under attack. Indeed, focusing on short-term profits often substantially weakens a company's defensive position.

Take one of the simplest ways to increase profits: reducing costs. This is a logical and popular approach to building profits. It isn't complicated; cutting costs leads to better margins, and better margins lead to higher profits. The challenge is that cutting costs is easier said than done. On many occasions, there is a slight trade-off involved: quality declines slightly with each cost savings move. In other cases, the flexibility of a business falls; a company that installs high-speed, superefficient production lines will usually find it more difficult to make changes to the product. Both of these dynamics weaken the defensive position of the company. Declining quality opens up space for a competitor to introduce a superior product that will delight customers. Lower production flexibility makes it harder for an established player to adjust quickly and capitalize on changes in the market.

Price increases are another way to drive profits. Indeed, pricing is arguably the finest technique for building profits of an established business; a price increase is certain, quantifiable, and immediate, and it can have a huge impact on profits. Pricing also can signal quality. The problem, however, is that price increases open the door for competition; with high margins, there is plenty of room for competitors to offer a significantly lower price and high quality while still being profitable.

Trimming marketing spending can boost short-term profits, too. This approach isn't complicated, at least in theory: simply identify the marketing spending with the lowest short-term return on investment and then cut it. This quickly increases profits; sales might fall a little, but the negative impact is often far less than the positive financial impact of lower spending. A different approach is to reallocate spending, moving money from tactics with a low short-term return to tactics with a high short-term return. Spending remains flat, but sales increase, which translates into higher profits. Managers looking to deliver strong results often start with the marketing spending.

Moves to optimize marketing spending, however, can also damage a business and make it vulnerable to attack. One problem is that many of the tactics with a high short-term return actually weaken a business. A short-term price discount, for example, might be highly effective at moving units and driving sales. But discounts encourage customers to focus on price, not quality. Similarly, offering your sales force a large incentive for hitting the month's targets might get them fired up and lead to good sales figures, but it doesn't encourage them to focus on building strong relationships with customers by spending the time to really understand their needs.

The bigger problem is that many of the marketing initiatives that strengthen a business deliver modest short-term returns. When the focus is on short-term profits, this spending is the most likely to be cut. This includes items such as advertising, customer service programs, and loyalty programs.

A focus on short-term results does two things. First, profits often increase, as cost savings, spending cuts, and price increases all combine to substantially build margins and profits. However, the secondary and frequently overlooked result of this focus is that the business becomes much more vulnerable to competitive attack; there is now room in the category for a competitor who provides a quality product at a good price.

This isn't to suggest that companies should strive to deliver poor results. A company struggling financially is vulnerable. With weak financial performance, a defense may not be possible at all because cash is so tight.

The key is balance. Managers should work hard to build efficiency and deliver good results. At the same time, the core of a business needs to be strong. If a company is able to trim manufacturing costs by 18 percent, for example, a portion of this cash should go back into the business to strengthen customer service, to improve the product, to enhance customer and staff loyalty, or even to reduce prices and give customers a better deal.

There are two ways to encourage a balanced approach: values and incentives. Values matter enormously; a company that fundamentally believes in building a strong, enduring brand will generally be in a stronger position defensively than a company that mainly celebrates short-term results. Incentives are perhaps more important, however, because incentives have a huge impact on behavior; executives have to be rewarded for building and defending the business, not just for boosting short-term profits.

To endure, companies need to balance the short-term needs of a business with the long-term strategies that help them stave off competitive attacks.

CREATE A REPUTATION FOR DEFENDING

Perhaps the single most important thing a company can do to prevent an attack is to create a reputation for defending. If a company is known to defend aggressively, the chances that a new entrant can justify the initiative are reduced; people won't attack a company that is certain to ferociously defend its business at all costs. This dynamic is very powerful, and it's one reason why developing a defensive culture is important for the long-term success of any organization.

To prevent attacks, a company should create the perception that it is strong, willing to defend, and equipped with the tools to do so effectively. The logic is simple: new entrants will be less likely to attack a strong player than a weak one.

In an established market, new entrants almost always watch and study the established players. This is one of the reasons why entering an established category is so compelling; a potential new entrant can examine what is currently in the market and identify gaps and opportunities.

This means that the established players can quite easily send a message to potential new entrants. A company that talks about the importance of defense and discusses all its new innovations in the works will appear to be a less attractive target. On the other hand, a company that primarily talks about short-term profit growth driven by supremely high margins will invite competition.

There is a delicate balance, of course. Companies that appear too confident and too strong may actually invite attacks, because they might appear complacent. Brushing aside competitive threats by declaring that "We are so strong, we're not particularly worried about what someone else might do in this market" simply invites new entrants eager to prove you wrong.

RETAIN YOUR PEOPLE

Every category is unique. Making commercial airliners is very different from running a roofing company, and these businesses are quite different from selling tacos. While many of the theories and concepts are consistent across industries, there is a very large body of industry-specific knowledge. Someone who has worked in flooring for ten years knows a remarkable amount about how that industry operates: the customer dynamics, the service challenges, the margin structure, and the pricing.

For this reason, many new entrants rely on people who already know the industry. The entire new product venture might have been created by people with category expertise. If this isn't the case, it is quite likely that the people who started the venture hired experienced people: seasoned sales executives, smart operations people, and gifted finance executives. For example, Nespresso,

Nestlé's blockbuster coffee brand, has recently been under attack from a new company that was launched by someone who used to work in the Nespresso business. This is a rather scary situation, because your attacker knows precisely how the business works and where you are vulnerable.

One way to avoid attacks is to retain your people. A company that has high staff turnover, replacing individuals every few years, will inherently make it easier for new entrants to attack. If an industry is full of people with experience looking for work, it will be easy for new entrants to assemble a strong team.

It is important to retain the most capable senior leaders, of course; these are the true players. Holding on to a gifted general manager is an obvious priority for any business. But it is a mistake to focus only on high-potential general managers. The bigger opportunity is retaining the average players, the solid contributors who know the industry and do a good job. These are the individuals who can help your competitors put together a strong launch plan. This is true across functions; holding on to a good salesperson is as important as keeping good customer service representatives.

Retaining people is a big topic; you can read books covering this issue. But creating a culture of retention and encouraging long careers is critically important in the quest to limit competitive attacks.

DON'T HELP YOUR POTENTIAL COMPETITORS

It doesn't make any sense to help your competitors. This is a fairly obvious point; your goal should be to make life as difficult as possible for anyone trying to attack your business.

The more difficult it is for a competitor to enter your industry, the less likely it is that someone will do it. If it is expensive to develop a certain technology, for example, people will think twice about making the investment. And if it is hard to understand a particular set of consumers, then it is less likely that competitors will do it.

Amazingly, though, companies frequently help competitors attack their business. For example, Dannon yogurt contracted with Agro-Farma, a start-up yogurt company, to produce yogurt for Dannon's Stonyfield Farm brand. These revenues helped Agro-Farma get started and then launch the Chobani brand of Greek yogurt. Chobani then went on to become one of the top brands in the yogurt category, stealing significant market share from Dannon. In a sense, Dannon partially funded the competitor's attack.

Licensing is one way companies encourage competitive attacks; the established player makes its unique technology available to new entrants. This move generates revenues in the form of fees, and it often delights the end users, since they can now work with multiple companies. But licensing makes life much easier for the new entrant. For example, for many years watch giant Swatch sold complicated mechanical watch movements to competitors, thereby reducing the barriers for new companies to enter the market and compete with Swatch's high-end brands. Not surprisingly, Swatch recently took steps to end the practice, much to the consternation of its competitors.

Apple has always been very reluctant to enter into licensing deals; the company owns its key technology and protects it ferociously. This makes it much more difficult for new entrants to attack the Apple franchise.

Another dangerous approach is to create joint ventures that involve sharing technology and market insights. In the short term, this makes good sense, because the joint venture generates cash flow and profit. But in the long run, the partner company may well become a viable competitor. Many companies have encountered this problem in China; in return for access to the enormous market, foreign companies have shared key technologies with emerging competitors.

The high-speed rail industry faced this very problem. Industry leaders, such as Alstom, Siemens, and Bombardier, partnered with local firms in China to gain access to the fast-growing market. Unfortunately, the Chinese firms then learned how to manufacture their own trains and quickly became viable independent competitors. Chinese firms such as China South Locomotive & Rolling Stock Industry Corporation then brought to market competitive products at much lower prices. China's Ministry of Railways explained the situation to *The New York Times*: "China's railway industry produced this new generation of high-speed train sets by learning and systematically compiling and re-innovating foreign high-speed train technology."[5]

Another way companies help competitors is by sharing information, either publicly, at industry conferences and gatherings, or privately. Giving a major address at a market research conference titled, "Customer Insights that Make a Difference," might be a coup for the market research manager involved, but it could well reveal key insights that will help competitors. Serving on boards is another problematic approach. Google's CEO Eric Schmidt served on Apple's board of directors until August 2009, which is a little odd in light of the fact that

Google launched a competitor to the iPhone in January 2010, just five months later.

LAYING THE GROUNDWORK

In the movie *Home Alone,* Macaulay Culkin, concerned that robbers were about to attack his house, worked diligently to prepare, setting an elaborate series of traps. When the bandits then attacked, he was ready. He unleashed one trap after the next and saved the house (and himself).

Preparation is critical in any defensive battle. Companies that defend well have often prepared for a very long time, just as armies will prepare at length for a skirmish. Many defensive tactics take time to execute. It is impossible to secure patents and trademarks in a few weeks. Creating a strong, motivated sales organization is time-consuming; you can quickly hire salespeople, but training them, motivating them, and getting them to work together takes time. Customer and channel loyalty doesn't just happen. Brands don't appear. New technology doesn't just develop itself.

To defend well, a company must have the capabilities and tools in place, and developing these takes time and effort. So it is important to think about defense and take steps to prepare even when a company isn't under attack.

In particular, companies should do the following to prepare.

CREATE FEAR

One of the most important things a senior executive can do to prepare a company for a defensive battle is to create fear. A company that is worried about competition will be ready to defend.

People often frown on fear; it seems weak and cowardly. Strong leaders are brave and proud, courageously moving forward toward a greater future. They aren't scared and fearful—or at least that's a common image of leadership.

In the world of defense, however, fear is almost essential, because fear battles complacency. If you're worried about the competition, you will be on your toes. Intel's CEO Andy Grove embraced this emotion in his appropriately titled book, *Only the Paranoid Survive*: "It is fear that every evening makes me read the trade press reports on competitors' new developments and leads me to tear out particularly ominous articles to take to work for follow-up the next day...fear can be the opposite of complacency."[6] Harvard professor

Rosabeth Moss Kanter echoes this thought: "Do you think the world is out to get you?" she says. "Go ahead, be a little paranoid. That's my management tip for today."[7]

Complacency is an enormous problem. An organization that is comfortable and successful will be slow to react. Carlos Fernandez, CEO of the brewing giant Grupo Modelo, believes that people should always be worried. He notes, "You always have to be concerned about the brands you manage. If you feel really comfortable, it's the start of disaster."[8]

Very often, the more successful a company is, the more reluctant it will be to defend when needed. Strategist Jim Collins warns that success itself creates problems: "Success creates pressure for more growth, setting up a vicious cycle of expectations; this strains people, the culture, and systems to the breaking point; unable to deliver consistent tactical excellence, the institution frays at the edges."[9]

Leaders, then, must constantly remind people to be on edge, to fear the competition, and to avoid complacency. As Collins observed, "Like great artists or inventors, visionary companies thrive on discontent. They understand that contentment leads to complacency, which inevitably leads to decline."[10]

FOCUS ON COMPETITIVE INTELLIGENCE

It is impossible to defend against a new product if you don't see it. For this reason, competitive intelligence should be a priority for any company. Looking for potential changes in the industry and competitive threats is a task that should never end.

Companies that become too inwardly focused are particularly at risk when it comes to identifying competitive threats. If a business manager spends most of her time focused on delighting her boss and her boss's boss, then there is a very good chance she will miss a threat on the horizon. Kellogg marketing professor Phil Kotler warns that this is a common downfall for companies, noting that "losing companies fail to monitor new technologies, new lifestyles, new competitors."[11]

It can be hard to see competitive threats, especially before the product hits the market or when the competitor is small. Consulting firm McKinsey recently completed a survey of business executives around the globe and found that only 23 percent of companies learned about competitive innovations in time to respond before they hit the market.[12] This is a disconcerting figure.

The problem is that the biggest threats are hard to see. They are the innovations that indirectly impact your business early on, such as a niche product that has the potential to grow into a major new product. These new products might succeed, and the risk is that you don't actually see them until it is too late.

So a company needs to proactively monitor the industry. This means it needs to have people out in the market, working to understand customer needs and looking for innovations. It is critical to have a broad perspective to identify and evaluate a range of ideas and identify the most threatening ones.

Competitive intelligence isn't failsafe; even the strongest companies miss things. As Phil Kotler said at a recent marketing conference, "You'll always be surprised. But you'll be less surprised if you have a peripheral vision."[13]

SET THE RIGHT INCENTIVES

People generally do what they are rewarded for. If people get positive feedback for doing something in particular, they are likely to do it again.

This is true for kids, certainly; if I give my son Charlie ice cream for playing well at his piano recital, he is more likely to focus on practicing for the next one. If I praise Claire for getting good grades in math, then she will probably spend more time on math.

This is also true for business executives; to a large degree incentives drive action. If an executive has a big incentive to cut costs, she will cut costs. If he is given a big incentive to build strong brands, he will try very hard to build strong brands.

As a result, setting the right incentives to ensure that defense is a priority is an important task. The basic question: what do we want our people to do? The wrong incentives will lead to the wrong behavior.

At many companies, managers are rewarded for focusing on growth—usually profit growth. Incentives are largely based on a simple question: were you able to grow your business?

The problem with this sort of incentive is that it doesn't encourage people to worry about defense. If there is little reward for focusing on protecting the core business, managers won't spend much time on it. Why invest in competitive intelligence? If the priority is growth, the money should go to product development and innovation, not into the basic business.

Indeed, a strong focus on profit growth actually provides the wrong incentive when it comes to defense, because managers are rewarded for taking a risk on the core business in order to fund the new products and move forward with growth initiatives. Cutting back support on the base business to fund a big new product launch makes perfect sense if your incentive is to grow. It makes little sense to reduce new product investment to invest in the stable base business.

In a growth-oriented firm, supporting the base business makes very little sense indeed. In the best case, you manage to maintain the business, and this isn't a win. So even if you execute well, you fail to deliver against your objectives. Only a manager lacking common sense would do this.

Supporting growth initiatives, however, makes perfect sense. You might manage to grow, successfully gaining acclaim and rewards: a good bonus, praise from senior management, and perhaps a promotion. You might not grow, of course, but you would probably be rewarded for trying; everyone knows that not all growth initiatives succeed, and most new products fail. In a sense, failing with the new product is the expected outcome, so there is relatively little risk.

Even when being attacked, there is a bias toward spending on the growth initiative if this is where the incentive lies. A successful new product is a clear win. If the gains are offset by a competitive attack, then this is just an unfortunate competitive situation.

If a company provides incentives for managers to deliver short-term financial targets, the managers will work hard to achieve this goal. And if the incentives are big enough, managers do whatever it takes. This is the situation at many companies today; the short-term incentives are enormous. As Disney's CEO Bob Iger lamented in a recent interview, "Unfortunately, all too often we're measured on near-term results. That seeps into compensation strategies. Clearly, executives today are overcompensated for what they deliver short-term and undercompensated for their long-term investment."[14]

The truth is that profit growth goals should be just one of a range of criteria for incentives. Protecting a base business is important, so incentives should support this. Market share, competitive intelligence, and defensive moves should all be rewarded. Given the financial realities of a business, the majority of incentives should focus on protecting the base business from competitive attack, not on short-term profit growth.

CREATE CUSTOMER LOYALTY

Perhaps the best way to defend an established business is to have loyal customers who love your product or service and aren't willing to switch.

Strong customer loyalty has two positive effects in terms of defense. First, attacking companies may be less likely to go after a company with loyal customers for the simple reason that it will be difficult to get much traction. Loyal customers are less likely to consider alternative products and will be reluctant to try new entrants. This means that any new competitor must factor this into its launch proposition, including perhaps exceptionally high levels of sales support or advertising spending for the new product. And this means it will be harder to get the new product proposition to work, so it will be less likely the new product will be launched at all. It would be easy to attack Internet shoe retailer Zappos, but no one does this for an obvious reason: Zappos delights its customers with legendary service. How do you get a Zappos customer to switch? I suspect the answer is quite simple: you don't.

Second, customer loyalty makes it easier to defend a business. Your loyal customers might alert you to a competitive launch, and when it occurs, they are likely to stick with you. When you add defensive programs, these customers will respond quickly, making the programs highly effective. A program aimed at rewarding customers, perhaps a "buy two get one free" deal, will be very attractive for your loyal customers; they will take advantage of the deal.

Building customer loyalty, then, is a wonderful way to prepare for a defense. The goal is to ensure that your customers like your product or service and aren't looking to switch. Of course, ideally your customers are ready and willing to stand up and defend your product, so they can also explain to their friends why there is no need to consider an alternative.

There are many ways to build customer loyalty; many people have written books on the topic. But there are three important approaches to consider. The first and most important is providing exceptional customer service. This is a combination of concentrating on delivering a positive experience and recovering when there are service gaps. The second approach is to reinforce the product proposition, reminding customers again and again why your product or service is different and superior. This validates their decision to work with you. Finally, it is critical to maintain product quality. The simplest way to lose customer loyalty is to sell an inferior product or service; in the short run your customers might not notice, but eventually they will.

BUILD CONNECTIONS WITH GOVERNMENT OFFICIALS

Government officials can play a very important role in a defensive situation; rules and regulations can effectively prevent competitors from gaining access to a market by simply excluding them or forcing them to deal with high taxes or onerous regulatory burdens.

Securing favorable regulations, however, requires that you can reach and communicate with key officials. An executive who picks up the phone and calls up her local government representative out of the blue isn't likely to get through. Even if she does get through, her concerns aren't likely to be taken seriously. But if the government contact knows and likes the executive, it is a totally different story. It is even better if the business leader helped out the politician a few times in the past.

The problem is that it takes time and money to build these critical connections; companies that invest in this effort have more options when it comes time to defend.

CREATE INTELLECTUAL PROPERTY BARRIERS

Intellectual property can play a very important role when it comes to defense; patents and trademarks can be effective tools because they may prevent a competitor from entering the market. Even if they don't, they can form the basis of an effective defensive program that makes life very difficult for the new entrant.

Creating these barriers, however, takes time and effort. You can't secure a patent in a week, and you can't claim a trademark by simply filing a form. The only way to get strong intellectual property defenses is to diligently set about building and defending patents and trademarks over time.

Companies focused on building a strong defensive intellectual property position work at it diligently. They focus on securing trademarks by employing unique phrases as much as possible and avoiding descriptors that are hard to protect. They invest in R&D and then file for patents, or they acquire companies with patents. And once they have patents and trademarks, they aggressively defend them.

A strong legal team is critical, of course; it is worth it to spend the money to hire excellent attorneys, and it is also worth engaging a top-notch firm to assist with the effort. Good lawyers are expensive but often well worth the cost.

Building intellectual property is an investment in the long run; the benefits show up over time, not in the short run. Securing a trademark on a particular ingredient, for example, isn't likely to drive an enormous boost in sales tomorrow. If an attacker shows up down the road, however, the trademark might be a very important part of the defensive plan.

ENGAGE THE CHANNEL

As we've learned, blocking distribution is a particularly effective form of defense; a competitor who can't secure space in the distribution channel can't generate sales and won't survive. For this reason, it is important to build strong relationship with channel partners. The stronger your connection with your distribution channel, the more likely you will be successful at keeping a competitor out if need be. As Harvard professor Michael Porter observed, "The more limited the wholesale or retail channels are and the more that existing competitors have tied them up, the tougher entry into an industry will be."[15]

There are many ways to create a positive relationship with a distribution channel. The core, of course, is being fair and honest in your interactions. If your distributors trust you, they will be quick to warn you about competitive activity and less likely to pick up a competitive brand.

NEVER STOP DEFENDING

Defense is a never-ending battle. People are always looking for new things, so threats are likely to appear with some regularity. If your business is visible and attractive, the threats may come quickly. The specific battles come and go, as people try to break in and succeed or fail, but the task goes on. Defending well requires a mind-set of proactive vigilance and continuous preparation.

The task of defending never stops.

Chapter 14

DEFENSIVE STRATEGY FOR INNOVATORS

IN 2008 ATHLETIC APPAREL COMPANY Under Armour entered the mainstream athletic shoes category, launching a line of cross training sneakers. CEO Kevin Plank was supremely confident about the new products and had invested a large part of the company's marketing budget in a launch plan that included a $4.4 million Super Bowl commercial. He told a reporter from *The New York Times,* "Under Armour controls its own destiny. We believe there are better fabrics, better technology, and better innovations...people are going to try us."[1]

Unfortunately for Under Armour, Nike put together an aggressive defensive campaign. The company launched a similar line of cross-training products a month before Under Armour's product introduction, invested heavily in marketing, and worked closely with key retailers.

Under Armour ended up with a disappointing 1 percent share of the athletic shoe market.[2] Plank's analysis of the situation wasn't entirely accurate. In the end, Under Armour's destiny was determined in large part by the defender, Nike.

All too many innovators make the same mistake. Companies launching new products tend to focus on playing offense: securing financial support, finalizing the product design, and figuring out how to make people aware of their great new idea. The emphasis is on bringing the new product to life.

Indeed, many entrepreneurs scoff at defensive strategy prior to launch. "We don't worry about the competition," they proclaim. "We worry about delighting our customers. By meeting customer needs in an innovative way, we will build revenue and market share and profits."

This is a huge miss. Defensive strategy is a critically important topic for anyone bringing a new idea to market; you need to understand how defensive strategy works and then seriously consider how it will affect your launch. Indeed, any innovator who isn't thinking about defense is taking an enormous risk.

Defense is important for people launching new products for two reasons. The first is quite simple: if you are launching a new product, you need to consider how the established players are likely to respond to your move and how they might defend. This is particularly important if you are attacking an established category with well-entrenched and financially strong players. Ignoring their likely defensive efforts is not a smart idea.

The second reason defensive strategy matters so much is that a successful innovator will have to think about defense as soon as the new product begins to take off. Once the venture is up and running, new competitors will likely appear, and this will force the innovator to react. The game quickly shifts from simply driving growth to balancing growth and defense.

PLAN FOR THE DEFENSE

If you're an innovator, it is essential to consider how the established players will respond to your launch. If you can anticipate the defensive effort, you can plan for it and deal with it more effectively. There are several critical things to remember.

ASSUME THAT THERE WILL BE A DEFENSE

Anyone launching a new product should start with the assumption that the established players will defend, and that they will do so aggressively. Indeed, the established companies may spend far more trying to kill you than you'll spend trying to succeed. There are enormous financial incentives for an established player to assemble and execute a big defensive effort. For them, defending aggressively is a completely rational course of action; they have a lot to lose.

In addition, the established players begin the battle with all sorts of advantages: they have experience and expertise, customer relationships, brand loyalty, and technological capabilities. Perhaps most important, they have deep pockets and a big incentive to use these resources to defend.

The defensive effort will probably be nasty and tough; the established company will attempt to squash the new product at every point in the launch process, doing whatever it takes to prevail. The defensive tactics won't be polite or elegant or fair. This isn't the refined sport of golf; it is street fighting in the marketplace where your competitor will attempt to scratch your eyes out and smash you on the head with a beer bottle while you're looking the other way. The existing players may try to hire your best people, drag you into court, spread rumors about your product, destroy your supply chain, tear down your posters, and create a price war.

All of this probably seems wrong to you, the innovator. After all, you're just trying to make the world a better place through clever thinking and big ideas. The concept that an established player would spend millions of dollars trying to destroy your company seems fundamentally unjust. The notion that competitors will simply copy your work feels unethical. Andrew Mason, the CEO of Internet deal site Groupon, made the point eloquently in a recent interview. He lamented, "We spent two years of pivoting and trying different things before we landed on this model. The clones completely lifted everything that we were doing. They'd just call all of our accounts. They were just drafting all the success that we had. I'm new as a businessperson. I used to be a music major. In that world, they call it plagiarism. In business, they call it competition."[3] The reality is that while copying might feel unethical companies do it all the time.

I recently spent the day with a fellow who created a new cleaning products company; he was enthusiastic, positive, and committed to making the world a better place for his customers and his employees. It was simply inspiring. But I knew that even as we were talking, his competitors, large and well-funded global companies, were almost certainly developing plans to squash his company and put it out of business or perhaps to bring the company to the edge of bankruptcy before buying it at a discount price.

The legal system will likely provide little help. The actions of an established player might be legally and ethically questionable. Unfortunately, pursuing these things in court takes time and money. By the time the legal system issues a ruling and a case works its way through the appeals process, your new venture will have succeeded or, more likely, failed.

It is essential to set reasonable expectations. Creating a new product proposition that doesn't factor in the likely defensive effort is almost always a problem; when the defense kicks in—as it almost certainly will—it will slow sales, and the new product will likely miss the financial forecast. Any new product proposition should assume that the established players will defend; if things work out well and for some reason the established player doesn't defend, then you will be ahead of plan, and that is a happy thing indeed.

ANTICIPATE YOUR COMPETITOR

If you're an innovator entering a new market, the message is simple: know your competitor and plan accordingly! If you know your new product will be met by a big defensive effort, you can create plans that address what you think your competitor might do. Consultants Kevin Coyne and John Horn recommend thinking about three questions: "Will the competitor react at all? What options will the competitor actively consider? Which option will the competitor most likely choose?"[4]

If you believe there's a good chance the established players will take steps to block your distribution build by signing agreements with channel partners, then you need to either sign the distributors first, provide a greater incentive, or look for a different distribution system. If you think the established players will load up customers with loyalty incentives, you may need to move faster than anticipated to get in front of the defensive efforts at loading up. If you think the established players will tear down your posters and signs, then you probably need to order some extras.

Understanding the defender is critical because with smart thinking you can plan for the defense or avoid it entirely. Frontier Airlines, for example, began operations at Denver International Airport. This was an unlikely choice for a new airline because it was (and remains) a major hub for global giant United Airlines. But Frontier figured out that it could avoid provoking United by scheduling flights at odd times and limiting service to certain cities; if Frontier flew to Los Angeles just twice a day, for example, United didn't defend on the route. The cost of defending would have been very high for United, and Frontier wasn't a big risk. By understanding United's view of defense, Frontier grew and thrived. Frontier's key learning, according to planning director Sean Menke, was simple: "It's vitally important to understand the mind of your opponent."[5]

DEFEND AGAINST THE DEFENSE

Anyone launching a product into an established category should expect to see the established players react and mount a vigorous defense, so at a minimum you need to plan for the defense. An even more powerful approach is to defend against the defense.

The logic here is quite strong: if a company launching a new product can block the defensive effort, then the launch has a greater chance of succeeding. In some ways this is no different than the tactics used in the game of American football: a well-placed block can slow a defender, giving the offensive running back a shot at an open field.

There are two main ways to limit a defensive strategy: block the defender and capitalize on the power of public relations.

BLOCK THE DEFENDER

To block a defense, a new entrant needs to consider the likely defense tactics and then consider ways to negate them. For example, the attacking company can buy up industry-specific marketing vehicles before the established player is aware of the attack. When the established player tries to defend, some of the most powerful options will be off the table. Alternatively, the new entrant might dramatically increase spending when the defense is likely to occur, so that the new product message gets through regardless.

Razor giant Gillette (now part of Procter & Gamble) employed this approach when launching its new razor, the Fusion. This major new product introduction was a clear threat to Schick, Gillette's key rival, and Gillette was planning to spend hundreds of millions on the product's launch. The team at Gillette could safely assume that the executives at Schick would develop a defense plan.

The classic defense in a category like razors is to block trial by loading consumers; giving people a new razor will naturally reduce their interest in buying yet another new razor. So in the weeks leading up to the Fusion launch, Schick would likely try to issue coupons with big savings in a bid to ramp up sales, load consumers, and hurt initial sales of the Fusion. Just slowing the Fusion's initial sales would be a big benefit for Schick, because it might discourage the Gillette sales force or its distributors and force the Fusion business team to revise the financials in light of the slow start.

The team at Gillette knew all this; Schick's defense was almost certain. To block their rival's efforts, Gillette proactively bought all the space in the Sunday coupon sections of most major media outlets. Gillette then ran a simple message in block letters: "Fusion is coming." This message added little real value to the launch. Indeed, it wasn't at all clear what Fusion was; the creative didn't show a razor or someone shaving. It could have been for a new cell phone service or a credit card. On its own, then, this made no sense; it was a waste of money. But by buying all the coupon space, Gillette ensured that Schick couldn't offer coupons and load up consumers. This left the field open for Fusion.

Another way to block the defense is to embrace tactics that are difficult or impossible for the established player to copy. The easiest thing for any defender to do is simply copy the new entrant's strategy. Employing unique tactics makes this harder to do. Jet Blue, a US airline that entered the market in 1998, employed this approach to build awareness and drive trial. The company offered a $599 "all-access ticket" for the month of September 1999. People who bought the ticket could fly for a month anywhere Jet Blue flew for free. This was a brilliant move; it generated a huge amount of excitement and publicity for Jet Blue, and it highlighted all the destinations in the new airline's network. It also was impossible for established players such as American Airlines and United Airlines to match it; the cost would be far too high.

USE THE POWER OF PUBLIC RELATIONS

Public relations can be an important tool for a new entrant. News organizations tend to embrace the challenger, the upstart, and the underdog. Innovators can use this to their advantage by pitching stories that will attract attention to their new ideas and new company.

In addition, new entrants can use the power of publicity to limit the established players' defensive efforts. When a large, entrenched company attempts to defend, the innovator can draw attention to the defensive activities, declaring them illegal or unethical. When done well, this creates a number of positive outcomes for the new entrant. First, it attracts attention. Building awareness is a critical task for any new product, so getting publicity in this fashion can be valuable. Second, it can help build the new entrant's brand image as an innovative, good-natured company (as opposed to the big, nasty established player who resorts to strong-arm tactics to squash innovators). Third, the negative publicity may force the established player to back away in order avoid further scrutiny.

The master of this approach is Richard Branson, adventurer and founder of the upstart Virgin Atlantic Airways. As Virgin expanded in the early 1990s, Branson found himself on the receiving end of a very aggressive defense effort by British Airways. The campaign was highly effective at damaging Virgin, so Branson publicly attacked British Airways and its CEO, Lord King, for what he called "dirty tricks." When King denied the charges, Branson created a bit of an uproar by suing him for libel. Branson explained his approach, stating "King was effectively calling me a liar, so I sued him."[6] The case eventually settled out of court, but Branson's public response was highly effective at building Virgin and limiting what British Airways could do.

Innovative cleaning products company Method was similarly effective in addressing a defensive effort from Clorox. The legal team at Clorox sent Method a formal letter in 2010 accusing the firm of violating a Clorox trademark on a "flower design." The letter asked Method to cease and desist from using flower designs. This would have forced Method to redesign much of its packaging and marketing materials, a costly task for a new firm. In response, Method founders Eric Ryan and Adam Lowry created a website and video where they responded publicly to the charge. They posted the formal legal letter from Clorox and explained that they didn't think anyone could trademark a flower, saying, "Own the daisy? That's ridiculous." They also invited people to vote on who precisely should own the daisy—Clorox, Method, or nobody.[7] Their strategy was very effective; it helped build Method by attracting publicity and positioning the brand as friendly and innocent and made Clorox look like a stodgy firm run by a bunch of lawyers. Not surprisingly, the team at Method didn't hear anything further from the attorneys at Clorox.

SECURE INTELLECTUAL PROPERTY

There is no question that intellectual property is a key area for new businesses. Anyone preparing to launch a new business needs to focus on establishing and defending trademarks and patents. Martin McCourt, the CEO of vacuum cleaner upstart Dyson, says bluntly, "Patents lie very much at the heart of what we do. We spend an absolute fortune on our patents."[8]

The reason is this: If your new business gains any traction at all, established players will try to defend, and one of the simplest ways to defend is to copy the idea. And if your launch succeeds, other new entrants will attack your idea, trying to participate in the emerging opportunity. For these reasons, securing patents and trademarks is critical because they can help you defend your idea—and your new business.

A word of caution: Don't be fooled into assuming that because you've filed a patent, you're fully protected from your competitors. This is rarely the case; you must enforce patents and trademarks for them to have any impact—and this takes time, resources, and strategic focus.

PROTECT INFORMATION AND ACT QUICKLY

If you are a new entrant launching a product in an established category, working quickly and limiting the flow of information are paramount to catching your competition unawares. A company will only react if it sees a new development and believes it is worthy of a response; if you are stealthy and quick, you can fly under the radar and delay a defensive action.

PROTECT INFORMATION

The longer a new entrant can remain invisible, the more time it has to make headway before the defensive effort kicks in. If an established player hears about a new entrant 18 months before the planned launch, it has plenty of time to react. In the worst case, the established player will simply copy the idea and rush it to market before the new entrant is even close to launch. As a result, it is critical to maintain confidentiality throughout the product planning process.

All too many entrepreneurs are eager to discuss their ideas. They are often in search of funding and support, so they are quick to increase their visibility by giving talks at conferences, guest lecturing at business schools like Kellogg and Wharton, and granting interviews to the trade press.

This is usually a bad idea; getting lots of publicity in the very early stages of a new product launch can accelerate the defensive process. And hyping the idea (by perhaps proclaiming, "We're going to become the dominant player in the beer industry") will substantially increase the chances that the established players will take action to make sure that this never occurs.

There is an appropriate time for publicity, of course. When the new product hits the market, it is essential to build awareness and trial, so generating attention and excitement is critical. Indeed, without a bit of attention the new product is destined to fail.

The challenge is to carefully manage the flow of information, laying low and preserving confidentiality during the development phase and then getting attention during the launch. Reversing this sequence of events is a problem.

Maintaining confidentiality isn't easy; it requires a focus on secrecy, limited information sharing, and careful consideration of what actually can be communicated publicly. Simply using nondisclosure agreements is rarely sufficient; people will readily sign them, but their use is limited. Employees need to understand the importance of keeping things quiet, and key information should only be shared among a small group of people.

Few companies manage information as well as Apple: the company is noto-
riously secretive during the product development process and then masterful at
getting publicity once a product is ready. Apple goes to extremes to keep things
quiet. Adam Lashinsky, an editor at *Fortune*, studied the company in depth. He
noted that Apple is uniquely protective of information, saying, "All companies
have secrets, of course. The difference is that at Apple everything is a secret."[9]

Apple employees understand that confidentiality is critical; releasing secret
information will quickly lead to termination. But Apple goes further; the company routinely blocks off certain areas of its corporate campus for key projects, limiting access to just a few people. Major decisions about the business are
made by a small group of top executives, with operating groups organized by
function. This means few people see the full picture. Jon Rubinstein, a former
senior executive at Apple, explained the company's approach in an interview
for *Business Week*: "We have cells, like a terrorist organization. Everything is
on a need-to-know basis."[10] Apple also hires people for dummy positions; new
employees often don't know what they are working on until they get started.

When a product is ready, however, Apple attracts enormous attention. An
Apple product announcement is a major media event, partly because the company is so good at keeping things quiet. In March 2012, for example, Apple
managed to get every major media outlet in the United States to report that the
company was going to make a product announcement, even though the actual
news was just a new version of the iPad.

GO FAST

A new entrant's biggest advantage is speed, the ability to move quickly to capitalize on the potential of an idea. This is critical for success because the faster a
new entrant moves, the harder it is for an established player to defend.

In particular, the need for speed changes over the life of a new entrant.
When a new company is very small, speed is less important; the top priority
must be getting the proposition right. In the initial phase, being small is a good
thing because you are then not a threat to the big players. A company selling
in a just a few stores or a smaller city won't seem like a problem. Yogurt giant
Dannon, for example, completely ignored Chobani when it first entered the
market because the new brand was sold only in a few stores on Long Island.

Once the new company begins to grow significantly, speed becomes essential. At some point the established players will react. Dannon unleashed a

massive defense effort once Chobani became one of the leading brands in the market, but Chobani had a period of time when it could grow without facing a major defensive campaign. Once Dannon engaged in the fight, further growth would be tough to achieve.

It can take a long time for a big, established company to get a defensive program into the market. The firm has to learn about the new entrant, evaluate it, and decide to defend. Then the team has to develop the plan, secure funding, and execute the plan. In a large organization with multiple layers of management this process can take a very long time.

This gives a new entrant an opportunity. Ideally, the new company moves so quickly that the established player is never really able to catch up; by the time the defense plan kicks in, the innovator has enough of a presence in the market that it is difficult to dislodge. This was exactly what happened with Chobani.

Entrepreneur Mike Cassidy, the founder of Internet start-up Xfire, notes that speed was critical to his success: "For the first year, we were launching an updated version of Xfire every two weeks. That makes it very difficult for a competitor to keep pace, because even if they decide, 'Wow, that's a product we have to reckon with,' for most larger companies it takes them quite a while to put together an analysis of how to compete and have meetings and design a competitive product."[11]

For a new entrant hoping to avoid encountering a massive defensive effort, speed is essential once the product gets moving.

CHOOSE YOUR STRATEGY WITH CARE

Picking the right strategy is critical; there are multiple ways to bring a new product to market, and selecting the optimal approach is essential. One of the reasons strategy matters so much is that your launch strategy will likely have an impact on the defensive reaction you will encounter. If you directly attack a big established player, for example, you will likely face a vicious defensive effort. Finding a less threatening approach is far more promising.

DON'T ATTACK THE CORE

Many companies launch new products by going head-to-head with the existing firms. This strategy involves launching a good product into a well-developed market. The item often is of high quality with a reasonable price. This feels like a winning proposition. The new entrant usually supports the launch with an aggressive communications effort to build awareness, along with a strong promotions and sales effort to secure trial and repeat.

This strategy, called "attack the core," is one of the most common ways that companies introduce new products. Unfortunately, it is rarely successful. DHL, for example, directly attacked shipping giants UPS and FedEx with this strategy in a bid to become the third big player in domestic shipping in the United States. The launch was a disaster; DHL lost billions before finally giving up on the initiative. Japanese pharmaceutical giant Eisai launched the proton pump inhibitor Aciphex, an effective product backed up by solid clinical trial results, into a well-established category and secured a disappointingly small portion of the market. Microsoft spent billions of dollars on Bing, a respectable search engine, and failed to make significant headway against industry leader Google. Best Foods launched a perfectly good line of salad dressings, attacking established brands including Hidden Valley Ranch (Clorox) and Kraft. This launch failed, too.

An attack-the-core strategy is rarely successful for all sorts of fairly obvious reasons. First, trial will be expensive; while you can get people to try the new product, it will be costly, since the new product isn't dramatically different. Securing distribution will also be expensive (and challenging) because established players are well-entrenched in the channels and have strong relationships with distributors. The business will build slowly, because you're fighting to change customer habits and routines.

Perhaps the biggest reason this strategy rarely is successful is that established players will usually defend, and they will do so effectively. This strategy in particular is likely to spark a defensive reaction because these launches look threatening; the spending is high and the product proposition is good. The established players will likely regard it as a direct attack (which in many cases it is), and they will take action. Attacking the core is a bit like walking up to someone on the street and punching the person in the nose. When you do this, you will likely meet with a reaction.

Defending against one of these new products is a relatively easy; the established company simply invests heavily in blocking distribution and trial. This will slow up the new product's momentum, and slowing the launch is often enough to kill the product entirely.

Nonetheless, strategies attacking the core are appealing; the opportunity is usually clear, and the execution hurdles are modest. All you really need is a bit of optimism, and you're underway. But anyone considering this type of strategy must factor in the likely defensive response. In many cases, the defense will be such that even the most promising new product launch quickly loses steam and is promptly abandoned. As Procter & Gamble CEO A. G. Lafley observed, "We have learned that head-on, World War I–like assaults on walled cities generally end with a lot of casualties."[12]

CONSIDER A NICHE

Niche strategies are far more attractive than those attacking the core, simply because established players are less likely to defend against a niche launch. The threat seems smaller, which reduces the defensive risk.

With a niche strategy, the new entrant identifies an underserved segment of the market and focuses on reaching this group. The niche might be defined by industry segment, geography, age, or attitude. There are hundreds of different possible niches.

Niche launches are feasible because there are always underserved segments in a market; there is no market where everyone is delighted with the existing items. As a result, there is almost always an opportunity to better meet customer needs and steal market share.

Perhaps the best aspect of this strategy is that an established player may consider the new product to be a small threat and not worthy of substantial defensive spending. There is a good chance the existing brands won't react at all. Established players must pick their battles; they can't defend against everything. This presents a big opportunity for the new niche entrant. Jim Koch, founder of craft brewer Boston Beer Company, believed that his company could survive in a high-end, premium niche. He observed, "Could a giant do what we do? It's not impossible. It's difficult because it's not what they're good at. They're good at cost-effectively mass-producing beers that appeal the mass market. They could make craft-styled beers if they put their minds to it. But it's hard for a big company to care about such specialized products."[13] Koch predicted that the beer giants would not defend heavily against a small company entering a specialized craft beer niche, and he was largely correct.

The big question with a niche strategy is one of size: is the niche big enough to support a business? The established players might be right when they declare the niche launch to be a very modest threat.

The best niche launches are those that are bigger than they look. If a niche appears small, then the new entrant can lock it up without competitive response. If it turns out to be much bigger than expected, there is an opportunity to claim the market before the established players recognize it. Whole Foods and Tesco are wonderful examples of this dynamic. The US grocery industry is intensely competitive, with numerous strong and well-funded competitors. Entering this category with a strategy to attack the core—for example, by introducing a new line of traditional grocery stores—would be a huge challenge. Indeed, British retail giant Tesco has learned this the hard way; the company entered the market in 2007, launching a chain of stores called Fresh & Easy. The company had almost two hundred locations by 2011 and managed to lose £700 million, a remarkable figure.[14]

In contrast, Whole Foods employed a niche strategy. John Mackey, Renee Lawson Hardy, Craig Weller, and Mark Skiles founded the company in 1980 in Austin, Texas. At the time they had just one store that sold organic and natural products in a supermarket format. Prices were high, and the selection was unique. Whole Foods carried organic and natural products and didn't carry many products from the big, global manufacturers.

The company gradually expanded to additional locations, spreading across the United States and then into other countries. In 2011, Whole Foods had 310 stores, with annual sales of over $10.1 billion and profits of $343 million.

The astonishing thing about the growth of Whole Foods was that the established grocery players simply watched it happen; they didn't mount a serious defense. The reason, of course, was that Whole Foods was focused on just a small piece of the market, namely, customers who would pay premium prices for organic foods. It wasn't a direct threat to mass grocers.

When large players do choose to defend, they can make life very difficult for new entrants. The power of a niche strategy is that the launch appears to be small and inconsequential and thus not worthy of a defense.

CONSIDER CHANGING THE RULES

Many of the most successful new product launches fundamentally shift an industry; the new entrant introduces a new feature, technology, or business model and manages to create a change in the dynamics of the market. This approach, changing the rules, is a promising approach to new product strategy.

Changing the rules requires companies to embrace the idea of a market-driving strategy, a new way of thinking about marketing and competition.

Both attacking-the-core strategy and that of establishing a niche are based on the idea of market focus. The basic concept is fairly simple: customers have needs, and competitors fight to best meet customer needs. Customers evaluate the offerings in the market and buy the solution that best meets their need. Products change as customer needs change, and companies battle to keep up.

Meeting customer needs is a good idea; you can't go too far wrong if you give your customers what they want. But market focus has some rather significant problems, too. One of the biggest is that market focus tends to lead to convergence, as all the existing players in a market converge on the same point. Each company spends time talking with customers, and this research yields similar results. Each company then develops similar products, focused on customer needs. The market then is saturated with very similar competitive offerings that have little or no differentiation in the eyes of the consumer. A market like this can easily become a price battle, where margins are squeezed as companies compete on price.

Market focus also assumes that customers actually know what they want. This is a very dangerous assumption to make, because customers usually have no idea what they actually would like in terms of products or services. People know what they have, and when asked they generally request more of the same, often at higher quality and lower prices. They can't identify new features and benefits. Yet another problem is that market focus is always looking backward; the assumption is that what people want today is what they told you they wanted *yesterday*. This is a very dangerous assumption because things change quickly in this world.

Market driving is a very different theory; it suggests that instead of just meeting customer needs, companies should think about shaping a market and influencing the needs. The insight behind market driving is that in many industries customers learn about new developments primarily from the companies that are in the industry.

Driving a market can be very successful; when it works, a company is able to shift a market so that customers value what the new entrant provides. The reason market-driving strategy often succeeds is that the established players often don't react to these new product introductions. This lack of a defense gives the new entrant an opening; it is possible to steal market share without getting a big defensive reaction.

This is how Dyson managed to succeed in the vacuum cleaner market. Inventor James Dyson, disappointed with the performance of his vacuum cleaner, spent 14 years developing a new type of vacuum cleaner, one that didn't use bags to filter the air. He took his new technology to the established players, such as Hoover, who turned him down, declaring it a feeble idea. As Dyson's CEO Martin McCourt recalled, "One by one they told him to get lost."[15]

Frustrated, Dyson decided to launch the product on his own. He invested heavily in marketing, patiently explaining to people why existing vacuums didn't work well and why his vacuum was superior because it didn't rely on a bag. In his introductory commercial he explained the situation: "Ever since the vacuum cleaner was invented, it has had a basic design flaw. Bags, filters—they all clog with dust and then lose suction. The technology simply doesn't work. So I spent fourteen years developing one that does."[16]

The established players didn't defend vigorously until Dyson had gained a major portion of the market, and by then it was largely too late. Dyson is now the top selling brand of vacuum cleaners in the United States, the United Kingdom, and Japan because James Dyson changed the conversation with consumers and changed the market to fit his product.

AFTER THE LAUNCH: PREPARE TO DEFEND

Innovators tend to gloss over the topic of defense, and it's understandable that defense is not the first thing entrepreneurs think about. Here's a case in point: I've worked with dozens of student teams working on new products during my time at the Kellogg School of Management. They tend to be very excited about the product and the market potential. But they don't think much about defense. When I ask how they will defend their business propositions, I frequently get two responses: they will file for a patent or create network effects. But as we've learned, patents and network effects are rarely sufficient to protect a new idea.

Indeed, people bringing new products to market tend to focus on the opportunity and the challenge of securing customers. During the launch, the focus is rightly on optimizing the launch, getting the product right, developing and implementing a strong marketing plan, and securing financing for the introduction.

But any successful new entrepreneur *will* have to worry about defense, and usually sooner than expected. Once your new product gets a start, other competitors will likely appear, and they will be focused on getting a piece of the new market you've created. At Facebook, for example, competition is a huge concern. Andrew Bosworth, one of the first people to join Facebook, observed in a recent interview, "God forbid we spend a single day not trying to prepare for tomorrow's Facebook."[17] Nespresso, Nestlé's highly profitable and fast-growing coffee system, now has more than fifty competitors.[18]

The problem is that defense is particularly difficult for new companies. New businesses go through a phase when they are particularly vulnerable to attack: when the new product has launched but before it has reached critical mass. This is a delicate time, because the new product is growing but still small, so resources are tight and there is a temptation to focus much more on growth than on defense. The new venture, however, has to attack and defend at the same time.

Innovators simply must spend time identifying competitive threats and preparing to mount defensive efforts. It's all about balance. Growth is critical, of course, because the new company has to secure new customers if the venture is going to succeed. Getting trial and repeat is clearly an essential task. But defense is also important to protect the gains. As with any business strategy, there is no perfect answer, and much depends on the competitive environment you are entering. Some new businesses should focus mainly on growth, with little emphasis on defense. Other new businesses should spend much more time thinking about defense, making it as critical a priority as growth efforts.

For every new business, however, defense is a topic that matters.

Chapter 15

A CAUTIONARY WORD ABOUT COMPETITION LAW

By Stephen Calkins[1]

SOME ATTORNEYS MIGHT TELL YOU not to buy this book, and if you insist on buying it anyway, to hide it and not let anyone, especially not a government enforcer or a potential plaintiff, see you reading it.

They have a point. The European Commission's official guidance in this area of the law calls for attention to, among other things, "direct evidence of any exclusionary strategy."[2] In one well-known monopolization case, the jury instructions said that, to "sum up," the jury should decide whether the defending firm had engaged in activities that "were designed primarily to further any domination" of a market.[3] The last thing a defense lawyer in any jurisdiction wants is a photo of the chief executive's office with a book such as this one prominently displayed.

No defense lawyer wants a judge or jury to learn that one of a defendant corporation's high-ranking officials when speaking about rivals said that he wanted to "flush these turkeys" and "cut off [their] air supply."[4] The European Commission candidly states that it is more likely to intervene where there is "direct evidence of any exclusionary strategy."[5] Having a valid business reason for your actions is critical. As the en banc Third Circuit declared, "A monopolist will be found to violate § 2 of the Sherman Act [which protects against monopolies] if it engages in exclusionary or predatory conduct without a valid business justification."[6] No matter what action you take in the course of defending your market, your defense lawyer would much prefer that the moves you make have been justified as necessary to improve quality, protect consumer interests, keep costs down, etc., rather than as a volitional act intended to harm a rival.

So my first piece of candid advice is to avoid referring to this book and to any antirival thinking in written presentations and especially in e-mails. Really.

With that out of the way, let's take a quick tour through the relevant law so that you'll be able to navigate some of the legal terrain. Remember that these are just general guidelines; you should never undertake a defensive effort without the direct involvement and advice of your legal team.

The applicable statutory standards are brief but relatively uninformative. The US Sherman Act, Section 2, declares that it is unlawful to "monopolize" or "attempt to monopolize." Similarly uninformative is the classic statement of illegality in the United States: Unlawful monopolization consists of "(1) the possession of monopoly power in the relevant market and (2) the willful acquisition or maintenance of that power as distinguished from growth or development as a consequence of a superior product, business acumen, or historic accident."[7] The US Federal Trade Commission can challenge "unfair methods of competition," but in most cases the commission interprets that language to mean the same thing as the Sherman Act.

The law in Europe offers more detail but still raises more questions than answers. Article 102 (formerly Article 82) of the Treaty on the Functioning of the European Union declares: "Any abuse by one or more undertakings of a dominant position within the internal market or in a substantial part of it shall be prohibited as incompatible with the internal market in so far as it may affect trade between Member States." And then it offers not especially helpful examples of abuse.[8] Many other countries, including Brazil, China, India, Israel, Japan, Mexico, Russia, South Africa, and South Korea, similarly prohibit abuse of a dominant position. But what is abuse of a dominant position? This isn't clear.

PRACTICAL REALITIES

Since the law governing anticompetitive behavior is fairly gray, it is helpful to look at some of the practical realities so that you can make informed decisions when formulating a defense plan.

COMPETITION LAW INVOLVES CIVIL LIABILITY, NOT CRIMINAL LIABILITY

First, and most important, monopolization/abuse of dominance competition law is almost entirely a matter of civil, not criminal, liability. Criminal penalties are reserved for the most egregious of competition violations: cartels, price fixing, horizontal market allocation, and bid rigging. The United States famously enforces this type of antitrust violation with criminal penalties, including jail time, as do a slowly increasing number of countries including Australia, Ireland and the United Kingdom. In the aggregate, the world competition community has agreed that the most serious violations involve agreements between companies, rather than the conduct of a single firm. Single-firm conduct is almost always a lesser offense, with less moral opprobrium and lesser penalties.

This is not to say that civil liability is necessarily trivial. The financial costs may be significant indeed. The European Commission fined Intel €1.06 billion in 2009 for what it saw as improper rebate practices (Intel appealed), and Microsoft paid €497 million in 2004, also for alleged abuses of dominance. The US antitrust agencies don't usually levy civil fines, but any meaningful monopoly case is virtually certain to be followed by a wave of private legal actions with potentially large damage awards. The famous Microsoft antitrust case resulted only in a court order—otherwise known as prospective "injunctive relief"—but thereafter Microsoft faced lawsuits in all or almost all 50 states. And all of this legal maneuvering requires paying antitrust lawyers at quite lofty rates.

Moreover, the real cost of these suits is often not measured in dollars or euros but in time, distraction, and constraint. When Bill Gates was preparing to be deposed and thinking about the litigation, he was *not* thinking about how best to move Microsoft forward. Ironically, pundits have long speculated about whether Microsoft was able to *become* Microsoft because IBM was immersed in its own legendary antitrust case during Microsoft's rise, and some have wondered whether Google was able to become Google because Microsoft itself was distracted. Now Google, facing its own antitrust challenges, is forced to consult antitrust lawyers as well as engineers as it plans various strategic moves. Might someone else step in to fill the void while Google is otherwise occupied? Court orders constrain companies, but so does the distraction of simple scrutiny.

The other real cost is in reputation. Once legal enforcers decide that a company is a bad actor, they subsequently take this into account. A company known to act maliciously to harm consumers will face more scrutiny when attempting to win approval for a merger than another company might face. A complaint about a "known" bad actor will receive more credence than the same complaint about a company with a better reputation. Reputations change, of course—but they matter.

YOU HAVE A PROBLEM ONLY IF YOU ATTRACT ATTENTION

Whereas substantial mergers have to be notified to one or (usually) multiple governments, other conduct normally does not. Bring out a new brand, lower a price, flood the market, launch an ad campaign, bad-mouth a competitor—none of that requires action by or attention from an antitrust/competition enforcer. It may or may not be secret, but there is a difference between just being not secret and causing enforcers to take notice. Most of the defensive conduct discussed in this book does not necessarily require notice to or approval from any governmental body.

This means that to calculate the risk, you must examine the likelihood that your actions will attract serious scrutiny. Action discussed in detail on the front page of the *Washington Post* or the *Financial Times* is considerably more risky than action that goes unmentioned in the press. Action that harms a company disinclined to involve the government is less risky than similar action that harms a politically well-connected firm that won't hesitate to lobby effectively for relief. Government antitrust/competition agencies universally try to "do the right thing," but if politically powerful forces are calling for action, the "right thing" surely requires attention to the issue. And, conversely, if no government agency focuses on some activity, well, there won't be a government challenge. A private party could sue in the United States, but only if there is motivation to bring the suit; private antitrust litigation is markedly less common elsewhere.

In addition, there are very few government monopoly or abuse of dominance cases. One of the two US federal antitrust agencies, the Department of Justice Antitrust Division, filed not a single monopoly case during fiscal years 2001–2010,[9] and it filed only one in fiscal year 2011. The other US antitrust agency, the Federal Trade Commission, files only a handful cases per year. Foreign enforcers similarly file few cases. The vast bulk of government antitrust and competition cases involve challenges to mergers or cartels. The point is not that there is no legal risk—there are several government cases each year as well as scores of private US cases—but that concerns about litigation risks should be seen in context.

ANTITRUST LAWS ARE DIRECTED AT SINGLE FIRMS ONLY IF THEY HAVE MARKET POWER OR DOMINANCE

If you didn't work for a firm with a certain amount of market dominance, you probably would not be reading this book. But it's important to remember that antitrust and competition laws are overwhelmingly directed at collective actions. Without some kind of an agreement, whether to merge and to take coordinated business action, there is rarely a role for antitrust or competition law—and if a single firm lacks market power and dominance, antitrust has nothing to say about unilateral actions. At one time General Motors had to devote significant time to making sure it did not violate the monopoly laws, but those days are (unfortunately for long-time GM shareholders) long past.

Specifically, the Sherman Act Section 2 bars "monopolization" and "attempts to monopolize." "Monopoly power" has been defined as "the power to control prices or exclude competition."[10] It also has been described as the power to charge substantially above the competitive price levels for a significant period of time. In practical terms, plaintiffs are usually required to define a product and geographic market and show that the defendant has a very high market share, such as 70 percent. Anything less than 50 percent is likely to lead to a quick exit from a US court. The offense of "attempt to monopolize" requires, among other things, proof of a "dangerous probability" of achieving monopoly power. Here, too, defendants can win quick exits if market shares are too low, for example, 30 percent or perhaps even 40 percent. And apart from low market share, defendants can win by proving that entry is easy, demand is elastic, or there are other reasons why consumers cannot be exploited.

Nations other than the United States, too, are concerned principally with coordinated behavior and mergers, but the threshold for concern about single-firm behavior is lower than in the United States. This can be seen partly in the wording of legal statutes that address dominance rather than monopolization. In the EU, "dominance" is defined "as a position of economic strength enjoyed by an undertaking [a business], which enables it to prevent effective competition being maintained on a relevant market, by affording it the power to behave to an appreciable extent independently of its competitors, its customers and ultimately of consumers."[11] In theory, the European Commission may challenge "collective dominance" by two or more firms, but this rarely happens. Dominance is not likely to be found where market shares are below 40 percent, but unlike in the United States, in Europe plaintiffs usually don't have to prove extremely high market shares. Easy entry can prevent liability, but the defendant firm's own conduct can be seen to create barriers to entry; this is not the US approach.

Regardless of whether a plaintiff has to prove a very high market share (United States) or just a substantial share (most other countries), it obviously matters how the court defines a product and geographic market. In a way, branded soft drinks compete with milk, coffee, juice, and tap water, and if the "market" included all beverages, even Coca-Cola would have a modest market share. Enforcers commonly think in terms of the approach used to evaluate mergers, which asks whether a sufficient number of consumers would switch products in response to a small but significant and nontransitory price increase. This approach is analytically imperfect when considering an alleged monopoly— maybe consumers would switch in response to an increase, but only because the product is already priced at a monopoly level—but the approach often proves helpful in analysis. If competitors and consumers view the market as broad, it is likely to be found to be broad. And if that means that a firm's market share is modest, the firm is not likely to be unduly troubled by a monopolization/dominance challenge.

From a planning perspective, the problem is that you cannot always be sure in advance how a market will be defined. In the famous *Microsoft* monopolization case, the market was found to be Intel-compatible operating systems, worldwide, thus excluding Apple and browsers. In an FTC merger challenge, Staples and Office Depot were found to compete in a market for office superstores that excluded Target, Wal-Mart, local stationery stores, etc. A more broadly defined market obviously reduces the chance that monopoly power or dominance will be found. One cautionary note: although by no means legally conclusive, it is never helpful to an antitrust/competition defense to have company officials freely tossing around words like "market" and "dominate." Be careful what you write down or type in an e-mail.

ENFORCERS TRY TO AVOID INTERFERING WITH EFFICIENCY AND INNOVATION

At least in theory, no antitrust enforcer wants to interfere with innovation and increased efficiency and consumer welfare. Build a better mousetrap, and you won't break any laws. No matter how anticompetitive your intent—"we plan to drive our last remaining competitor into the sea and then raise prices to the ceiling!"—if your actions are legitimate, all will be well. No matter your intent, if you proceed by building the best product or providing the best service, no enforcer would want to challenge you.

As the US Supreme Court stated in *Verizon Communications v. Law Offices of Curtis V. Trinko, LLP,* "[t]he mere possession of monopoly power, and the concomitant charging of monopoly prices, is not only not unlawful; it is an important element of the free-market system.... To safeguard the incentive to innovate, the possession of monopoly power will not be found unlawful unless it is accompanied by an element of anticompetitive *conduct.*"[12] The trick is to determine what conduct, viewed after the fact with perfect hindsight, will be found to have been anticompetitive. But firms are always free to point up legitimate business justifications.

Countries other than the United States also consider justifications. The European Commission explicitly recognizes this, but adds that a dominant firm would have to show efficiencies (such as improved quality or reduced costs), show that there were no less competitive alternatives, show that the benefits outweigh the harms, and show that the challenged conduct did not remove most or all sources of competition. Depending on how they are applied, these can be quite challenging standards—but they provide talking points about possible justifications.

THERE ARE OTHER LAWS

Courts limit antitrust's reach in part because questionable conduct that harms a rival could be subject to challenge under a host of laws beyond antitrust/competition laws. Obvious examples would include business tort/commercial wrong litigation, advertising law, trade law, intellectual property law—it is a long list. Defense lawyers point to these options to argue against expanding the reach of competition laws, which can be a comfort. It is also a caution, of course, and we mention it in part so you don't forget that there's more in play than just competition law. The best way to steer clear of legal issues is to work closely with your legal team.

LAWFUL CONDUCT

So what kind of conduct can turn a lawful monopoly into unlawful monopolization (or be sufficiently predatory to support the attempted monopoly offense)? What constitutes an abuse of a dominant position? There is no simple answer.

As the court in the famous *Microsoft* monopolization case explained: "Whether any particular act of a monopolist is exclusionary, rather than merely a form of vigorous competition, can be difficult to discern: the means of illicit exclusion, like the means of legitimate competition, are myriad. The challenge for an antitrust court lies in stating a general rule for distinguishing between exclusionary acts, which reduce social welfare, and competitive acts, which increase it."[13] Or, as the same court said three years earlier, "'Anticompetitive conduct' can come in too many different forms, and is too dependent upon context, for any court or commentator ever to have enumerated all the varieties."[14]

The search for a single, workable test has thus far eluded competition scholars and enforcers, although not for want of trying. For a time the United States Department of Justice advanced a "no economic sense" test, condemning only those few actions that would make no sense but for their ability to lessen competition and harm rivals. But that time has passed, and today the Justice Department and the FTC are slightly more aggressive. The leading US antitrust treatise uses a balancing test, defining exclusionary conduct as acts that "(a) are reasonably capable of creating, enlarging, or prolonging monopoly power by impairing the opportunities of rivals; and (b) that either (b.1) do not benefit consumers at all, or (b.2) are unnecessary for the particular consumer benefits that the acts produce, or (b.3) produce harms disproportionate to the resulting benefits."[15]

Guidance from the European Commission explains that it is concerned about "anti-competitive foreclosure" where "effective access of actual or potential competitors to supplies or markets is hampered or eliminated as a result of the conduct of the dominant undertaking [firm] whereby the dominant undertaking is likely to be in a position to profitably increase prices to the detriment of consumers."[16] EC Guidelines set forth that when the commission is reviewing allegedly exclusionary conduct, it considers a long list of factors, including:

- "the position of the dominant undertaking"
- "the conditions on the relevant market"
- "the position of the dominant undertaking's competitors"
- "the position of the customers or input suppliers"
- "the extent of the allegedly abusive conduct"
- "possible evidence of actual foreclosure"
- "direct evidence of any exclusionary strategy."[17]

What that list does not provide, of course, is a clear, simple test.

One conceivably important distinction between the United States and most of the rest of the world is that US antitrust law condemns only conduct that is exclusionary and not conduct that is exploitative. Under US law (and ignoring the role of politics, public relations, and ethical constraints on defensive efforts), there is nothing legally wrong with charging a monopoly price. Europe and many other jurisdictions, by contrast, are concerned to some limited extent with exploitation as well as with exclusion. At least in theory and according to government language, directly exploiting consumers by, for instance, charging excessively high prices can be unlawful in many countries.[18] But in truth such cases are sufficiently rare that they do not merit more than brief acknowledgment here.

QUESTIONABLE PRACTICES

If no single test distinguishes hard competition from unlawfully exclusionary conduct, how can you determine what not to do in a defensive effort? At this point, experts are reduced to proceeding practice by practice. Slowly we are developing an understanding of what kind of aggressive pricing, refusals to supply, exclusive dealing, and so on are lawful in various jurisdictions. This isn't ideal, perhaps, but that is where we are.

Let's briefly examine predatory pricing, bundled pricing, tying, exclusive dealing, loyalty rebates, refusals to deal, use of government, and questionable tactics.

PREDATORY PRICING

It is almost impossible to price too low in the United States. So-called predatory pricing is unlawful only when it is below marginal or average variable cost (courts use different measures) *and* there is a dangerous probability of "recoupment," meaning that the dominant firm is likely to earn back all sacrificed revenues with interest by charging sustained supracompetitive prices. Defendants point to ease of entry or relatively modest market shares and persuade judges to toss cases out of court. From time to time there is some grumbling about the this law, but thus far the substance has withstood attack, and this does not seem likely to change. Canada, too, requires a showing of recoupment.

Other countries are slightly more aggressive, in particular by not emphasizing the importance of proving recoupment. The European Commission asks whether an equally efficient competitor is prevented from competing; it makes this determination by examining whether there is below-cost pricing (usually considering "average avoidable cost" or "long-run average incremental cost"). Where pricing *is* below cost and could foreclose an equally efficient competitor, then the commission will consider this along with other relevant factors to decide whether to intervene. And case law would seem to allow a challenge even to pricing merely below average total cost where it is "part of a plan for eliminating a competitor."[19]

BUNDLED PRICING

Although the law is in flux, dominant firms have a little less flexibility when it comes to bundled pricing, in which a discount depends on purchasing multiple products. In one well-known case, this issue arose when 3M faced competition in supplying 3M-produced private label tape. 3M responded by offering substantial discounts keyed to purchases of a total bundle of 3M products, which included both 3M's branded tape and its house-brand tape. The court found that the substantial discounts made it impossible for a rival not offering the same array of products to compete and said there was evidence that 3M intended first to lessen the role of private label tape and then raise prices. Although that particular lawsuit was resolved (against 3M), the law did not come away with a clear standard to apply to bundled discounts—and, of course, bundled pricing is very common. The leading US approach today is the "discount attribution" rule, where one allocates the entire discount to the competitive product(s) and then determines whether pricing would be below average variable cost.[20] The European Commission asks whether the bundled rebate is so large that "equally efficient competitors offering only some of the components cannot compete."[21] This usually means asking whether the incremental price for the second product is above the long-run average incremental cost while also considering justifications and efficiencies. The Korean Fair Trade Commission has also found bundling to be an abuse of a dominant position. All enforcers, however, recognize that bundled pricing is a common and normally procompetitive practice.

TYING

"Tying," where the purchase of one product is conditioned on another, can be similar to bundling. In the United States, tying is rarely challenged as monopolization although any agreement that is unreasonably anticompetitive could be attacked. The European Commission has condemned tying as an abuse of dominance, notably in the 2007 *Microsoft* case. The commission is particularly concerned about longer lasting ties and ties that allow for price increases or make entry more difficult. Other countries, such as Canada and India, specifically ban certain tying practices.

EXCLUSIVE DEALING

Exclusive dealing (requiring a distributor or retailer not to carry competing brands) is another frequently practiced tactic that can be procompetitive and clearly lawful. There are legitimate reasons to want a retailer not to stock rival brands. In one example, a hearing aid company's advertising drove potential customers to its dealers to have their hearing tested, and the firm quite reasonably did not want those customers steered to rival models that had not born the advertising expense. But where exclusive arrangements have made access to the market notably harder, without any efficiency benefit, they have been condemned.[22] The European Commission has explained that an important factor is the ability of a rival firm to compete—for instance, if there are capacity constraints or a "must stock" item involved. Both Europe and Japan have condemned exclusive arrangements that were practical rather than contractual, such as when a dominant firm in frozen foods might restrict the use of a display freezer it supplied. Short-term arrangements are easier to justify than long-term ones.

LOYALTY REBATES

Loyalty rebates have been met with varying levels of concern in different parts of the world. Rebates can include volume discounts, discounts for specified percentage shares of purchases, or retroactive rebates based on share of purchases (for example, attaining the 90 percent mark for purchases of a product from the dominant supplier will result in a rebate for all of that year's purchases). The leading US case treats these types of rebates as just another form or aggressive pricing and allows them unless they are below an appropriate measure of cost and result in a dangerous probability of recoupment.[23]

More recently, US enforcers have shown greater concern about the practice and have started to regard it as potentially equivalent to exclusive dealing. And Europe and other jurisdictions view loyalty rebates with much greater skepticism. The European Commission has shown special concern about substantial retroactive rebates that make it difficult for rivals to compete for what the commission views as the "contestable" part of the business. More specifically, the commission tries to determine whether a dominant firm's "effective price"— the normal price minus the loyalty rebate to be lost by switching—is below its "average avoidable cost" (similar to average variable cost).[24]

REFUSALS TO DEAL

The United States has been quite strong in its recognition of even a dominant firm's freedom to choose the parties with which to do business. It would be very unusual for a firm to lose a refusal to deal case in the United States. One notable exception is the 1985 Supreme Court case of *Aspen Skiing Co. v. Aspen Highlands Skiing Corp.*[25] In this case, the dominant ski area ended a two-area lift ticket and went so far as to refuse to accept cash-equivalent payments for lift tickets, solely to frustrate its rival's attempt to put together an alternative package. Since there had been successful joint marketing, and this was such a clear incursion of a short-run loss for long-run lessening of competition, it was condemned. But ever since then the case has stood as the exception, not the rule.

In contrast, the freedom to refuse to deal is a somewhat less hallowed concept in other parts of the world. The European Commission considers whether the product or service at issue is "objectively necessary" to be able to compete and whether the refusal is likely to eliminate effective competition and lead to harm for consumers.[26] The commission is likely to be more troubled by interruption of supply than refusal to initiate supply. Even intellectual property can be the basis for a refusal to deal challenge in an exceptional situation.[27] The law elsewhere in the world continues to evolve. For instance, China prohibits refusals to sell "without justification," but what this means in practice remains to be seen.

The above examples refer to relatively "pure" refusals to sell. If a seller refuses to sell unless the buyer promises not to buy from anyone else, that would be exclusive dealing, not a simple refusal to deal. A threat by a monopolist to cut off any seller or customer who patronizes a new rival also could raise exclusive-dealing-type issues.[28]

What if a dominant firm operates at two levels—say, wholesale and retail— with rivals at the second level dependent upon it for supply? Can it raise its wholesale price while keeping its retail price constant, thus "squeezing" any rival trying to compete at the retail (only) level? In the United States, courts are unlikely to act against this unless they were to conclude that the pricing was predatory or there was a duty to deal with the rival, neither of which is very likely.[29] Elsewhere the matter is less clear. In particular, two recent decisions of the European Court of Justice have recognized price squeezes as potential stand-alone violations.[30] Where the pricing is such that it does not allow an equally efficient competitor to compete in the second market, this could be an abuse of dominance. Such cases continue to be unusual, but not nearly as hard to imagine overseas as in the United States. And the rest of the world follows Europe more than the United States.

(MIS)USE OF GOVERNMENT REGULATION AND SELF-REGULATION

Among the more effective ways to block rivals is to use government restrictions such as zoning, licensing, and intellectual property laws. Antitrust/competition lawyers view these as different from other questionable practices in two ways. They can be seen as less vulnerable to challenge because, after all, the dominant firm is merely exercising its rights to petition the government. If harm occurs, the argument goes, it is caused by the government, not the dominant firm, and dominant firms have the same rights to petition as others firms. On the other hand, misuse of government can be seen as making companies *more* vulnerable to antitrust/competition challenges because it is seen as more plausibly anticompetitive and more likely to harm consumers. Misuse of government has been characterized as "cheap exclusion," which is inexpensive for the dominant firm and unlikely to benefit consumers and thus of greater concern to enforcers. As a general matter, genuine attempts to influence governments, even for purely anticompetitive purposes, are protected. Questionable tactics designed to influence government also can enjoy immunity, but here the lines can be difficult to draw.[31]

Most alleged harm stemming from intellectual property laws is not subject to successful challenge under competition laws. Intellectual property laws offer the promise of lessened competition as the carrot to inspire innovation, and there is nothing unlawful about enjoying the fruits of that government-granted right to exclude. Nor is it common that use of intellectual property—for instance, through licensing—results in the finding of a violation. The most important exception to this pattern is that the enforcement of a fraudulently obtained patent can easily be part of a successful competition law challenge.[32]

The other pattern frequently associated with successful challenges concerns abuse of a standard-setting organization. Were a dominant firm to deceive a standard-setting organization and trick it into requiring use of the dominant firm's patented technology, for instance, that could possibly form part of a successful competition challenge. Acquisitions of patents, just as those of any other asset, also can be subject to competition review. Recently, the European Commission has been expressing concern about using collections of patents to "hold up" an industry and threaten to ban products, but it is too early to tell where this will go.

OTHER QUESTIONABLE TACTICS

As noted above, there are many ways to try to exclude, and most any of them can be questioned under the antitrust/competition laws. Most, however, will be found to be lawful. Introduce a new product? Hire away a key employee? Run arguably misleading advertising? All are probably lawful. Even dominant firms are allowed to compete—hard and aggressively—on the merits. On the other hand, there *are* limits. When a dominant firm embarked on a campaign to keep out rivals by physically removing and destroying its display racks, which were critical to competition, a jury found this action to have crossed the line.[33] So also it would be hard to justify a dominant firm's hiring away a key employee and paying him or her to retire and promise never to work for a rival.

DEALING WITH LEGAL UNCERTAINTY

That leaves us, unfortunately, where we started, with some uncertainty— the kind of uncertainty that is inevitable in a system with general standards enforced by fallible humans. It bears repeating that the above long list of conduct that could be subject to challenge in one jurisdiction or another does not mean that successful monopoly or abuse of dominance cases are common. Far from it: they are relatively rare. Coordinated, not unilateral, conduct is at the core of competition law. Indeed, one could argue that standards are vague precisely because successful challenges are so rare. The above list, and, indeed, this chapter, does not mean to prohibit anything; rather, it merely raises red flags of caution where it would be wise to consider whether to consult expert counsel.

The best advice is probably to use some common sense. Don't use flamboyant rhetoric. Avoid militaristic language and analogies. Always have a procompetitive story to tell, and if there really isn't any way to describe your conduct as helping consumers, or improving quality, or lowering costs, or encouraging innovation, or anything else you would be comfortable mentioning to an enforcement official, think at least twice before proceeding. Avoid unnecessary publicity. Don't make unnecessary enemies. Nurture a reputation as a reasonable firm and a good corporate citizen. And do all this while also following the advice of the other chapters of this book.

Just don't let anyone see you reading it.

ACKNOWLEDGMENTS

MANY PEOPLE HELPED WITH THIS book; my big problem is that it is difficult to thank them all.

I am in particular debt to my brother, Stephen Calkins, for supporting this project and contributing a chapter. This topic is a delicate one; I am grateful that he agreed to share his perspective. He wrote his chapter while relocating from Detroit to Dublin; I know it was not easy for him to find the time.

I spoke with many marketing executives while researching this topic, and they provided invaluable insights. It simply would not have been possible to create the book without their ideas and experiences; defensive strategy is a shadowy world. John Anton, Wilder Baker, David Bardach, Carter Cast, Tom Cutler, Dallas Diggs, Doug Gluck, Paul Groundwater, Brian Kelly, Rick Lenny, Sergio Pereira, Dennis Powell, Gary Rawlings, Mark Shapiro, Amy Shulman, Andrew Stein, Dave Tuchler, David Vinjamuri, James Weldon, Steve Yanovsky, and many others all provided input. Roland Jacobs, Art Middlebrooks, Mike Marasco, and Greg Wozniak provided particularly notable support. I connected with many of these executives through the Marketing Executives Networking Group (MENG). I am lucky to be part of this group of talented professionals.

My students at Northwestern University's Kellogg School of Management and at Kellogg's partner schools around the world contributed substantially to this project. They challenged my thinking and shared their experiences. Teaching these gifted individuals is a challenge and a joy. A few students made particularly notable contributions, including Dave Brenner, Daniel Young, Guillermo Olivera Salcedo, and Sharam Sadeghi.

My faculty colleagues at the Kellogg School of Management helped develop these concepts, especially the professors who teach the marketing strategy course with me: Greg Carpenter, Lakshman Krishnamurthi, and Julie Hennessy.

Professors Eric Anderson, Jim Anderson, Adam Galinsky, Kent Grayson, Phil Kotler, Eric Leininger, Keith Murnighan, Derek Rucker, Bob Schieffer, Brian Sternthal, and Alice Tybout also helped me refine my thinking. Professor Holger Ernst, at WHU, Otto Beisheim School of Management, provided useful input on innovation and creativity. Subarna Ranjit, my administrator, helps me keep things moving forward every day. My research associates, Dhruv Koul and Maria Turner, helped me gather and make sense of the cases discussed in this book. Dean Dipak Jain, now at INSEAD, supported my teaching and research at Kellogg for many years. I am grateful to Kellogg Dean Sally Blount for her encouragement and inspiration.

The team at Palgrave Macmillan has been supportive throughout this project. Laurie Harting, in particular, provided the spark that got this book moving forward and has been encouraging during the writing process. My agent, David Hale Smith, provided valuable guidance and helped make this book happen.

This is the third time I've worked with Patty Dowd Schmitz on a book project. She went through every chapter several times and provided terrific advice and guidance; she challenged my thinking, helped with the overall structure, provided good ideas, and significantly improved the copy.

Finally, I give special thanks to my parents, Evan and Virginia Calkins, for teaching me the joy of tackling projects and to my family, Carol, Claire, Charlie, and Anna, for their encouragement and good cheer. They make life meaningful and fun.

NOTES

1 INTRODUCTION

1. Gary Hamel, "Reinventing the Technology of Human Accomplishment," University of Phoenix Distinguished Guest Video Lecture Series, accessed March 12, 2012, on www.youtube.com/watch?v=aodjgkv65MM.
2. Reddi-wip print ad.
3. Bill Walsh with Steve Jamison and Craig Walsh, *The Score Takes Care of Itself* (New York: Portfolio/Penguin, 2009), 83.
4. Michael Porter, "The Five Competitive Forces that Shape Strategy," *Harvard Business Review* 86, no. 1 (January 2008): 25.
5. Greg, Farrell, "Return of the Barista-in-Chief," *Financial Times,* March 22, 2010, 12.
6. Adam Lashinsky, "Palm Fights Back (Against Apple)," *Fortune*, June 8, 2009, 88.
7. Walsh, 209.
8. Quote retrieved from http://www.great-quotes.com/quote/139616, last accessed March 12, 2012.
9. BBC documentary, *40 Minutes,* accessed March 12, 2012, on www.youtube.com /watch?v=Dr0cQ84VgQA&feature=related.
10. Jack Trout, *Trout on Strategy* (New York: McGraw-Hill, 2004), 57.
11. Steve Yanovsky, interview, February 7, 2012.
12. Charles Forelle and Don Clark, "Intel Fine Jolts Tech Sector," *The Wall Street Journal*, May 14, 2009, 1.

2 THE THREAT

1. Martin Peers and Nick Wingfield, "Blockbuster Set to Offer Movies by Mail," *The Wall Street Journal*, February 11, 2004, D1.
2. Blockbuster 2008 Annual Report, 4.
3. Alyssa Abkowitz, "The Movie Man," *Fortune,* February 2, 2009, 24
4. Stephen Gandel, "How Blockbuster Failed at Failing," *Time*, Sunday, October 17, 2010, www.time.com/time/magazine/article/0,9171,2022624,00.html, last accessed March 12, 2012.
5. John Anton, presentation at Kellogg School of Management, November 4, 2011.
6. Andrew Grove, *Only the Paranoid Survive* (New York: Crown Business, 1999), 3.

7. Laura Mazur and Louella Miles, *Conversations with Marketing Masters* (New York: Wiley, 2007), 20.
8. Brewer Hamish, "Delivering Real Results for More Demanding Customers," *NRF Stores,* www.jda.com/file_bin/news/JDA_Brewer_STORES.pdf, last accessed March 12, 2012.
9. Ilya Gutlin, interview, March 3, 2011.
10. *Forbes,* "The World's Billionaires," www.forbes.com/wealth/billionaires, last accessed March 12, 2012.
11. Jack Trout, *Trout on Strategy* (New York: McGraw-Hill, 2004), 61.
12. Al Ries, "Want to Expand Your Business? You Should Narrow Your Focus," *Advertising Age,* May 9, 2011, 15.
13. Jack Neff, "P+G Plots Growth Path through Services," *Advertising Age*, March 22, 2010, 22.
14. Bradford C. Kirk, *Lessons from a Chief Marketing Officer* (New York: McGraw-Hill, 2003), 153.
15. Luke Johnson, "There is Only One Way to be a Success," *Financial Times,* August 10, 2011, 8.
16. Trout, *Trout on Strategy,* 132.
17. Grove, *Only the Paranoid Survive,* 3.

3   THE FINANCIAL CHALLENGE

1. Bob Parsons Blog, Episode 47, http://www.bobparsons.me/dat/articles/captions/_404_CC.BP.Blog47.txt, last accessed May 24, 2012.
2. Charlie Rose, "Charlie Rose Talks to Reed Hastings," *Bloomberg Businessweek,* May 9–15, 2011, 26.
3. Michael E. Porter, *Competitive Strategy* (New York: The Free Press, 1980), 99.
4. Paul Groundwater, interview, July 2, 2010.
5. Andrea Felsted, "All Lined Up," *Financial Times*, January 6, 2012, 7.
6. BBC Documentary, *40 Minutes,* www.youtube.com/watch?v=glxNi1esupU&feature=related, last accessed March 12, 2012.
7. BBC documentary, *40 Minutes,* www.youtube.com/watch?v=Dr0cQ84VgQA&feature=related, last accessed March 12, 2012.

4   KNOW YOUR ENEMY

1. Willie Pietersen, *Reinventing Strategy* (New York: Wiley, 2002), 82.
2. Kevin P. Coyne and John Horn, "Predicting Your Competitor's Reaction," *Harvard Business Review* 87, no. 4 (April 2009): 96.
3. Keith Johnson, "What Kind of Game is China Playing?" *The Wall Street Journal,* June 11–12, 2011, C3.
4. Paul Groundwater, interview, July 2, 2010.
5. David Barboza, "One Entrepreneur's Rival in China: The State," *The New York Times,* December 8, 2011, 1.
6. Sun Tzu, *The Art of War,* new translation by Ralph D. Sawyer (New York: Fall River Press, 1994), 232.
7. Coyne and Horn, 97.

5   COMPETITIVE INTELLIGENCE

1. Andy Serwer, "P&G's Covert Operation," *Fortune*, September 17, 2001, http://
   money.cnn.com/magazines/fortune/fortune_archive/2001/09/17/310274/index
   .htm, last accessed March 13, 2012.
2. Fred Vogelstein, "Search and Destroy," *Fortune,* May 2, 2005, 74.
3. Jonatha Schwartz, "If You Want to Lead, Blog," *Harvard Business Review* 83, no.
   10 (November 2005): 30.
4. Emma Hall, "Lagnado Adds a Strong Shot of Creativity to Spirits Category,"
   Advertising Age 82, no. 24 (June 13, 2011): 30.
5. "Israeli Raid Called Off After Facebook Slip," *USA Today*, March 5, 2011, 4A.
6. Randy Hlavac, "Social Monitoring: 'Eavesdrop' on your High Value Markets –
   and your Competitors – In the Social Web," Marketing Executives Networking
   Group webinar, November 2, 2011.
7. Anonymous, "Confessions of a Corporate Spy," *Details,* December 2009, 77.
8. H. Keith Melton, "What? Me, Worry?" *Harvard Business Review,* 83, no. 10
   (November 2005): 26,
9. Ibid.
10. Ariel Kaminer, "In-Flight Entertainment," *The New York Times Magazine,* October
    23, 2011, 24.
11. Ameet Sachdev, "P&G Admits Unilever Garbage Search," *The Chicago Tri-
    bune,* September 1, 2001, http://articles.chicagotribune.com/2001–09–01/busi
    ness/0109010181_1_unilever-hair-care-dumpster, last accessed March 13, 2012.
12. Jack Welch with John A. Byrne, *Jack: Straight from the Gut* (New York: Hatchette
    Book Group, 2001), 346.
13. Ibid.
14. Strategy and Competitive Intelligence Professionals website, www.scip.org/resources
    /content.cfm?itemnumber=601&navItemNumber=533, last accessed January 3, 2012.
15. Christopher Hinton, "Marsh & McLennan Sells Kroll for $1.13 Billion," *Market-
    watch,* June 7, 2010, http://www.marketwatch.com/story/marsh-mclennas-sells-
    kroll-unit-for-13-billion-2010–06–07, last accessed March 13, 2012.
16. Serwer, "P&G's Covert Operation."

6   THE KEY QUESTION

1. The Japan Lawletter, "US Imposed 45% Tariff on Imported Motorcycles," July–
   August 1983,: www.japanlaw.info/lawletter/july83/ase.htm, last accessed March 13,
   2012.
2. Roger L. Martin, "Don't Get Blinded by the Numbers," *Harvard Business Review*
   89, no. 3 (March 2011): 38.
3. Paul Groundwater, interview, July 2, 2010
4. Mike Krzyzewski with Donald T. Phillips, *Leading with the Heart* (New York:
   Business Plus, 2000), 103.
5. Michael E. Porter and Mark R. Kramer, "The Five Competitive Forces that Shape
   Strategy," *Harvard Business Review* 84, no. 12 (December 2006).
6. Beth Kowitt, "The Man Powering up GE," *Fortune,* December 26, 2011, 65.
7. Jim Collins and Jerry I. Porras, *Built to Last* (New York: HarperCollins,
   2002), 188.

8. Ron Adner and Daniel C. Snow, "Bold Retreat: A New Strategy for Old Technologies," *Harvard Business Review* 88, no. 3 (March 2010): 80.

9. Spencer E. Ante, "Avoiding Innovation's Terrible Toll," *The Wall Street Journal*, January 7–8, 2012, B2.

10. Clayton Christensen, "How Will You Measure Your Life?" *Harvard Business Review* 88, no. 7 (July–August 2010): 50.

11. Andrew Grove, *Only the Paranoid Survive* (New York: Crown Business, 1999), 117.

12. Bill Walsh with Steve Jamison and Craig Walsh, *The Score Takes Care of Itself* (New York: Portfolio/Penguin, 2009), 46.

13. Clayton Christensen, *The Innovator's Dilemma* (New York: HarperCollins, 2000), 226.

14. Dan Ariely, "Is it Irrational to Give Holiday Gifts?" *The Wall Street Journal*, December 17–18, 2011, C3.

15. Stephen Denny, *Killing Giants* (New York: Portfolio/Penguin, 2011), 223.

16. Kevin P. Coyne and John Horn, "Predicting Your Competitor's Reaction," *Harvard Business Review* 87, no. 4 (April 2009): 97.

17. Allstate website, www.allstate.com/about.aspx, last accessed January 5, 2012.

18. Paul Groundwater, interview.

19. Jason Zweig, "Ignoring the Yes-Man in Your Head," *The Wall Street Journal*, November 14–15, 2009, B1.

20. Keith J. Murnighan, *The Art of High-Stakes Decision Making* (New York: Wiley, 2002), 170.

21. P. C. Wason, "On the Failure to Eliminate Hypotheses in a Conceptual Task," *Quarterly Journal of Psychology* 12 (December 1960): 129–40.

22. Clifford R. Mynatt, Michael E. Doherty, and Ryan D. Tweney, "Confirmation Bias in a Simulated Research Environment: An Experimental Study of Scientific Inference," *Quarterly Journal of Experimental Psychology* 92, no. 1 (1977): 85–95.

23. Martin A. Tolcott, F. Freeman Marvin, and Paul E. Lehner, "Expert Decision Making in Evolving Situation," *IEEE Transactions on Systems, Man and Cybernetics* 39, no. 3 (May/June 1989): 606–15.

24. James Anderson, presentation at the Kellogg School of Management, March 21, 2011.

25. Gary Rivlin, "The Problem with Microsoft," *Fortune*, April 11, 2011, 46.

26. Grove, *Only the Paranoid Survive,* 112.

27. Christensen, *The Innovator's Dilemma,* 228.

28. Lucy Kellaway, "Talk Like a Loser and You Might End up a Winner," *Financial Times*, February 14, 2011, 12.

29. Kellaway, "Talk Like a Loser and You Might End up a Winner," 12.

30. "CEO Wisdom," *Bloomberg Businessweek,* May 30–June 5, 2011, 22.

31. Cameron Anderson and Adam D. Galinsky. "Power, Optimism, and Risk-Taking," *European Journal of Social Psychology* 36, no. 4 (2006): 511–36.

32. Grove, *Only the Paranoid Survive,* 20.

7 PLANNING THE DEFENSE

1. Dallas Diggs, interview, February 7, 2012.

2. Eric Ryan, presentation, December 7, 2011.

3. Clayton M. Christensen, *The Innovator's Dilemma* (New York: HarperCollins, 2000), 43.

4. Mike Krzyzewski with Donald T. Phillips, *Leading with the Heart* (New York: Business Plus, 2000), 103.
5. Jim Collins, *How the Mighty Fall* (New York: HarperCollins, 2009), 123.
6. Martin Peers, "Colgate Lowers Profit Expectations," *The Wall Street Journal*, September 21, 2004, A3.
7. Collins, 80.

8   STOPPING THE LAUNCH

1. Sun Tzu, *The Art of War*, new translation by Ralph D. Sawyer (New York: Fall River Press, 1994), 177.
2. Joseph T. Hallinan, "Bank One CEO Dimon Finds His Patience Pays Off in the End," *The Wall Street Journal*, January 15, 2004, A10.
3. Becky Yerak, "Washington Mutual Steps Back," *Chicago Tribune*, September 8, 2006, Section 3, 3.
4. Richard Lapper, "Brewers Tap Into South Africa," *Financial Times*, March 31, 2010, 20.
5. Anjali Cordeiro, "P&G Targets India for Expansion Push," *The Wall Street Journal*, June 23, 2010, B6.
6. Jack Neff, "P&G Tests Revival of Eagle Snacks Brand," *Advertising Age,* January 5, 2004, http://adage.com/article/news/p-g-tests-revival-eagle-snacks-brand/97273/, last accessed March 13, 2012.
7. Dave Brenner, interview, June 6, 2011.
8. Neff, "P&G Tests Revival of Eagle Snacks Brand."
9. Oded Shenkar, "Imitation is More Valuable than Innovation," *Harvard Business Review,* April, 2010, 28.
10. Stefan Stern, "The Outsider in a Hurry to Shake Up His Company," *Financial Times*, April 15, 2010, 12.
11. Michael E. Porter, *Competitive Strategy* (New York: The Free Press, 1980), 86.
12. Jeanne Whalen, "Astra Loses Bid to Overturn Fine," *The Wall Street Journal*, July 2, 2010, B4.

9   BLOCKING DISTRIBUTION

1. Paul Groundwater, interview, July 2, 2010.
2. David Kesmodel, "Fight Brews in Craft Beer," *The Wall Street Journal*, April 27, 2011, B8.
3. Nicola Mawson, "South Africa: SAB Pulls Out All Stops to Stay On Top," *AllAfrica*, January 13, 2009, http://allafrica.com/stories/200901130140.html, last accessed March 26, 2012.
4. Carter Cast, interview, June 7, 2011.
5. Don Clark and Kara Scannell, "Parsing Intel's Impact on Dell," *The Wall Street Journal*, June 14, 2010, www.allthingsd.com/20100614/parsing-intels-impact-on-dell/, last accessed January 20, 2012.
6. Robert Berner, "P&G: New and Improved," *Bloomberg Businessweek,* July 7, 2003. http://www.businessweek.com/magazine/content/03_27/b3840001_mz001.htm, last accessed May 25, 2012.

7. Cast, interview.

8. Daniel Young, interview, June 20, 2011.

9. Ann Zimmerman and Timothy W. Martins, "Wal-Mart Tries to Unmask Foes," *The Wall Street Journal*, September 23, 2010, B1.

10. Ann Zimmerman, "Rival Chains Secretly Fund Opposition to Wal-Mart," *The Wall Street Journal,* June 7, 2010, www.online.wsj.com/article/SB1000142405274870487 56045752804142188878150.html, last accessed January 20, 2012.

11. Jorge Fernandez Roncagliolo, "Legally Blondes: The War between 'Cristal' and 'Brahma,'" *The Peruvian Lawyer,* www.theperuvianlawyer.com/?p=20, last accessed February 2, 2012.

12. Daniel Michaels, "Jets Fuel Germany Air Fight," *The Wall Street Journal*, June 9, 2010, B1.

13. Christian Oliver and Kang Buseong, "Seoul Acts to Help Safeguard its Small, Local Businesses," *Financial Times*, August 15, 2011, 14.

14. Jennifer Levitz, "4 out of 5 Dentists Think They Should Whiten Teeth," *The Wall Street Journal*, November 16, 2011, B1.

15. Dexter Roberts, "Closing for Business?" *Bloomberg Business Week,* April 5, 2010, 37.

16. Roberts, 36.

17. John Taglibue, "To Avoid Tariffs, Pasta Makers Come to U.S.," *The New York Times,* March 5, 1998, www.nytimes.com/1998/03/05/business/international-business -to-avoid-tariffs-pasta-makers-come-to-us.html?pagewanted=all&src=pm, last accessed January 19, 2012.

18. Barilla website, retrieved from: www.fundinguniverse.com/company-histories/ Barilla-G-e-R-Fratelli-SpA-Company-History.html, lLast accessed January 19, 2012.

19. Gary Rawlings, interview, February 8, 2012.

10 LIMITING AWARENESS

1. Rich Thomaselli, "Big Pharma Finds Way into Doctors' Pockets," *Ad Age* 76, no. 38 (September 19, 2005), http://adage.com/article/news/big-pharma-finds-doc-tors-pockets/104651/, last accessed March 13, 2012.

2. "Bank One is Bear's 'Presenting Partner,'" *Sports Illustrated,* June 24, 2003, http:// sportsillustrated.cnn.com/football/news/2003/06/24/bears_ap/, last accessed March 13, 2012.

3. Matt Townsend and Holger Elfes, "Adidas' Big Money Defense Against Nike," *Bloomberg Businessweek*, May 17–23, 2010, 22.

4. Gary Rawlings, interview, February 8, 2012.

5. Jonathan Weisman, "Rivals Crowd Romney Kickoff," *The Wall Street Journal*, June 2, 2011, A6.

6. "Perry and the Republican Party," *Financial Times*, August 15, 2011, 6.

7. Jack Trout, *Trout on Strategy* (New York: McGraw-Hill, 2004), 34.

8. Lee Gomes, "Intel Turns to a Stunt as Challenger AMD Beats it to the Market," *The Wall Street Journal*, September 29, 2003.

9. HP Advertisement, *The New York Times,* July 13, 2009, B3.

10. "Judge Denies Pepsi Bid to Block Ads," *The Wall Street Journal,* August 6, 2009, B2.

11   PREVENTING TRIAL

1. Jon Hilkevitch, "New Kid on the Tarmac," *The Chicago Tribune,* May 26, 2011, 25.
2. Hilkevitch, 25.
3. David J. Bryce, Jeffrey H. Dyer, and Nile W. Hatch, "Competing Against Free," *Harvard Business Review* 89, no. 6 (June 2011): 108.
4. Robb Montgomery, "Chicago Sun-Times Ends Red Streak Edition," *Editorsweblog,* December 20, 2005, http://www.editorsweblog.org/newspaper/2005/12/chicago _suntimes_ends_red_stre.php, last accessed March 13, 2012.
5. Stephen Denny, *Killing Giants* (New York: Portfolio/Penguin, 2011), 88.
6. Lucy Kellaway, "Copying is the Mother of all the Best Inventions," *Financial Times,* November 7, 2011, 14.
7. Karen Dillon interview of A. G. Lafley, "I Think of my Failures as a Gift," *Harvard Business Review* 89, no. 4 (April 2011): 87.
8. Thomas Catan, "Gore-Tex Faces Antitrust Probes," *The Wall Street Journal,* June 22, 2011, B2.
9. Janet Morrissey, "Can the Builder of Ticketmaster Now Unseat It?" *The New York Times,* June 12, 2011, 7.
10. Apple presentation, March 2, 2011, www.ebongeek.com/2011/03/05/the-steve-jobs-ipad-2-presentation/, last accessed January 30, 2012.
11. Jeanne Whalen, "Glaxo's HIV-Drug Ads Draw Critics," *The Wall Street Journal,* August 25, 2008, http://online.wsj.com/article/SB121961241070167309 .html?mod=rss_Health&utm_source=feedburner&utm_medium=feed&utm_cam paign=Feed%3A+wsj%2Fxml%2Frss%2F3_7089+%28WSJ.com%3A+Health%29, last accessed March 13, 2012.
12. Tara Parker-Pope and Jonathan Friedland, "Whistle-Blower: P&G Calls the Cops as it Strives to Expand Sales in Latin America," *The Wall Street Journal,* March 20, 1998, A1.
13. Sergio Pereira, interview, March 5, 2012.

12   FIGHTING REPEAT

1. Todd J. Behme, "Walgreens to Buy Drugstore.com," *Chicago Tribune,* March 24, 2011. http://articles.chicagotribune.com/2011–03–24/business/ct-biz-0325-wal greens-drugstore-20110324_1_drugstore-com-chief-executive-greg-wasson-wal greensm, last accessed January 31, 2011.
2. Mintlife blog, "Why Mint.com + Intuit is a Big Idea," September 14, 2009, http:// www.mint.com/blog/updates/why-mint-com-plus-intuit-is-a-big-idea/, last accessed January 31, 2012.
3. Claudia Penteado, "Brazil's Northeast Goes form 'Land of Laziness' to Next China," *Advertising Age* 82, no. 24 (June 13, 2011): 10.
4. Ashlee Vance, "When Its Mainframes are Threatened, I.B.M. Strikes Hard," *International Herald Tribune,* March 23, 2009, 10.
5. Carter Cast, interview, June 7, 2011.
6. Daniel Roberts, "Under Armour Gets Serious," *Fortune,* November 7, 2011, 153.
7. Cast, interview.

8. Jeff Bezos, interviewed by Julia Kirby and Thomas A. Stewart, "The Institutional Yes," *Harvard Business Review* (October 2007): 79.

9. Oded Shenkar, "Imitation is More Valuable Than Innovation," *Harvard Business Review* 88, no. 4 (April 2010): 28.

10. Mike Esterl, "Tropicana Swaps Carton for Carafe," *The Wall Street Journal*, February 17, 2011, B6.

11. Stephanie Thompson, "Kraft Struggles to Find Right Recipe for Meals," *Advertising Age*, 74, no. 23 (June 9, 2003): 4.

12. Max Colchester, "Discounted E-Books Spark Outcry From French Shops," *The Wall Street Journal*, September 24, 2010, B1.

13. James R. Hagerty and Bob Tita, "Whirlpool Accuses Samsung, LG of Dumping Washers," *The Wall Street Journal*, December 30, 2011, http://online.wsj.com/article/SB10001424052970204632204577130483950517346.html, last accessed January 31, 2012.

14. Emily Maltby, "Name Choices Spark Lawsuits," *The Wall Street Journal*, June 24, 2010, B13.

15. MSNBC.com, "Mattel Awarded $100 Million in Bratz Lawsuit," August 27, 2008, http://www.msnbc.msn.com/id/26410627/ns/business-us_business/t/mattel-awarded-million-bratz-lawsuit/, last accessed February 1, 2012.

16. Stephanie Strom, "Trademarks Take on New Importance in Internet Era," *The New York Times*, February 20, 2012, www.nytimes.com/2012/02/21/business/battle-over-pretzel-crisps-shows-value-of-a-brand.html?pagewanted=all, last accessed February 28, 2012.

13   DEFENSE NEVER ENDS

1. Michael E. Porter, *Competitive Strategy* (New York: The Free Press, 1980), 98.

2. Carter Cast, interview, June 7, 2011.

3. MSNBC.com, "Toys"R"Us Acquires High-End FAO Schwarz," May 28, 2009, http://www.msnbc.msn.com/id/30976981/ns/business-retail/t/toys-r-us-acquires-high-end-fao-schwarz/, last accessed January 31, 2012.

4. David Jolly, "In Paris, One Luxury Retailer Is Suspicious of the Intentions of Another," *The New York Times,* November 26, 2010, B3.

5. Norihiko Shirouzu, "Train Makers Rail Against China's High-Speed Designs," *The Wall Street Journal,* November 18, 2010, A20.

6. Andrew Grove, *Only the Paranoid Survive* (New York: Crown Business, 1999), 118.

7. Noted and Quoted, *HBS Alumni Bulletin*, June 2011, 5.

8. David Kesmodel, "Corona Brewer Drinks to Family Business," *The Wall Street Journal*, March 14, 2011, B4.

9. Jim Collins, *How the Mighty Fall* (New York: HarperCollins, 2009), 63.

10. Jim Collins and Jerry I. Porras, *Built to Last* (New York: HarperCollins, 2002), 187.

11. Laura Mazur and Louella Miles, *Conversations with Marketing Masters* (New York: Wiley, 2007), 18.

12. Kevin P. Coyne and John Horn, "Predicting Your Competitor's Reaction," *Harvard Business Review* 87, no. 4 (April 2009): 93.

13. Phil Kotler, presentation at the Kellogg School of Management, September 15, 2011.

14. Adi Ignatius, "Technology, Tradition, and the Mouse," *Harvard Business Review* 89, no. 7 (July–August 2011): 116.

15. Michael Porter, "The Five Competitive Forces that Shape Strategy," *Harvard Business Review* 86, no. 1 (January 2008): 5.

14   DEFENSIVE STRATEGY FOR INNOVATORS

1. Elizabeth Olson, "Expanding in Athletic gear in a Tough Economy," *The New York Times*, August 2, 2008, B2.

2. Daniel Roberts, "Under Armour Gets Serious," *Fortune,* October 26, 2011, http://management.fortune.cnn.com/2011/10/26/under-armour-kevin-plank/, last accessed March 26, 2012.

3. Kara Swisher, "What's the Deal?" *The Wall Street Journal,* June 6, 2011, R8.

4. Kevin P. Coyne and John Horn, "Predicting Your Competitor's Reaction," *Harvard Business Review,* Volume 87, Number 4, April 2009, 92.

5. Scott McCartney, "Upstart's Tactics Allow it to Fly in Friendly Skies of a Big Rival," *The Wall Street Journal,* June 23, 1999.

6. Martyn Gregory, "Battle of the Airlines," *The Independent,* January 12, 1993, http://www.independent.co.uk/news/uk/battle-of-the-airlines-lord-king-was-calling-me-a-liar-so-i-sued-him-martyn-gregory-reports-on-bas-dirty-tricks-campaign-which-he-uncovered-as-producerdirector-of-thames-televisions-this-week-programme-1478013.html, last accessed March 14, 2012.

7. Method website, "Vote Daisy," www.votedaisy.com, last accessed March 14, 2012.

8. Martin McCourt, presentation at the Kellogg School of Management, September 15, 2011.

9. Adam Lashinsky, "The Secrets Apple Keeps," *Fortune,* February 6, 2012, 86.

10. Lashinsky, 92.

11. Stephen Denny, *Killing Giants* (New York: Portfolio/Penguin, 2011), 49.

12. A. G. Lafley interview by Karen Dillon, "I Think of My Failures as a Gift," *Harvard Business Review,* Volume 89, Number 4, April 2011, 87.

13. Denny, 33.

14. Andrew Gumbel, "Tesco Still Searching for Magic Formula to Make America Pay," *The Guardian,* January 18, 2012, http://www.guardian.co.uk/business/2012/jan/18/tesco-magic-formula-united-states, last accessed March 14, 2012.

15. McCourt, presentation.

16. Dyson television ad.

17. Miguel Helft and Jessi Hempel, "Inside Facebook: How Does the Social Media Giant Really Work?" *Fortune,* March 19, 2012, 116.

18. Haig Simonian and Louise Lucas, "Nestlé and Starbucks Set for Turf War," *The Financial Times,* March 6, 2012, 21.

15   A CAUTIONARY WORD ABOUT COMPETITION LAW

1. Professor of law, Wayne State University Law School, and former general counsel to the Federal Trade Commission. At various times in the recent past, I have served as a member of the Competition Authority of Ireland, have been of counsel

at the global law firm Covington & Burling, and have been associate vice president of Wayne State University. This chapter is written entirely in my personal capacity and the views expressed herein are not the views of the Competition Authority, Covington & Burling, and/or Wayne State University. Although largely written earlier, this chapter will be published during my service with the Competition Authority, and thus I especially wish to emphasize that these are the views of an academic prior to appointment. I also must note that this is just a brief introduction to a subject on which whole books and lengthy reports have been written. See ABA section of *Antitrust Law, Monopolization, and Dominance Handbook* (2011); U.S. Department of Justice, *Competition and Monopoly: Single-Firm Conduct under Section 2 of the Sherman Act* (2008) (later withdrawn). Whenever there is any doubt, legal counsel should be consulted.

2. Guidance on the Commission's Enforcement Priorities in Applying Article 82 of the EC Treaty to Abusive Exclusionary Conduct by Dominant Undertakings (2009/C 45/02) ("EC Guidelines") at § 20.
3. Aspen Skiing Co. v. Aspen Highlands Skiing Corp., 472 U.S. 585, 597 (1985).
4. Olympia Equipment Leasing Co. v. Western Union Telegraph Co., 797 F.2d 370. 379 (7th Cir. 1986) (nonetheless finding for defendant); United States v. Microsoft Corp., 1998–2 Trade Cas. (CCH) § 72,261 at 20 (D.D.C. 1998), *aff'd*, 165 F.3d 952 (D.C. Cir. 1999).
5. Guidance on the Commission's enforcement priorities in applying Article 82 of the EC Treaty to abusive exclusionary conduct by dominant undertakings (2009/C 45/02) ("EC Guidelines").
6. LePage's, Inc. v. 3M, 324 F.2d 141, 151 (3d Cir. 2003) (en banc).
7. United States v. Grinnell Corp., 384 U.S. 563, 570–71 (1966).
8. "Such abuse may, in particular, consist in:
   (a) directly or indirectly imposing unfair purchase or selling prices or other unfair trading conditions;
   (b) limiting production, markets or technical development to the prejudice of consumers;
   (c) applying dissimilar conditions to equivalent transactions with other trading parties, thereby placing them at a competitive disadvantage;
   (d) making the conclusion of contracts subject to acceptance by the other parties of supplementary obligations which, by their nature or according to commercial usage, have no connection with the subject of such contracts." Article 102.
9. DOJ Antitrust Division Workload Statistics FY2001–2010, available at http://www.justice.gov/atr/public/workload-statistics.html
10. United States v. E.I. duPont de Nemours & Co., 351 U.S. 377, 391 (1956).
11. EC Guidelines.
12. 540 U.S. 398, 407 (2004).
13. United States v. Microsoft Corp., 253 F.3d 34, 44–45 (D.C. Cir. 2001) (en banc).
14. Caribbean Broadcasting System, Ltd. v. Cable & Wireless PLC, 148 F.3d 1080, 1087 (D.C. Cir. 1998) (reversing in part the district court's dismissal of complaint and holding that radio station's claim that defendants made misrepresentations to advertisers and the government in order to protect its monopoly stated valid claim).
15. 3 *Areeda & Hovenkamp Antitrust Law* § 651a, at 72 (2d ed. 2002).
16. EC Guidance at § 19.
17. EC Guidance at § 20.
18. See Article 102, quoted in note 8.

19. Akzo Chemie BV v. Commission, Case C-62/86, [1991] ECR I-3359 (European Court of Justice).

20. See Cascade Health Solutions v. PeaceHealth, 515 F.3d 883 (9th Cir. 2008).

21. EC Guidelines § 59.

22. See, for instance, United States v. Dentsply Int'l, 399 F.3d 181 (3d Cir. 2005).

23. See Concord Boat Corp. v. Brunswick Corp., 207 F.3d 1039 (8th Cir. 2000).

24. EC Guidelines at IV.A.b. For an enforcement decision resulting in the leading broadcaster's promising that discounts would no longer depend on the share of advertising committed to it, see Decision of the Competition Authority of Ireland (Case COM/10/02), RTÉ's Conduct in the Market for Television Advertising (Jan. 17, 2012).

25. 472 U.S. 585 (1985).

26. EC Guidance § 81.

27. See Joined Cases C-241/91 P and C-242/91 P Radio Telefis Eireann (RTE) and Independent Television Publications Ltd (ITP) v. Commission (Magill) [1995] ECR 743; Case C-418/01 IMS Health v NDC Health [2004] ECR I-5039.

28. See Lorain Journal Co. v. United States, 342 U.S. 143 (1951); *In re Pool Corp.* (FTC proposed consent order Nov. 21, 2011).

29. See Pacific Bell Telephone Co. v. LinkLine Communications, Inc., 555 U.S. 438 (2009).

30. See Case C-52/09 Konkurrensverket v. TeliaSonera Sverige AB, judgment of February 17, 2011; Case C-280.08 P Deutsche Telekom Ag v. European Commission, judgment of October 14, 2010.

31. As for the government itself, genuine state action in the United States cannot be successfully challenged under the US antitrust laws, but the situation is a little different in Europe, where nations are not permitted to undermine the Treaty excessively. The Court of Justice has held that it is unlawful for a member state "to require or favour the adoption of agreements, decisions or concerted practices contrary to Article [81] or to reinforce their effects, or to deprive its own legislation of its official character by delegating to private traders responsibility for taking decisions affecting the economic sphere." P. Van Eycke v. ASPA, [1988] ECR 4769, § 16.

32. See Walker Process Equipment, Inc. v. Food Machinery Corp., 382 U.S. 172 (1965).

33. Conwood Co. v. United States Tobacco Co., 290 F.3d 768 6th Cir. 2002).

INDEX

acquisition, 101, 152–3, 159–60, 177, 207–11, 222, 252, 264
   and distributors, 159–60
action focus, 134–5
Actonel, 200–1
Acuvue, 17
Adami, Norman, 142
Adidas, 178
Adner, Ron, 100
Advertising Age, 147
Agro-Farma, 226
Ahold, 166
Aldi, 122
Allstate, 109–10
Alstom, 227
Amazon, 7, 80, 109, 212
AmBev, 166–7
AMD, 162, 180
American Airlines, 183–4
Amgen, 70
Anderson, Cameron, 115
Anderson, Jim, 113
Anheuser-Busch, 147, 160, 177, 208
"anti-competitive foreclosure," 258
antitrust laws, 9, 97, 253–9, 263–4
Anton, John, 15
Antonio Payet, Jose, 166
AOL's "free trial" campaign, 123
Apple, 7, 17, 91, 113, 125, 199, 227, 243, 256
ArcelorMittal, 16–17

Ariel del Plata, 201
Ariely, Dan, 106
Armstrong, Tim, 114
Army War College, 51
Arnault, Bernard, 222
Art of Shaving, 220
Article 100 of the Treaty on the Functioning of the European Union, 252
Aspen Skiing Co. v. Aspen Highlands Skiing Corp, 262
attacking-the-core strategy, 244–8
Auchan, 121
awareness
   and competition law, 254
   limiting, *See* awareness, limiting
   and new products, 120, 122
awareness, limiting, 122, 173–82
   and block and limit, 176–9
   and Elbert Alpine Energy example, 174–5
   and filing a complaint, 181–2
   goal of, 173–4
   and government regulations, 182
   and heightening the challenge, 182
   and key marketing vehicles, 176–8
   and outspending, 178–9
   and planning defensive strategy, 123
   and similar news, 179–81

Bacardi, 71

Backus, 166–7

Bakersfield Citizens for Local
        Control, 166

Ballmer, Steve, 113

Bank One, 140, 178

Barboza, David, 53

Barilla, 49–50, 168–71

Barilla, Pietro, 50

Battle of Gettysburg, 120

Becton Dickinson, 63

Beer Store, 160

Best Buy, 64

"best defense is the best
        defense," 26–7

Best Foods, 245

Bezos, Jeff, 211

Bing, 245

Blockbuster video, 13–15, 60

blocking, 17, 103, 105, 109, 119, 124,
        130, 137–53, 155–72, 176,
        178–80, 182–203, 205–18,
        222, 234, 238–40, 245, 263
    awareness, 122, 173–82
    See also awareness, limiting
    the defender, 239–40
    distribution, 119, 130, 155–72, 216,
        234, 238, 245
    See also distribution, blocking
    launches, 137–53
    See also launch, preventing
    repeat, 205–18
    See also repeat, blocking
    trial, 183–203, 205, 245
    See also trial of new product,
        preventing

blogs, 69–71, 91, 148

Boise Cascade, 51

Bombardier, 227

Boniva, 200

Borden, 168

Boston Beer Company, 246

Bosworth, Andrew, 250

brand protection, 13–27, 193–4
    and the Blockbuster story, 13–15
    and constant attack, 15–16
    and defense versus growth, 24–6
    and the economics of
        defense, 18–23
    and limiting product trials, 193–4
    and the motivation gap, 23–4
    and new product success, 17–18

Branson, Richard, 15–16, 183, 240–1

Bratz, 217

Bridgestone, 193

British Airways, 7, 17, 34, 240–1

Buffet, Warren, 16

bulletin boards, 70–1

bundled pricing, 260

bundling portfolios, 162–4

Bush, George W., 127

business team, relying on, 81–2

Business Week, 243

Café Pharma, 70

Calkins, Stephen, 11

Calpino, Barry, 113

cannibalization, 150, 221

careers, and defensive strategy, 93–5

Carrefour, 121–2, 158

Cassidy, Mike, 244

Cast, Carter, 161, 210–11, 220

Catalent Pharmaceuticals, 63

CBS marketing, 8

Chicago Bears, 178

Chicago Sun-Times, 189–90

Chicago Tribune, 189–90

Chicken Helper Oven Favorites,
        215–16

China, 47, 50–2, 168, 227, 252, 262
    Ministry of Railways, 227
    strategy thinking, 50–1

China South Locomotive &
        Rolling Stock Industry
        Corporation, 227
"Chinese walls," 84
Chobani, 106, 226, 243–4
Christensen, Clay, 104, 106,
        113–14, 125
Chrysler, 17–18
Churchill, Winston, 127
Cialis, 177
Cirque du Soleil, 17, 92
Cisco, 98
civil liability, 253–4
Clorox, 96, 146, 195, 241, 245
CNBC, 148
CNN, 114
Coca-Cola, 159, 181, 191, 193, 207,
        213, 220, 256
Colgate, 131
Collins, Jim, 128, 135, 229
Competition Authority of Ireland, 11
competition law, 251–65
    and attention, 254
    and civil liability, 253–4
    and common sense, 264–5
    and efficiency, 256–7
    and lawful conduct, 257–9
    and legal uncertainty, 264–5
    practical realities of, 252–7
    and questionable practices,
        259–64
competitive intelligence, 57, 59–86,
        125, 142–5, 229–30
    challenge of, 59–60
    and "know your enemy," See
        "know your enemy"
    and legal and ethical boundaries,
        75–8
    locating and securing, 60–75
        See also securing competitive
        intelligence

and long-term strategy, 229–30
and market research tests, 142–5
as never-ending, 86
organizing for, 81–6
    See also organizing for
        competitive intelligence
using, 78–81
    See also using competitive
        intelligence
competitive intelligence
        group, 82–3
competitors
    financials of, 62–3, 79–80
    helping, 226–8
    information on, See competitive
        intelligence; "know your
        enemy"
    product of, 61–2
ConAgra, 2, 98, 103, 161
Connecticut State Dental
        Commission, 168
Cook, David, 13, 15
Cook, Tim, 7
Cool Whip, 2–4
copying, 8, 15, 88, 111, 171, 179–81,
        190–2, 199–200, 207, 211–13,
        237, 240–2, 268
    products, 8
    strategy, 88, 240
copyright filings, 73
Covington & Burling, 11
Coyne, Kevin, 50, 53, 238
CPC, 168
Craigslist, 188–9
creating fear, 228–9
Crest, 17
Cristal, 166
Crystal Pepsi, 191
Culkin, Macaulay, 228
customer loyalty, 231–2
customer service, 201–3

Dannon, 106, 226–7, 243–4

Davidson, Arthur, 87

Davidson, William, 87

defend or not?, 87–116
  and key questions list, 116
  reasons not to defend, 95–104
    See also resisting defensive
      strategy
  reasons to defend, 89–95
    See also using defensive strategy
  and "too little too late," 104–15
  and the wrong reasons, 101–4

defense decision tree, 94

defense planning, 117–35, 236–8
  and action focus, 134–5
  and avoiding perfection, 131–2
  and the competitive response,
    133–4
  and embracing uncertainty,
    124–6
  and financials, 130–1
  and five critical steps, 120–4
  and innovators, 236–8
  and limiting damage, 133
  and picking your spot, 120–4
  and rallying the team, 126–8
  and setting the right objectives,
    129–30
  and speed, 117–19

defensive strategy
  and awareness, *See* awareness,
    limiting
  and brand protection, *See* brand
    protection
  and competition law, *See*
    competition law
  and competitive intelligence, *See*
    competitive intelligence
  and decision-making, *See* defend
    or not?
  difficulty of, 109–10

and distribution, *See* distribution,
    blocking
  economics of, 18–23
  and evaluating threats, 116
  and the financial challenge, *See*
    financials
  and growth, 24–6
  for innovators, *See* innovators,
    and defensive strategy
  introduction to, 1–11
  as "invisible" strategy, 6–7
  and "know your enemy," *See*
    "know your enemy"
  and launch, *See* launch, preventing
  and the law, *See* law/legal
  as long-term, *See* long-term
    defensive strategy
  matters, 4–6
  planning, *See* defense planning
  power of, 2–3
  prevalence of, 5
  and product trial, *See* trial of new
    product, preventing
  and reasons to defend, 89–95
  resisting, *See* resisting defensive
    strategy
  and repeat, *See* repeat, blocking
  using, *See* using defensive strategy
  and "watch and wait," 115–16
  works, 91

defense versus growth, 24–6

Del Monte Foods, 95

Dell, 162

Delta Airlines, 183

Denizen, 150

Denny, Stephen, 107

The Desert News, 188–9

"destroyyourbusiness.com" teams
    (DYB), 80–1

DHL, 105, 245

Dick's Sporting Goods, 121

Diggs, Dallas, 118
Dimon, Jamie, 140
Disney, 231
distribution/distributors, 35, 43–5,
        51, 60–5, 81, 90–1, 98, 103,
        109, 114, 119–24, 128, 130,
        133, 144, 155–72, 216, 234,
        238, 245
    acquiring, 159–60
    channel, 234
    and competitive intelligence, 64–5
    blocking, See distribution,
        blocking
    and distributors, 64–5
    and new product launch, 120–3
distribution, blocking, 119, 130,
        155–72, 216, 234, 238, 245
    and acquiring distributors,
        159–60
    approaches to, 158–9
    and bundling portfolios, 162–4
    and caution, 172
    and government support, 167–71
    and in-store battles, 164–6
    and key channel partners, 160–2
    and long-term defensive
        strategy, 234
    and new products, 171–2
    and operational barriers, 166–7
distributors, See distribution/
        distributors
dominance (EU), 251–65
"doom loop," 26, 35
Drugstore.com, 207
Duke University, 91
Dusty Chimney Sweep financials
        example, 33–4
DYB, See "destroyyourbusiness.
        com" teams
Dyson, 17, 105–6, 241, 249
Dyson, James, 249

Eagle snacks line, 147–8
eBay, 208
Eckert, Bob, 217
economics of defense, 18–23
efficiency, and competition law,
        256–7
Eisai, 70, 245
Elbert Alpine Energy Bars example,
        174–5
Eldorado, 177
Eli Lilly, 98–9
Ellison, Larry, 16
Emirates Airline, 167
Emory University, 111
employees, 8, 47, 67–9, 74, 76, 78,
        83–5, 90, 97, 166, 217, 225–6,
        230–1, 237, 242–3, 264
    and competitive intelligence, 67–9,
        83–5
    current and former, 67–9,
        76, 78
    hiring away, 8, 90, 264
    incentives, 230–1
    retaining, 225–6
espionage, 8, 76
ethics, 8, 68, 75–8, 85, 159, 166, 192,
        237, 240, 259
European Commission antitrust law,
        251–65
"Evanston Oatmeal"
        example, 18–22
exclusivity agreements,
        197–8, 262

Facebook, 6, 8, 70–1, 208, 250
FAO Schwarz, 222
Febreze, 113
FedEx, 17, 105, 245
Fernandez, Carlos, 229
Financial Times, 25, 82, 114, 179,
        192, 254

financials, 29–37, 55–6, 79–80,
        130–1
    building, 79–80
    destroying, 32–5
    gathering information on, 55–6
    and making money, 29–31
    and momentum, 35–6
    and new entrants' rationales, 31
    and planning defense, 130–1
first mover, 17–18, 148
Fisher College of Business (Ohio
        State University), 212
five steps in defense planning, 120–4
    building distribution, 121–2
    and the defensive choice, 124
    and developing and testing, 121
    and gaining trial, 122–3
    and generating awareness, 122
    and securing "repeat," 123–4
flexibility, 47, 85, 126, 183–4,
        223, 260
Flip, 98
Forbes, 16
Ford, 17–18
Fortune, 243
the four Ps, 43–5, 61
    See also place; price; product;
        promotion
frame of reference, 42–3
Fresh & Easy, 247
Frisbie, John, 168
Frito-Lay, 144, 147–8, 165, 217
Frontier Airlines, 238
FTC, See U.S. Federal Trade
        Commission

Galinsky, Adam, 115
game playing, 80–1
game theory, 6
Gates, Bill, 16, 69, 253
Gatorade, 181–2

Geico, 109–10
General Electric (GE), 51, 65, 80,
        92, 137
General Mills, 214–16
General Motors (GM), 17, 255
Germany, 41, 69, 127, 150, 167–8, 177
Germanwings, 150
Gillette, 46, 220, 239–40
    Fusion, 239–40
Girl Scouts, 97
Glad, 190–1
GlaxoSmithKline, 201
Go (game), 50–1
Go Daddy, 30
Gomes, Lee, 180
Good Times Home Rentals (GTHR)
        example, 185–7
Google, 69, 97, 227–8, 245, 253
Goose Island brewery, 208
Gore-Tex, 197
government support
    and blocking distribution,
        167–71
    and long-term defensive
        strategy, 232–3
Great Britain, 7, 17, 32, 34, 127, 155,
        183, 240–1, 247
greed, 222–4
Groundwater, Paul, 32, 48, 52,
        111, 155
Groupon, 123, 199, 237
Grove, Andy, 15, 27, 105, 116, 228
growth
    bias, 107–8
    and defense, 24–6
    words, 25
Grupo Modelo, 229
GTHR example, See Good Times
        Home Rentals
guojin mintui, 53
Gutlin, Ilya, 16

Haben, Mary Kay, 215
Habitat for Humanity, 6
Hainer, Herbert, 178
Hamburger Helper, 214–16
Hamel, Gary, 1
Hardy, Renee Lawson, 247
Harley, William S., 87
Harley-Davidson, 87–9, 216
Harvard Business Review, 50, 100
Harvard University, 5, 32, 42, 62, 92,
    104, 106, 113, 125, 151, 219,
    228–9, 234
Hasting, Reed, 30
Healthy Choice, 103, 161–2
Hefty, 190–1
Heinz, 85
Hellmann, 6, 188, 194
Hermes, 222
Hewlett-Packard (HP), 180
Hidden Valley Ranch, 96, 245
high-speed rail industry, 227
Hilton, 150
Hitler, Adolf, 127
HIV market, 201
Hlavac, Randy, 71
Home Alone, 228
Home Depot, 17, 100–1
Honda, 17–18, 87–9
Hoover, 106, 249
How the Mighty Fall (Collins), 135
HP, *See* Hewlett-Packard
Hua Cheng, 53–4
Huggies, 17, 200
Hurd, John, 50

IBM, 101, 209, 253
Iger, Bob, 231
Ikea, 16
incentives, 160–2, 230–1
    and blocking distribution, 160–2
    and long-term strategy, 230–1

industry analysts, 66–7
information gathering, *See*
    competitive intelligence;
    "know your enemy"
Ingersoll Rand, 32
innovators, and defensive strategy,
    235–50
  and acting quickly, 243–4
  and anticipating your
    competitor, 238
  and "attacking the core," 244–8
  and blocking the defender, 239–40
  and changing the rules, 247–9
  and choosing strategy with care,
    244–9
  and defending against defense,
    238–41
  and intellectual property, 241
  and niche strategies, 246–7
  and planning for defense, 236–8
  and post-launch defense, 249–50
  and protecting information, 242–3
  and public relations, 240–1
The Innovator's Dilemma
    (Christensen), 113–14
in-store battles, 164–6
Intel, 9, 15, 27, 99, 105, 116, 162, 180,
    253, 256
intellectual property, 56–7, 199, 233
  barriers, 233
International Flavors and
    Fragrances, 63
Internet, 69–71, 74–5
Intuit, 207
iPad, 113, 199–200, 243
iPhone, 113, 227–8

Jergens, 24
Jesus, 207
Jet Blue, 240
job postings, 68–9

Jobs, Steve, 199
Johnson, Carl, 95
Johnson, Luke, 25
Johnson, Rahsaan, 184
Johnson & Johnson, 118
JPMorganChase, 140

Kaminer, Ariel, 77
Kamprad, Ingvard, 16
Kanter, Rosabeth Moss, 228–9
Kawasaki, 88
Kellaway, Lucy, 114, 192
Kelleher, Herb, 16
Kellogg School of Management
    (Northwestern University),
    6, 15, 42, 62, 112–13, 229,
    242, 249
key attribute, 42–3
Killinger, Kerry, 140
Kimberly-Clark, 200
King, Lord, 240–1
Kirk, Brad, 24
Knight, Phil, 17
"know your enemy," 39–58, 238
    and the basics, 39–43
    and financials, 55–6
    and the four Ps, 43–5
    and innovation, 238
    and intellectual property, 56–7
    and knowing who's really
        attacking, 51–5
    and the launch, 41
    and the legal/regulatory
        environment, 57
    and motivation, 48–51
    and other industry players, 57–8
    and positioning, 41–3
    and source of sales
        volume, 45–8
    and the supply chain, 47–8
    and timing, 40–1

Kobe Delight Oyster and Clam salad
    dressing, 212–13
Koblenz Classics, 41, 139
Koch, Jim, 246
Kodak, 180
Kohlberg Kravis Roberts, 115
Korean Fair Trade Commission, 260
Kotler, Phil, 15, 229–30
Kraft Foods, 2–3, 95, 103, 113, 145,
    161–2, 181, 188, 194, 214–16,
    222, 245
    Oven Classics, 214–16
Kravis, Henry, 115
Krenicki, John, 92
Kroc, Ray, 7
Kroes, Neelie, 9
Kroll, 83
Krzyzewski, Mike, 91, 127

Lafley, A. G., 89, 164, 195, 246
Lagnado, Silvia, 71
Lai, David, 51
Laker, Freddie, 34–5
Laker Airways, 34–5
Lakshmi Mittal, 16
Laliberte, Guy, 92
Land o'Lakes, 103
Lashinsky, Adam, 243
late entrants, 17–18
launch
    of different products, 194–5
    and post-launch defense, 249–50
    preemptive, 148–50
    preventing, See launch, preventing
    of similar products, 188–92,
        211–17
launch, preventing, 137–53
    and agreements, 152–3
    and commitment to defense,
        138–42
    and destroying the test, 142–3

and Koblenz Classics example,
139–40
and the legal system, 150–3
and making threats, 146–8
methods for, 138–50
and operational barriers, 151–2
and preemptive launches, 148–50
law/legal, 9–10, 22, 57, 68, 73–8, 81,
96–7, 119, 140–1, 150–1, 159,
162, 166–7, 181–2, 192, 217,
233, 237, 241, 252–65
and antitrust law, *See* antitrust
laws
and competition law, *See*
competition law
and competitive intelligence, 75–8
and the decision to defend, 96–7
and defensive strategy, 9–10
and innovators, 237, 241
and intellectual property, 56–7
and legal filings, 73–4, 81
and limiting awareness, 181–2
and preventing launches, 140–1,
150–1
and uncertainty, 264–5
Lawn Doctor, 217
Leclerc, 121
Lee, Robert E., 120
Lenovo, 84–5, 101
Levitra, 177
LG Electronics, 216
licensing, 168, 226–7, 263
Lilienfeld, Scott, 111
Lincoln Medical example, 163
LinkedIn, 70–1
Lipitor, 17, 94
Live Nation, 197
long-term defensive strategy, 90–1,
116, 219–34
and competitive intelligence,
229–30

and creating fear, 228–9
and customer loyalty, 231–2
and the distribution channel, 234
and gap-filling, 220–2
and government officials, 232–3
and greed, 222–4
and helping competitors, 226–8
and incentives, 230–1
and intellectual property, 233
laying the groundwork for, 228–34
and licensing, 226–7
and long-term problems, 90–1
and preventing attacks, 219–28
and reputation for defending,
224–5
and retaining employees, 225–6
low-margin businesses, 15
Lowry, Adam, 241
loyalty rebates, 261–2
Lufthansa, 150, 167
Lululemon, 17, 92–3, 105
LVMH, 222

Macintosh computer (Apple), 113
Mackey, John, 247
Mark, Reuben, 131
market research tests, 72–3, 142–5
destroying, 142–5
market share loss, and risk, 18–23
Marketing Synergy, 71
Marriott, J. Willard, 93
Marriott Corporation, 93
Mars, 15
Marsh & McLennan, 83
Mason, Andrew, 237
Mattel, 217
McCourt, Martin, 241, 249
McDonald, Bob, 24
McDonald's Corporation, 7, 14, 144
McKinsey, 108, 229
Meade, George Gordon, 120

Media Markt, 64, 177
Melton, H. Keith, 76
Menke, Sean, 238
Merck, 94
Method, 122, 241
methodology, 10–11
MGA Entertainment, 217
Microsoft, 16, 69, 97, 99, 113, 245,
        253, 256, 258, 261
Mint.com, 207
Minute Rice, 74, 172
Molson-Coors, 160
momentum, 35–6, 60, 91, 99, 131,
        169, 181, 185, 218, 245
monopoly (U.S.), 251–65
motivation, understanding, 48–51
    and behavior, 48–9
    and the corporate context,
        49–50
    and goals and objectives, 48–9
    and how people think, 50–1
    and who's attacking, 51–5
motivation gap, 23–4
Mt. Elbert, 174
Murnighan, Keith, 112

Nabisco, 97, 165
National Pasta Association, 170
Nespresso, 225–6, 250
Nestlé, 85, 168, 222, 225–6, 250
Netflix, 14–15, 30, 60
The New York Times, 53, 77, 201,
        227, 235
niche strategies, 58, 103, 105, 169–70,
        230, 246–8
Nike, 17, 149–50, 178, 211, 235
Nike Pro Baselayer, 149–50
Northwestern University, 6, 15, 42,
        62, 71, 112–13, 229, 242, 249
    See also Kellogg School of
        Management

objectives, 48–9, 129–30
Occupational Safety and Health
        Administration (OSHA), 74
Office Depot, 256
Ohio State University, 149, 212
Only the Paranoid Survive
        (Grove), 228
optimism, 114–15
Oracle, 16
organizing for competitive
        intelligence, 81–6
    and addressing needs, 85
    and the competitive intelligence
        group, 82–3
    and hiring external
        resources, 83–5
    and relying on the business
        team, 81–2
OSHA, See Occupational Safety and
        Health Administration
outspending, 178–9
ownership, 51–2
Oven Classics (Kraft), 214–16
Oven Favorites (General Mills),
        214–16
overconfidence, 110–14

P&G, See Procter & Gamble
P&L, See profit and loss statement
Palin, Sarah, 179
Palmisano, Samuel, 101
Pampers, 17, 200
Pan Am, 34
Parkay, 98
Parsons, Bob, 30
Patzer, Aaron, 207
Pepper, John, 60
PepsiCo, 17–19, 159, 191
Pereira, Sergio, 2–3, 202
perfectionism, 131–2
Perry, Rick, 179

Petco, 17

Pfizer, 94

Phoenix Consulting Group, 83

Phoenix Program, 83

Pietersen, Willie, 39

place, 43–5, 61

Plank, Kevin, 211, 235

Platform Solutions, 209

Polman, Paul, 149

Porter, Michael, 5, 32, 92, 151, 219, 234

positioning, 1–3, 26, 41–5, 61, 85,
    148–50, 191, 222–4, 237–41

  defined, 41–3

positioning statement, 42, 61

PowerPoint document, 75

predatory pricing, 259–60

pricing, 43–4, 61, 259–60

  defined, 43–4, 61

  predatory, 259–60

primary benefit, 42–3

Princeton Vanguard, 217

Pringles, 147–8

Procter & Gamble (P&G), 5, 24,
    60, 78, 89, 144–8, 164, 195,
    200–1, 220, 239, 246

product, 43–4, 61

profit and loss statement (*P&L*), 19,
    22, 51, 55–6, 79–80

promotion, 43, 45, 61, 73–5, 79,
    164–6

  and competitive intelligence,
    73–5, 79

  defined, 43, 45, 61

  in-store, 164–6

  reservations, 73

public relations, 6, 70, 73, 76, 97, 122,
    140, 185, 239–41, 259

  power of, 240–1

  risks, 97

purchasing, 61–3, 83, 124, 177, 184,
    196, 260

Quaker Oats, 18–22

Quandry Medical example,
    162–4

*Quarterly Journal of Experimental
    Psychology*, 112

questionable practices, and
    competition law, 259–64

  and bundled pricing, 260

  and exclusive dealing, 262

  and loyalty rebates, 261–2

  and misuse of regulation,
    263–4

  and predatory pricing, 259–60

  and refusals to deal, 262–3

  and "tying," 260–1

Quicken, 207

Quill.com, 202

rallying the team, 126–8

Rand, Ingersoll, 32

Rawlings, Gary, 178

reasons to defend, 89–95

  and capitalizing on a good
    idea, 92–3

  and effectiveness of defensive
    strategy, 91

  and learning and
    growing, 93

  and long-term interests, 90–1

  and managing your
    career, 93–5

  and protecting share and profit,
    89–90

  and sending a signal, 92

Red Eye, 189–90

Red Streak, 190

Redbox, 14–15, 60

Reddi-wip, 2–3

refusals to deal, 262–3

regulation, misuse of, 263–4

relative strength, 56, 158

repeat, blocking, 205–18
  and acquiring the new entrant, 206–11
  avoiding the situation, 218
  and filing suit, 216–17
  and government support, 216
  methods for, 205–11
  and reducing prices, 213–14
  and similar products, 211–16
repeat, securing, 120, 123–4
reputation for defending, 224–5
resisting defensive strategy, 87–9, 95–116
  and legal concerns, 96–7
  and not caring about the business, 97–8
  and other opportunities, 99–100
  and public relations, 97
  and short-term results, 104
  and small threats, 96
  if success is impossible, 100–1
  and "too little, too late," 104–15
  and validating a competitor's idea, 101–3
  and wanting a competitor, 98–9
  for the wrong reasons, 101–4
  if you're a small player, 103
risk, 18–23, 108–9, 115, 128, 133
  and ceding market share, 18–23
  and limiting damage, 133
  and optimism, 115
  and rallying the team, 128
  underestimating, 108–9
Roberts, Susan, 70
Romney, Mitt, 179
Rubinstein, Jon, 243
Ryan, Eric, 122, 241
Ryan Air, 17, 150

SABMiller, 142, 160
Safeway, 158, 166
Saint, Michael, 166

Saint Consulting Group, 166
sales volume, source of, 45–8
Samsung, 137, 216
Sapporo, 160
Schick, 42, 239–40
Schmidt, Eric, 227–8
Schultz, Howard, 5
Schwartz, Jonathan, 69–70
SCIP, *See* Strategic and Competitive Intelligence Professionals
securing competitive intelligence, 60–75
  and competitors' financials, 62–3
  and competitors' products, 61–2
  and distributors, 64–5
  and employees, 67–8
  and industry analysts, 66–7
  and job postings, 68–9
  and market research, 72–3
  and promotional vehicles, 73
  and regulatory and legal filings, 73–4
  and senior executives, 62
  and social media, 69–71
  and suppliers, 63–4
  and surprises, 74–5
  and trade shows, 65–6
  and where to look, 60–1
senior executives, 62
September 11, 2001, 127
Shenkar, Oded, 149, 212
short-term perspective, 49–50, 52, 96, 102, 104, 108–9, 119, 129–31, 163, 196, 222–5, 231, 261
Siegel's, 100–1
Siemens, 137, 227
Simpson, Martha, 151–2
SITA, 16
Skiles, Mark, 247
Slim, Carlos, 16
Smith, Fred, 17
SnackWell (Nabisco), 165

Snow, Daniel, 100
social media, 69–71
Sony, 107
Southwest, 16
speed, and defense, 117–19,
        132, 242–4
Spicy Mexican example, 171–2
Staples, 256
Starbucks, 5, 193
Starwood Hotels, 150
Stax (Frito-Lay), 147–8
Steam While Brewing, 160
Storch, Jerry, 222
Stouffers, 17
Strategic and Competitive
        Intelligence Professionals
        (SCIP), 83
Sun Microsystems, 69–70
Sun-Tzu, 53, 138
Super Bowl, 131–2, 177, 235
Super Shine example, 156–7
Supervalu, 166
suppliers, 40, 50, 63–5, 67, 81, 125,
        152, 258, 261
supply chain, 47–8
surprises, 74–5
Suzuki, 88
Swatch, 63, 227

target, 42–3
Target, 122, 256
Taylor, Greg, 160
Tesco, 32, 158, 247
test results, destroying, 142–5
Thailand, 46
threats, making, 146–7
3M, 260
timing, 40–1, 209–10
Titleist, 6
Tolcott, Martin, 112
Torengos, 6, 147–8
Toyota, 17–18

Toys"R"Us, 222
trade shows, 65–6
trademarks, 56, 73, 149–50, 192,
        216–17, 228, 233, 241
Trader, Ric, 217
Trane, 32
Treaty on the Functioning of the
        European Union, 252
trial, gaining, 120, 122–3
trial of new product, preventing,
        183–203, 205, 245
    and branding, 193–4
    and criticizing competition,
        199–201
    and customer service, 201–3
    and exclusivity agreements, 197–8
    and GTHR financial forecast
        example, 185–7
    and "killing trial kills product,"
        184–7
    and launching a different product,
        194–5
    and launching a similar product,
        188–92
    and loading up customers, 195–6
    and trial-building programs,
        198–9
    and ways to limit trial, 187–8
Tropicana, 39, 213
Trout, Jack, 7–8, 16, 26, 180
Twitter, 6, 8, 70
"tying," 260–1

uncertainty, embracing, 124–6
Uncle Ben's rice, 74, 172
Under Armour, 149–50, 211, 235
Unilever, 78, 142, 149, 188, 201, 220
United Airlines, 183–4, 238, 240
United States
    airline industry, 34–5, 183–4,
        238, 240
    antitrust law, 251–65

United States—*Continued*
 football, 239
 grocery industry, 247
 insurance market, 109–10
 motorcycle market, 87–8
 pasta industry, 168–71
 salad dressing industry, 144–5
 soda industry, 159–60
 tobacco industry, 182
United States v. Microsoft, 97, 253,
  256, 258, 261
UPS, 105, 245
U.S.-China Business Council, 168
U.S. Civil War, 120
U.S. Commerce Department, 170
U.S. Department of Justice Antitrust
  Division, 254
U.S. Federal Trade Commission
  (FTC), 11, 252, 254, 256, 258,
  277n1
U.S. Patent and Trademark
  Office, 73
U.S. Sherman Act, 251–2
using competitive intelligence, 78–81
 and competitors' financial
  statements, 79–80
 and game playing, 80–1
using defensive strategy, 87–95
 and capitalizing on a good idea,
  92–3
 and the effectiveness of
  defending, 91
 and learning and growing, 93
 and long-term interests, 90–1
 and managing your career, 93–5
 and protecting share and profit,
  89–90
 and reasons to defend, 89–95
 and sending a signal, 92

Verizon Communications v. Law
  Offices of Curtis V. Trinko,
  LLP, 257

Viacom, 13
Viagra, 177
Vietnam, 83
Virgin, 15–17, 183–4, 240
Virgin America, 183–4
Virgin Atlantic Airlines, 15–16, 240
Vittal, Gopal, 142

Wal-Mart, 109, 121, 161, 166, 256
Walgreen's, 207
The Wall Street Journal, 77, 140, 180
Walsh, Bill, 4, 7, 106
Washington Mutual, 140, 178
Washington Post, 254
Wason, Peter, 112
"watch and wait," 115–16
Watts, Roy, 7
Wayne State University, 11
wei qi (game), 50–1
Welch, Jack, 80
Weller, Craig, 247
Wendy, 144
Wharton School of the University of
  Pennsylvania, 62, 242
Whirlpool, 216
Whole Foods, 17, 93, 247
Willaume, Marc, 222
Wilson, Chip, 92–3
Wilson, Warren, 217
Wishbone, 212–13
W. L. Gore & Associates, 197
World War I, 246

Xfire, 244
Xigris, 98–9

Yamaha, 88
Yanovsky, Steve, 8
Yard Doctor Landscaping, 217

Zappos, 232
Zocor, 17
Zyman, Sergio, 191